FREEDOM, RESPONSIBILITY AND GOD

LIBRARY OF PHILOSOPHY AND RELIGION

General Editor: John Hick, H. G. Wood Professor of Theology, University of Birmingham

This new series of books will explore contemporary religious understandings of man and the universe. The books will be contributions to various aspects of the continuing dialogues between religion and philosophy, between scepticism and faith, and between the different religions and ideologies. The authors will represent a correspondingly wide range of viewpoints. Some of the books in the series will be written for the general educated public and others for a more specialised philosophical or theological readership.

FREEDOM, RESPONSIBILITY AND GOD

Robert Young

Lecturer in Philosophy, La Trobe University, Melbourne

M

First published 1975 by
THE MACMILLAN PRESS LTD
London and Basingstoke
Associated companies in New York
Dublin Melbourne Johannesburg and Madras

SBN 333 15976 4

Typeset in Great Britain by
PREFACE LIMITED
Salisbury, Wilts.
and printed in Great Britain by
LEWIS REPRINTS LIMITED
London and Tonbridge

For H, R, R and D

Contents

Preface

I lay no claim to great originality for many of the arguments employed in the course of this book. I do not think, however, that this need detract unduly from its usefulness. For one thing, it seems to many people antecedently improbable that any contribution to the topics discussed here will be both highly original and plausible. But, more importantly, since the book is conceived as, in part, a means of introducing to the ongoing debate those (from both philosophical and theological orientations) who are interested in these topics, it has seemed worthwhile to adopt the approach taken. Finally, because a further part of my purpose has been to convince my readers (including those already familiar with the literature), I have been reluctant to bypass good arguments just because I didn't think of them first, or couldn't presently see how to improve on them, or give them an original twist.

Not only have I been able to have recourse to the published work of others, I have been fortunate in being given much critical help and encouragement by friends and colleagues. The improvements they have suggested have reinforced my belief in the value of discussion and criticism in all (philosophical) enterprise.

Rodney Allen, Bruce Langtry and David Armstrong each read and commented in detail on drafts of one or more chapters. The interest and care they showed in reading my efforts have been greatly appreciated.

Jack Smart, Michael Bradley, John Kleinig and Robin Attfield each read and commented extensively on drafts of the whole essay. Their contributions to my thinking have improved the final product no end. Lastly, I must single out Greg O'Hair for his insightful criticisms of various drafts of the essay and for his much appreciated encouragement during the major period of the writing.

I would also like to express my appreciation to the editors of various journals for permitting me to draw on material presented in earlier, longer and more extensively footnoted versions of some of what follows: namely, *Journal of Value Inquiry*, vol. 8 (Chapter 2); *Second Order*, vol. 3 (Chapter 3); *Metaphilosophy*, vol. 4 (Chapter 5); *Mind*, vol. 83 N.S. (Chapter 11) and *Philosophia*, vol. 6 (Chapter 14).

A word of thanks is due to the University of Wales for the award of a University Fellowship for the period 1972 to 1974, which provided me with the freedom not only to prosecute my other research interests but to improve on the text of this book.

Finally, I want (inadequately) to acknowledge the role that the fellowship of H, R, R and D has played in providing me with a stimulating and loving environment in which to work.

May 1974   ROBERT YOUNG

1 Introduction

From the fact that 'x is sufficient for y' we may infer that 'y is necessitated by x'. This truth has caused consternation to many who fear that if there are any sufficient conditions for human actions and decisions, then these decisions and actions must be necessitated and human freedom and responsibility jeopardised.

Maybe it should go without saying that if this feeling is well-founded, belief in Christian theism becomes even more difficult to sustain. For human freedom and responsibility appear to be core concepts in Christian theism. The stress in Christian theism, for instance, on the culpability of human sinfulness seems to require that those who fall short in a culpable way, not be powerless to do otherwise.

It is well known that there have always been Christian theists who were prepared to hold men (including themselves) culpable before God, regardless of whether men could avoid sin, and who believed, furthermore, that in so doing they were being faithful to Scripture. Thus, some have said that God's choice is the sufficient and necessary cause of *whatever* finite and contingent events occur in the universe. Others have claimed that men are born with an irresistible tendency or bias toward sin. On either of these two accounts, questions clearly arise about the justice of God (or anyone else) holding men responsible for their decisions and actions. Those who advocate such claims have, of course, gone on to argue that God's just nature remains, in virtue of considerations we need not enter into here.

In this essay I shall be concerned with arguments purporting to move from the fact that certain conditions are sufficient for human decisions and actions, to the conclusion that such decisions and actions must therefore be necessitated and men not free. Should these arguments prove sound, it would appear that those in the former of the two

1

traditions of Christian thought just sketched, must concede a knock-down argument against their Christian belief. Obviously the soundness of such arguments as I shall consider would not serve to overthrow the second strategy, but it would surely be incumbent upon its adherents to indicate, however inadequately, why they believed God's just nature was not threatened. It is quite possible that adoption of this stance would remain unpromising apologetically, but that is another matter. Christian theists would still be well served by knowing what position they must embrace.

The arguments I propose to consider involve four different sorts of sufficient condition. The first argument hinges on the claim that the operation of certain laws of logic (notably the law of excluded middle and the principle of bivalence) is sufficient for certain outcomes and hence that these outcomes are necessitated. The universal operation of these laws entails the necessitation of all human actions and decisions.

The second argument appeals to the universal operation of antecedently sufficient causal conditions for all human actions and decisions.

The third invokes the twin Christian beliefs of God's infallible knowledge and his eternal nature, and then proceeds to claim that because God knows in advance what human decisions and actions will take place, his existence as one who possesses such attributes is sufficient for those decisions and actions.

Finally, I shall look at an argument which takes as its starting point the existence of an omnipotent deity and charges that his active power is ultimately sufficient for all that occurs including human decisions and actions, in that, roughly, God makes happen whatever he wants.

The upshot of each of these arguments is that whatever is sufficient for human decisions and actions, necessitates them, and renders them unfree. If any or all of the arguments is sound the picture certainly looks dismal for Christian theism, and perhaps devastating.

I have restricted my task to the four aspects outlined because these are relevant to the freedom of all men. There are other areas of interest to the Christian theist in connection with freedom, for instance, the relation between grace and freedom, but these areas involve only sub-classes of men (e.g. just believers). Furthermore, these issues cannot be looked at until the preliminary work is done in the four areas I shall discuss, because the question of the freedom of all men is logically prior for Christian theology.

The nature of my essay should now be clear, but there are two other matters on which I wish to comment. The first concerns a philosophical methodology which will recur in subsequent chapters. The second involves the structure of the book.

Human freedom seems to me to be an area in which there are no 'knock-down' arguments — or at least, none of which I am confident enough to apply the 'count'. Consequently I will often resort to claiming that arguments I use against other positions than my own, reveal that these alternative accounts are less *plausible* than mine. No doubt there will be many who will consider this an unsatisfactory method. Nevertheless, it seems to me a very important and common test of the strengths of rival positions. Furthermore, I shall always employ judgements of plausibility in connection with rational arguments, rather than just try to engage in intuition-swapping. I do not expect that everyone will agree with all my assessments of plausibility. However, I would be more than disappointed if rational men agreed with none of them.

Secondly, I wish to say something about the book's structure. In Chapter 2 I endeavour to provide a minimally helpful account of the notion of moral responsibility. This account will serve as a touchstone for the rest of my discussions though it will be tied most directly to the problem of freedom in relation to determinism.

In Chapter 3, I broach the subject of fatalism — this will involve consideration of the demands of moral responsibility in connection with the first of the four arguments previously mentioned.

In Chapter 4 the doctrine of determinism is spelled out. In Chapters 5 to 11 I shall put forward a number of distinct responses to the problem raised by the truth (if truth it be) of that doctrine. The second of the arguments previously isolated will thus be considered at some length. Greater length in fact, than each of the other arguments. Not only is the argument from determinism the one most feared by believers in freedom, it is the one that has received the greatest attention. In order to do justice to the ingenuity of the responses it must be dealt with at length.

In Chapter 12 I will be concerned with the third of the arguments — namely that from God's omniscient fore-knowledge.

Chapter 13 consists in a discussion of the doctrine of omnipotence as a prelude to consideration of the fourth argument, which I take up in Chapter 14.

2 Moral Responsibility

It is evident that the concept of 'moral responsibility' is profoundly important in discussions of human freedom. It is also evident that there is a wide variety of senses in which one can attribute responsibility for something to someone. A short list of the senses likely to be relevant in any investigation of moral responsibility would include causing something to happen, being answerable for it, being liable to certain favourable or unfavourable responses from others for it, being blameworthy or praiseworthy for it and being guilty of, but not necessarily blameworthy for, something.

The lack of any consensus about the requirements for moral responsibility *apropos* the problem of human freedom, cannot, I believe, be attributed to the difficulty of making a direct identification with one of these senses. I shall be arguing that it is too often assumed that there is not much more to the job of adequately characterising moral responsibility than advocating slick slogans. My aim in clearing away what I consider obstructions to the satisfactory characterisation of moral responsibility is, however, the positive one of trying to offer a minimally helpful account of the concept, which will be drawn upon in the remainder of the essay.

I

In the literature about moral responsibility and human freedom, one often finds displayed a conviction that it would be helpful to establish common ground on moral responsibility, but unaccompanied by any effort to furnish the common ground. Whether the lack of effort stems from the difficulties acknowledged in the task or from a failure in awareness of its centrality, does not really matter at the moment. It is important at this stage only to note this first attitude. Some of the debate is premised on a second and very different view, namely, that no such common ground could be furnished, because moral responsibility is to be defined persuasively, in accordance with varying moral outlooks. Thirdly, still others make legal conceptions paradigmatic for the discussion of moral responsibility. For them the problem in analysing moral responsibility is thought to be tied up with fashioning a conception sufficiently similar to the legal model (where the criteria are clearer) to be called 'responsibility', but sufficiently rational and autonomous to be called 'moral'.

I think we can begin to make some progress toward a working account of moral responsibility if these three stances are considered a little more closely. I will begin with the third one. Allowing that the practices of blaming and holding guilty are not univocal because we, for instance, blame the weather as well as people, it still seems reasonable to claim that moral responsibility is theoretically, though not always practically, fundamental (rather than ancillary) to such practices as blaming, holding guilty or punishing. On accounts of 'justice' which retain the notion of desert, unless a person is morally responsible for some act or omission, he cannot deserve blame, praise, reward, punishment and so on. On such a view moral responsibility is a necessary condition of the justice of a person's receiving what he deserves and, further, moral responsibility is a clear prerequisite for legal responsibility at least for all offences other than strict liability ones. (There are other accounts of justice which reject the notion of desert, though, and that rejection has an important bearing on the question of moral responsibility. For the moment I want to leave this dispute to one side, though I will shortly return to it.) Nevertheless, I am bound to acknowledge that legal theorists have perhaps given most consideration to the notion of responsibility. The doctrines of *mens rea*, strict liability and criminal insanity, for instance, are relatively firmly entrenched considerations in accounts of legal responsibility, even if they are all three problematic. No matter how much more advanced the state of the deliberations, though, the ancillary status of legal responsibility remains.[1] Further, more often than not our concern with moral responsibility is in no way tied to a concern about legal responsibility. Moral responsibility extends to praise, rewards, honours; to blame and guilt in non-legal contexts; and, in the theological sphere, to sin rather than crime. In contexts like these the criteria of legal responsibility do not seem to provide much guidance.

It may be of some help if we consider the other two approaches together because there is at least a measure of agreement between them about the *form* which an account of moral responsibility must take. Those who have not made much effort to complete the analysis have usually been satisfied with what they consider a necessary, even if not sufficient, account of moral responsibility. It is quite common in the literature for a writer to plunge headlong into a discussion of human freedom after a few terse remarks to the effect that provided a man 'could have done otherwise', the problem of moral responsibility poses no further worries. Fortunately, some of the participants in the debate about freedom have tried to go further. It would not be unreasonable to suggest that it is widely agreed that it is necessary (and perhaps also sufficient) for a man to be morally responsible for some act or occurrence, x, that he has done it or brought it about, *and* has done it or brought it about freely. (A similar, albeit not parallel, formula for 'omissions' could be easily devised.) I hope to show what modifications and riders to this formula are required.

Recently a number of writers who would accept something like the above form as spelling out some (and perhaps all) of the necessary conditions of moral responsibility, have gone on to claim that the *content* cannot be understood independently of one's moral convictions.[2] In particular, it is urged that the concept of freedom essential to the formula outlined cannot be fixed independently of one's moral outlook, especially in relation to the justice of holding persons responsible who could not help doing what they did *when* so holding them will usefully redirect their behaviour, and also *when* the moral gravity of a situation is crucial to our assessment of what a man could reasonably be required to do. For such writers the sense in which one speaks of moral responsibility reflects one's moral convictions. I shall try to illustrate this contention in the following paragraphs where I

outline and criticise the two most prominent characterisations of the content of moral responsibility supported in the
freedom and determinism controversy.

Many 'compatibilists' — those who believe it is quite consistent with an action's being freely performed that it be the
outcome of antecedently sufficient causal conditions — have
argued that a man is morally responsible for his acts if his
performance of them can be influenced or modified favourably by reward or punishment.[3] Some writers have advocated
the stronger view that it is a necessary (as well as sufficient)
condition of moral responsibility, that a man's behaviour be
modifiable. Quite often the thinking behind these two related
claims is that causality may be incompatible with freedom in
the sense required by moral guilt or blameworthiness, but
that all that follows from this is that these latter notions are
unacceptable. 'Libertarians' — whether contra-causal libertarians or agent-causation ones — believe, by contrast, that
actions cannot be both free and the outcome of antecedently
sufficient causal factors. Furthermore, they charge that our
normal use of the concept of moral responsibility presupposes that free actions cannot be determined.

It is my belief that even though the two preceding
accounts can handle some of the objections which have been,
or might be levelled at them, there remain some very
effective criticisms. One criticism of the modifiability thesis,
which is commonly made by libertarians, is that we can apply
sanctions to a well-meaning but dangerous person without
holding him morally responsible for his actions, even though
the sanctions effectively modify his behaviour. I think,
though, that a defender of the modifiability thesis can
accommodate such a case by saying one of two things.
Either, that the sense of moral responsibility here involves
holding someone morally blameworthy and thus, on pain of
begging the question against his analysis, which explicitly
excludes such a suggestion, must be dropped. Or, he could
say, that if the modifiability thesis does diverge at this point
from the popular view then that is so much the worse for the
unenlightened popular view. Likewise, against the criticism
that the behaviour of non-human animals is modifiable by
reward and punishment but yet such animals are not thought

to be morally responsible, he might say that they are responsible insofar as some degree of intentionality and rationality is attributed to them, but not thereby guilty or blameworthy. Finally, against the claim that we hold the dead responsible for certain things even though their behaviour is no longer modifiable, the modifiability theorist could probably say with some plausibility that our holding them responsible depends on the truth of the counter-factual that had they been punished they would have been altered in their behaviour.

Nevertheless, there are three powerful criticisms to which the modifiability thesis is open. Firstly, C. A. Campbell[4] (who believes the objections just looked at have greater force than I have suggested) has pointed out that often we are less inclined to hold someone fully responsible for an action in cases where we consider that features of his heredity or environment have played a considerable causal role. For example, a ghetto background or the having of an extra Y chromosome may well be relevant to the assessment of a person's responsibility for an action, quite apart from the possibility of modification by reward or punishment. As against this, the modifiability theorist would presumably have to say that such factors are relevant precisely because they bear on modifiability. Some empirical support would be needed at this point. The silence of modifiability theorists on such matters is regrettable and important, especially in connection with the stronger version of the modifiability thesis. Two points emerge at this stage, I think. First the modifiability thesis suffers from being too closely linked with the notion of punishment. Second, and for my purposes more importantly, the difficulty noted above requires some attention from advocates of the thesis.

A second problem arises where a man is justifiably thought morally responsible because he was able to do other morally relevant acts, but yet neither will be, nor would have been, affected by punishment. A conscientious objector to conscription for overseas war service would resent the claim that he is not morally responsible for his refusal to obey orders just because his stand is not modifiable by punishment. This difficulty counts against both versions.[5]

The third worry has even more force. Supporters of the modifiability thesis have found it congenial to view punishment as legitimate insofar as it is a measure of either (or both) reform or deterrence. Recall that the thesis is that if a judgement of moral responsibility will not affect behaviour in desirable ways, then there is no point in holding a person responsible. Now, in social situations the consequence of holding a person morally responsible in this sense may have effects on the behaviour of other people (e.g. deterrent ones). It isn't always noticed that on such a view the guilty are punished for purely instrumental reasons. Perhaps this point gets neglected because it is thought more frightening that where punishment is viewed in such an instrumental way it becomes acceptable to punish an innocent man, provided only that punishing him does have a deterrent effect. Persons are open to being treated as patients rather than agents, as means only, rather than ends. This counter-intuitive consequence is often covered up by the fact that it is only punishment as a measure of personal reform which adherents to the modifiability thesis discuss. Of course, one could swap one counter-intuitive consequence for another, namely, by saying that punishment can *only* be a measure of reform or by relegating justice to a place subservient to utility or some such teleological notion.

Does the libertarian claim mentioned previously, fare any better? It can meet at least one of the criticisms frequently raised against it. Very often it is said that libertarianism cannot satisfy the demands of moral responsibility because, in identifying free action with uncaused action, it really is identifying free action with randomness. But I want to suggest that once the several distinct senses of indeterminateness are unravelled, there is little plausibility in the claim that the libertarian conception of freedom boils down to nothing more than blind chance. Later, in Chapter 9, I shall develop in detail an argument for this claim. At the present moment I ask the reader to allow this so as to get a libertarian view of moral responsibility up for discussion.

Even so, the libertarian account fails on its own terms, namely as an account of the 'normal' use of the concept of moral responsibility. If there is a normal or popular attitude toward moral responsibility, it clearly does not license our absolving people from responsibility whenever it is discovered that their actions have causes.[6] It is true that some special or non-standard causal factors such as pathological urges or irresistible impulses are thought to absolve people from responsibility. That the normal use of the concept of moral responsibility does not rule out the possibility of standard causes, on the other hand, is easily seen. The knowledge we have of sexual drives and desires lends powerful support to the hope of providing a causal account of certain sexual behaviour. Even so, this knowledge does not normally lead to someone who commits an act of rape, for example, being absolved. Only when it is judged that the person laboured under an alien condition does the idea of absolution enter considerations. Thus as an account of our actual, normal practice, the libertarian view is inadequate.

Furthermore, the libertarian account seems to founder on the fact that there are no independent criteria for recognising the presence of contra-causal or agent-causation freedom. The absence of these criteria suggests that it is just a metaphysical assumption to which the libertarian is appealing. Any attempt to justify such an assumption in terms of its being required by our normal use of the concept of moral responsibility will, of course, just lead us back to the first worry. In Chapters 9 and 10 I will try to show that the metaphysical assumption is fraught with worries anyway.

II

I have tried to show the inadequacy of two approaches to the problem of filling in the content of moral responsibility. But there has been a noticeable and important difference in the criticism of each of the two approaches. In the one case – the modifiability thesis – I criticised the thesis as one which has been very frequently adopted by compatibilists. However, I nowhere suggested that it is the thesis which *must* be adopted by a compatibilist. By contrast I have argued that the libertarian attitude toward moral responsibility is inextricably tied up with the libertarian view of freedom. Indeed, I suggested that it is so bound up with it, that it seems to be a metaphysical presupposition of the libertarian view of responsibility that a man be free in an incompatibilist way.

Now it follows from the above remarks that it is possible for a compatibilist to maintain that the presence of antecedently sufficient (causal) conditions for an act, does not rule out such an act being free in the sense required for *moral* guilt and blame. It is clearly the case that most compatibilists have not wished to defend this more stringent position. The reasons for this are no doubt complex, but the two crucial influences seem to be the widely held belief that it would be contrary to enlightened *moral taste* to think in terms of moral guilt and blame (because justice as desert, as well as justice as fairness is obviously central to the stronger thesis), and the widespread acceptance of a non-cognitivist meta-ethic.

I do not have the space to argue against these influences. I can only assert that while I acknowledge that conceptions of moral responsibility do vary with particular moral outlooks, it does not follow that they are all adequate, any more than the truth of moral relativism follows from the mere diversity of moral opinions.

In arguing that a compatibilist need not adopt the modifiability thesis, it may appear that I am flying in the face of received opinion. Perhaps I am, but, if I am, it is well to recall that it is only *opinion* which I am opposing. Nowhere, to my knowledge, is there an argument — sound or otherwise — to the effect that a compatibilist must adopt a modifiability approach to responsibility. In the absence of an argument I can only reiterate that from the fact that *many* compatibilists have found the modifiability thesis congenial to their moral taste, nothing further follows for other compatibilists. One can admit that the normal view is more than accidentally linked to the view of responsibility, without conceding that there is some conceptual link.

I have tried to bring out something of the moral dimension of the problem of freedom. But it must be remembered that there is also a metaphysical dimension. One piece of evidence for this claim is the fact that compatibilists of differing moral convictions can agree that the presence of antecedently sufficient causal conditions for an act does not preclude its being free. Furthermore, hard determinists and libertarians can unite with those compatibilists who stress moral guilt and blame, in insisting that the question of moral responsibility goes beyond the question of the *usefulness* of praise or blame. Where they will part company, of course, is over the matter of whether one can have the power to act in a way deserving of moral praise or blame, when one's actions have causally sufficient antecedents. Thus the problem does not await only the resolution of certain disputes surrounding the relative strengths of competing moral systems. The problem has a metaphysical as well as a moral dimension.

III

In addition to considering the influence of moral convictions on the filling out of the formula cited earlier (and the diversity to which this gives rise), one must also pay heed to the important context of broad general agreement that exists about moral responsibility. This agreement is reflected in the belief that the slogan 'ought implies can' (and its contrapositive: 'cannot implies not-ought'), captures something indispensable for an adequate understanding of 'moral responsibility'. I propose to argue that this slogan goes wrong in an instructive way, but that by attending to its deficiencies we can learn something important about the requirements for morally responsible conduct.

There is a serious worry about the interpretation of the slogan.[7] Let's begin with the most obvious interpretation, namely that it means 'S ought to do A at time t implies that S has it in his power, at t, to do A at t'. Consider the following clear counter-example. Cedric has promised to marry Cynthia. But at the duly appointed time, t, he fails to show. As a matter of fact, he happened to be on a plane bound for Haiti at t. Clearly at t he cannot be present at the wedding ceremony since that is taking place, let us say, in Cambridge, England. Yet it is perfectly sensible to say that he ought to be there, and no doubt Cynthia would assert such a proposition. Even so it could be that a great injustice has been done to Cedric. If it turned out that he had been captured by the Tontons Macoutes he would have a good excuse and we would want to say that he really *couldn't* be at the ceremony. If, on the other hand, his presence on the plane was occasioned not by powerlessness but by disinclination to be present, then the slogan seems inadequate at least on the simple interpretation offered above. In this case Cedric remains a cad.

Cedric's problem at time t is powerlessness, but the trouble is that he remains responsible because he ought to have put himself in a position at time t where he would not be powerless (leaving aside the activities of the Tontons Macoutes from now on). In failing to perform the necessary preparatory acts, he renders himself powerless to be at the ceremony, but he does not render nugatory any ascription of moral responsibility. I don't think it will do to try and salvage the slogan by weakening it so as to mean 'S ought to do A at some time t implies that there was some time, at or before t, at which S had it in his power to do A at or by t'. Because, as Goldman has pointed out, this would take the teeth out of almost any attempt to exculpate by appeal to powerlessness. For leaving aside the possibility of ignorance, it is pretty plausible to consider that there is *some* time at which an agent possessed power to do most acts for which he is likely to be held responsible, or even not likely to be held responsible.

The upshot is that powerlessness is not an automatically exculpating fact, for there are instances of agents who are culpably powerless. There is obviously some truth in the 'ought implies can' slogan, since if a person was *never* able to perform an act — for example, crushing the Pentagon in his bare hand, or, less flippantly, stopping all racial prejudice — it would be pointless to say he ought to do the act. The difficulty is to make precise just what the limits of its use are. Much the same applies to that other over-exposed slogan, 'he could have done otherwise'. There is undoubtedly something of worth in it, but it does not help to bandy it about in an unexamined way as it frequently is in the literature. Cases of culpable powerlessness, such as that discussed above, cast doubt on the necessity for moral responsibility of a man's being able to do otherwise (at the time of an act). I wish also to cast doubt on the sufficiency of such a condition.

An agent may have the capacity and the opportunity to do some act and yet not be thought morally responsible for

failing to do the act, even though the particular act is the
right one to perform. Suppose that I promise to attend a
secret meeting to negotiate with the enemy in a wartime
situation. On my way to the destination I see a crowded bus
run over an embankment, so I decide to stop and try to help.
It turns out that no one has been seriously injured. But one
consequence of my stopping is my slightly late arrival at the
secret negotiation point. By the time I arrive the enemy
representatives have left, believing the deal to have fallen
through – peace is, as a direct result, slow in achievement.

Now it might be said that it is sufficient for my being
morally responsible for the continuation of hostilities that I
had the capacity and the opportunity to halt them. But this
is by no means clear-cut. Certainly it is more plausible to say
I am responsible *in some degree*. Yet the slogan 'he could
have done otherwise', does tend to obscure the importance of
degrees of responsibility by making responsibility seem an
'either-or' notion. Degrees of responsibility aside, though, we
often have the opportunity and capacity to do things which
are important and right but which require our doing other
things to which we are averse, or which are costly, or which
require us to forego valuable opportunities. The slogan tends
to obscure these considerations, too.

There is a third important difficulty, which is also relevant
to the 'ought implies can' slogan and to the formula given in
Section I. A man may have the capacity and the opportunity
to do some act but yet be ignorant that he has the power (or
opportunity) to do so. Whether or not such a man is morally
responsible for failing, for example, to do the act is likely to
hinge on the culpability or otherwise of his ignorance.

If a man's ignorance results from a refusal to raise certain
questions when, regardless of whether he expects the answers
to be palatable, he should have made any reasonable effort to
learn the answers, his ignorance is culpable. The importance
of the questions which those who carried out Hitler's orders
in the last world war should have asked, but frequently
didn't, is what underlines their culpability. At a less crucial
level there are countless instances of people who ought to do
certain things, who are quite capable of doing them, have
undefeated opportunity, but fail to because of ignorance of
one kind or another about their capacities and opportunities.

Ignorance, of course, can be important in questions of moral responsibility when it does not relate to possession of power or opportunity. One can be ignorant of *how* to do something, or ignorant of the *consequences* which an act one performs may generate. But the important point is that ignorance is not an automatic excuse, it may be culpable. (Perhaps I should add, though, that ignorance is often viewed as an extenuating or mitigating circumstance — a further indicator that any account of responsibility must allow for there being degrees of responsibility.)

IV

I have argued firstly that it is crucial to bear in mind the role that one's moral convictions play, in the assessment of the adequacy of any account of moral responsibility, and in particular that no account of moral responsibility which leaves to chance the demands of justice, where this includes the notion of desert, can be acceptable. My suggestion is, I believe, contrary to the moral taste of many compatibilists about freedom and determinism but not thereby inconsistent with the compatibilist programme. I have also claimed that a compatibilist position which takes account of the claims of justice is the most satisfactory standpoint. This will strengthen my hand when I later argue for a compatibilist account of freedom.

Secondly, I have tried to show that there are complications of a different order which take the gloss away from the apparently indispensable truth about moral responsibility embodied in slogans such as 'ought implies can' and 'he could have done otherwise'. On their most obvious, and I might add, most plausible, interpretations, these slogans fail to account for some vital cases in which persons are justifiably held responsible but in which the slogans are not fulfilled. This is particularly the case with culpable ignorance and culpable inability. Such cases cast doubt on the claim that these slogans embody necessary conditions for moral responsibility. Likewise, there seem to be clear-cut objections to their having the status of sufficient conditions. (Nevertheless, the slogans have some value as marking out, albeit roughly, something of the requirements for freedom in human endeavour. I shall often treat them as such.)

Another fact which emerged from investigation of these slogans is that they tend to overemphasise non-epistemic senses of the terms 'can' and 'could'. But, knowledge and ignorance can often play vital roles in the assessment of moral responsibility and this ought not to be obscured.

Finally, I have suggested that any account of moral responsibility must admit recognition of the fact that responsibility is as often a matter of degree as it is an 'either-or' affair.

Can a set of conditions approaching necessary and sufficient status be provided? I don't know whether such a set can be provided but I will try to formulate what seems to have emerged from the preceding discussion.[8] In the case of *acts*, the formula cited earlier in the chapter — it is necessary for a man to be morally responsible for some act or occurrence, x that he has done it or brought it about, *and* done it or brought it about freely — perhaps needs supplementing only by some reference to knowledge or belief.[9] For, one might be the free causal agent of an act and yet be excusably ignorant of the true nature of the act. This is to be distinguished from knowledge of the consequential effects of one's acts. We often are interested in the responsibility for such consequences. Even though I recognise the controversial nature of my claim, I think it is important to distinguish an act (such as throwing a dice) and its result (a number between 'one' and 'six' coming up), from the consequences of the act (sparking off a brawl and so on) because this often forms the basis for our distinguishing a man's causal responsibility from his moral responsibility.

The situation with failures to act, *omissions*, is perhaps a little trickier. It is probably true that in general our concern over moral responsibility relates more to omissions, because they highlight the question of responsibility more directly. Nevertheless, it is important not to be drawn in too much by the legal model, and begin thinking that moral responsibility is only important in connection with failures and omissions. I would suggest that for a person justifiably to be held morally responsible for an omission (whether for purposes of praise or blame), he must have omitted to do the act, he must have freely omitted to do the act, and his omission must either have been known to be such, or else have resulted from ignorance which would itself be culpable.

It remains now to assess the bearing of these findings on the four problem areas outlined in Chapter 1. My attention will be concentrated almost entirely on the question of the *freedom* of doing or omitting to do some act, or of making or failing to make some decision. It is obvious that questions about whether someone actually did or actually omitted to do something, or had knowledge of or was ignorant of certain pertinent facts, are empirical not conceptual ones.

3 Fatalism and Freedom

In this chapter I shall not be concerned with such popular kinds of 'fatalism' as can be found in the astrology columns printed in newspapers and magazines. I think that as a matter of fact such popular kinds of 'fatalism' strictly are just particular versions (and not very plausible ones at that) of the quite different doctrine of 'determinism'. This for the reason that the popular kinds allege that there are *empirically* sufficient conditions for all human decisions and actions (e.g. in the motions of the planets). By contrast, the philosophically formidable versions of fatalism are alleged to be supported by considerations of a formal or logical type alone. The thrust of such arguments is that there are *logically* sufficient conditions for all human decisions and actions. These versions appeal, therefore, to considerations which it is hard to imagine any intelligible world could lack, but whose presence would make any world containing them, fatalistic. The doctrine of fatalism is clearly then a more stringent one than is that of determinism, and the philosophically formidable versions of fatalism more stringent than the popular ones.

It is sometimes alleged that fatalistic conclusions can only be avoided at high cost, the cost, namely, of committing oneself to a number of metaphysical doctrines. After discussing several fatalistic arguments in Sections II and III, I proceed to a consideration of this allegation and in Sections IV to VII explore the putative metaphysical ramifications of avoiding the conclusions of the arguments discussed. In the final section I argue that it is not necessary to take on these metaphysical encumbrances because there are other less burdensome ways of avoiding fatalistic conclusions.

I

According to fatalists, men are not free with regard to any of their decisions or actions for the simple reason that the only

19

things a man *can* do are the things he *does* do. In order to forestall misunderstanding, it should be pointed out that this claim does not entail that all things will turn out as they will no matter which logically possible actions a man performs. Fatalists need not assert that the actions which men perform are the only logically possible ones open to them, but rather, that the only things a man can do are the things he does do.[1]

Hence if it is fated that Bannister will be the first 'four-minute miler', the fatalist would not claim that this would occur regardless of whether Bannister ever trained (presuming that the task would require such rigorous preparation) or of whether he regularly gorged himself on pastries, starches, beer and other fitness-undermining items. On the contrary the fatalist would say that if it is fated that he perform the feat, it will also be fated that he engage in the necessary training over an extended period and be not given to fitness-undermining habits. It is not denied that it is logically possible he fail to train, but it is denied that it is within his power to do so. The *prima facie* oddity of this last claim ought not to be used as evidence against fatalism for the reason that he lacks the power is that it is fated. Thus what we do and the effect that has on the future (the consequences of the action) are each equally fated.

The fatalist therefore counsels that we adopt the standpoint toward the future that we already adopt toward the past. Fatalism about the past, if we may legitimately so speak, is unexceptionable in that we do not think it sensible to speak of altering the past.

Altering the past would require that we could bring about a certain state of affairs at time t_1 and then so act at a later time t_2 that we produce a state of affairs empirically sufficient for the state of affairs produced at t_1, not having taken place.

II

It is sometimes argued that if the future were real, 'all laid out', then it could not be changed, just as the past cannot be changed. Moreover if the future were real then any statement about it would be true unless false. Thus if we believe that some of our decisions or acts are free ones, we should hold that before they occur they were not real and corresponding statements about them were neither true nor false. Consider an argument of this sort put forward by Aristotle.[2]

Suppose it were true now that there would be a sea-battle tomorrow. It follows there could not *not* be a sea-battle tomorrow (since in that case it would not be true now that a sea-battle would take place), hence tomorrow's sea-battle is *necessary*. Similarly, if it were false now that there would be a sea-battle tomorrow, the failure of tomorrow's sea-battle to occur would be necessary. But it is now either true or false that there will be a sea-battle tomorrow. Hence either tomorrow's sea-battle or its failure is necessary. Since the argument is easily generalised, whatever happens happens necessarily, and thus both chance and freedom are illusions. Before proceeding to consider ways of avoiding this undesirable conclusion we should note that there has been disagreement about the interpretation of Aristotle's discussion. There have been two main streams of interpretation, roughly that

(i) Aristotle holds certain propositions about the future to be neither true nor false,

and that

(ii) Aristotle holds every proposition to be either true or false — but in addition propositions about the present and the past (though not some at least about the future) to be necessary.

Even though it has seemed to most recent scholars that the first interpretation is not Aristotle's view[3] this will not preclude my discussing it. It has had many philosophical supporters and underlies two of the three competing views about the ontological status of the future which I discuss in Section IV.

For the moment it is a prior task to get clear about what is meant by 'necessity' in the argument outlined. It is not logical necessity (events are never logically necessary), nor causal necessity (for in Aristotle's sense a random or uncaused event can be necessary), nor epistemic necessity (since a completely unknown past event can be necessary). He says that 'whatever is, *when* it is, is necessary' which suggests a notion of temporal necessity or unavoidability, on the grounds that what has already happened cannot be prevented from happening.

Aristotle's argument then looks like this, where 'T' is used for 'it is true that', 'F' for 'it is false that' and 'U' for 'it is unpreventable that':

1. $Tp \rightarrow Up$ Premise
2. $Fp \leftrightarrow T \sim p$ Logical Truth
3. $Fp \rightarrow U \sim p$ From 1 and 2
4. $Tp \vee Fp$ Premise
5. $Up \vee U \sim p$ Conclusion

Clearly, however, it is a very long chalk from 'it is true that p' to 'it is unpreventable that p' (premise 1). Denying this premise enables us to escape the unwelcome conclusion. One might wonder whether anyone has ever argued for the truth of premise 1. Diodorus Cronus, a contemporary of Aristotle, did just that. He attempted to show that the possible is identical with that which either is or will be and hence that, if only what is or will be is possible, what neither is nor will be is impossible. Hence everything that is or will be is inevitable and unpreventable.[4] This argument clearly leads to fatalism because there can be no events which are possible but not necessary. This is, according to fatalists, not to be construed as a denial of a distinction between possible and necessary events, but as an assertion that the class of all simply possible events is empty.

Recently in e.g. his *Metaphysics* (Englewood Cliffs, N.J., 1963), Richard Taylor has updated these fatalistic arguments of Aristotle and Diodorus Cronus. He argues as follows: Let O denote that a naval commander issues a certain order at time t_1, and Q that a sea-battle takes place at time t_2. Assume that O is sufficient for Q, that is, that the issuing of the order at t_1 is a sufficient condition for the occurrence of the battle at t_2 (and further that $\sim O$ is sufficient for $\sim Q$). Then Q is clearly necessary for O and $\sim Q$ for $\sim O$. Taylor then goes on to assert the principle that no one can perform any action a necessary condition of which is absent, from which it follows that if $\sim Q$, then a necessary condition for O is lacking and the naval commander cannot issue the order

— that is, it is not possible that O. Similarly if it is the case that Q then it is not possible that not O. The argument can be formulated as follows, with 'M', as usual, standing for 'possibly'.[5]

1. $Q \rightarrow \sim M(\sim O)$
2. $\sim Q \rightarrow \sim M(O)$
3. $Q \vee \sim Q$

Therefore

4. $\sim M(\sim O) \vee \sim M(O)$

I noted earlier in the chapter that to be free to act (here to issue the order at t_1), one must both be able to issue it and able not to $(M(O). M(\sim O))$. Now 3 above is just the law of excluded middle, the flaw if there is one must lie in steps 1 and 2 (presuming for the moment that it is undesirable to have to resort to denying 3).

What is crucial in this argument is the principle that no one can perform any action, a necessary condition of which is lacking. This principle would seem reasonable where the kind of possibility in question is relative to a set of initial conditions. What of other cases? John Turk Saunders[6] has made a vital distinction which we must note before considering other cases. He has pointed out that past necessary conditions must be separated out from future necessary conditions. Provided that the necessary condition is a past or present one Taylor's principle seems acceptable. For example, if buying a ticket is a necessary condition for entry into a cinema then on those occasions when I have no money I not only *do not* obtain entry I *cannot*. On the other hand should a future necessary condition of my obtaining entry be lacking I *can* still gain entry. Suppose that having bought my ticket I am standing outside the theatre. My entering the theatre may be a sufficient condition for the usherette walking with me to seat A3. Hence the usherette's walking with me to seat A3 is a necessary condition for my entering the theatre. But if the usherette does not so walk with me this does not mean that I *cannot* enter the theatre, but merely that I *do not*.

What is wrong then with premises 1 and 2 of Taylor's argument is that the presence of, or absence of, any future necessary condition for the giving of the order at time t_1 by the naval commander (such as the non-occurrence of the battle at t_2) is quite irrelevant to his *ability* to give the order. All it is relevant to is whether he *in fact* gives the order. The issue as to whether he can make the order is relativised to time t_1 not t_2 and at t_1 he manifestly can choose to make the order or choose not to make it.

III

All is not over yet, however. Storrs McCall[7] raises the question of what we should say if the sea-battle fails to take place at time t_2 and if in addition it is true at t_1 that it will fail. Should we say that a necessary condition for the issuing of the order at t_1 is lacking and furthermore that it is a *present* necessary condition which is lacking? He makes reference to an argument on which Cahn often relies:

> If P has it within his power to render it false that *e* will occur tomorrow, then P has it within his power to alter the past, for he has it within his power to render it true that a proposition was false, whereas by hypothesis, the proposition was true. (p. 39)

One should notice that this argument is somewhat different from that of Taylor's and requires a different formalisation:

1. $T(Q) \rightarrow \sim M(\sim O)$
2. $F(Q) \rightarrow \sim M(O)$
3. $T(Q) \vee F(Q)$

Therefore

4. $\sim M(\sim O) \vee \sim M(O)$ where 'T' stands for 'it is true at t_1 that' and 'F' 'it is false at t_1 that'.

According to this more far-reaching argument if it is true at t_1 that there will be no battle at t_2, the naval commander cannot issue the order at all. McCall's escape from this fatalistic argument raises, in what is I think an instructive way, the issue of metaphysical commitments alluded to earlier in the chapter. He proposes that we look for the flaw in this argument not in 1 and 2 (for we can no longer deny these) but rather in 3. Apart from the limitation to time t_1 in the present argument, he wants to distinguish:

'T(Q) v F(Q)' (premise 3 of Cahn's argument)
and 'Q v ~Q' (premise 3 of Taylor's argument).

His reason for wanting to distinguish these is that the former states the principle of bivalence, the latter that of the law of excluded middle and it is his contention that it is within order to deny the former while asserting the latter.[8]

Thus McCall's contention is that the best way to avoid fatalism is to assert that some propositions referring to future events are neither true nor false. According to McCall, further benefits which accrue in the preservation of a logical asymmetry between past and future are associated with introducing into the objective four-dimensional world of modern science such notions as time's arrow, temporal passage and temporal becoming.[9]

IV

There are three competing theories about the ontological status of the future and two of them claim that some propositions referring to future events are neither true nor false. The first — sometimes dubbed 'the empty future theory' — says that the 'some' is to be understood as 'all'. The future is 'unreal' or 'not yet actual' and propositions about future events, particulars or states of affairs acquire truth values when the events or states occur or fail to occur. Future tense statements cannot be true or false, for that would require the existence of the relevant future states of affairs to make them true or false and there simply are no such states of affairs. If the future were real then any statement about it would be true unless false and, as we have seen, if this is the case then it may be argued that it could not be changed (i.e. fatalism must be true). Since the future, however, is precisely what within certain limits we can change, fatalism must be false, and along with it theories about the future and time which permit future-tense propositions to be true 'timelessly'. Furthermore, holding that the future is unreal accounts for the asymmetry of time because what is or has been real (present and past) cannot cease to have been real or to be real, whereas the future, being as yet unreal, can *become* real. Finally, in support of this theory, it is contended that we cannot succeed in referring to particular events or states of affairs about the future for they are not there to be designated.

Advocates of the second position about the future, who claim that some future tense statements cannot be true or false, concede that others may be true or false. Those parts which are as yet causally contingent are non-existent or unreal but those parts which are causally determined by the present or past are fully real now. Defenders of this theory use many of the same arguments as the empty future theorists. The main advantage of the halfway theory over it is, however, that the empty future theorist must deny that we have any empirical knowledge of the future, regardless of the extent to which it is causally determined. This is imcompatible with our strong belief that we do have some knowledge of the future (which is utilised in such fields as that of space exploration). Since, strictly speaking, to say that the occurrence of a relatively later event is determined *vis à vis* a set of relatively earlier events is only to say that there is a functional connection or causal law linking the properties of the later event to those of the earlier, it does seem that the empty future theory is somewhat implausible. I will shortly be considering some further problems for these two theories. Although the attack will mainly be directed at the more plausible halfway theory, some of the criticisms apply also to the empty future theory.

The third traditional competitor is 'the full future theory' which holds that the future, like the present and the past, is fully real, actual and determinate. The principle of bivalence is held to apply to all meaningful statements about the future unless, as can happen equally with those about the present and past, they are beset with vagueness or other flaws. Future particulars can, like past and present ones, be designated by referring expressions. It is the desire to avoid the alleged fatalistic consequences of this timeless truth approach which has led many to back one of its competitors. My procedure will be first, to consider whether it is the case that these competitors have the alleged explanatory advantages over the full future theory. Next, in Section VI, I shall consider whether the so-called 'generality of predictions thesis' offered in favour of non-full theories is acceptable. In Section VII, I will consider certain problems about causal laws and about relativity theory and discuss which theory they leave least damaged. Finally, in Section VIII, I will consider whether the full future theory does entail an effort-throttling fatalism or even the weaker thesis of universal causal determinism.

V

Empty future and halfway theorists assert that the asymmetry of past and future is not explicable simply in terms of the sort of specific causal and epistemic asymmetries to be mentioned below but is a matter of logical necessity.[10] Our modes of speech should be taken as subtle testimony to this necessity and not be considered of dubious force in establishing the asymmetry.

I will now endeavour to cast doubt on the claims of non-full theorists to the effect that non-full theories alone can account for such features of temporal asymmetry as

(i) The absence of a future analogue to 'trace' or 'memory'

(ii) the fact that we can so act as to falsify some predictions but not retrodictions

(iii) the fact that we can deliberate over future but not past conduct.

Firstly a distinction which has been made between 'temporal determinacy' and causal determinacy[11] may be appealed to by non-full theorists.[12] Temporal determinacy is a status reserved for present and past particulars which cannot be changed now or acted upon causally. Particulars possess causal determinacy if causally sufficient conditions for them already exist. A particular will be real at time t if, and only if, it is either temporally or causally determined as of time t. According to this proposal the 'becoming present' of events is a matter of becoming real in acquiring either kind of determinacy.

However, to say that something has temporal determinacy is simply to say it is present or past, hence cannot *explain why* things and events become present. At that rate causal determinacy must bear the brunt of the explanation. If it is recalled that halfway theorists agree that some events are already causally determined while yet future, it becomes clear that causal determinacy is not a sufficient condition of an event's being or becoming present. Appeal to temporal determinacy being of no assistance, it seems doubtful that this approach provides any explanation of temporal asymmetry. It may be, of course, that the less plausible empty future theory fares better here since it declares that to become real is to become present.

Other non-full theorists contend that the (supposed) impossibility of something's changing from being wholly real or determinate to being partly unreal or indeterminate explains the general unidirectionality of time. But it can be questioned whether this is really an explanation and not just an affirmation of a supposed *a priori* metaphysical truth. Gödel has argued for the empirical possibility of travel from future to past (in that a world line under a general relativity world model could bend back on itself) and such a possibility undermines the seeming *a priority* of this second non-full theory contention.[13]

A third claim is Storrs McCall's in 'Temporal Flux' that adoption of a timeless theory of truth 'is at variance with the ways we ordinarily speak and think about the future and about truth' (p. 273). Now I do not consider that an ordinary language argument can be as final as McCall obviously does (by the fact that this is the *only* argument he offers). Nevertheless one must consider its force even if one is not prepared to acknowledge any ultimate or knock-down significance for it. Consider a case that McCall discusses. A doctor, having just given a patient a pill, says 'There, *now* he'll get better'. In McCall's view what these words imply is that it is now true to say the patient will get better, whereas it would not have been true to say that a moment or two before. Rogers Albritton[14] had considered an exactly similar case and concluded that such a locution as 'it is now true that' is certainly a manner of speaking we adopt and that it means roughly 'it is causally ensured that' and its negation means simply 'it is not causally ensured that'.

What McCall considers ordinarily involved in the ways we speak and think about the future and about truth, Albritton considers 'eccentric' and 'not readily intelligible'. It is clear that the force of this third proposal, aside from any general methodological scepticism is hardly great enough to account for temporal asymmetry. Indeed there are those who claim it is only a linguistic convention that prevents us from calling a later event the cause of an earlier one.

It is not that there is increasing determinateness or richness as we 'go from past to future' but rather that this is just a way of speaking and not a deep metaphysical truth.

If, finally, some specific causal and epistemic asymmetries between past and future are considered we see again that it is hardly helpful to say that our knowledge of the past is so much more detailed than that of the future because the one is there to be known and the other not. For we undoubtedly do have some knowledge of the future and indeed a great ignorance about the past and yet this does not lead to our positing a partial unreality of the past! The full future theorist can (as we shall see) explain the present unknowability of most of the future by citing, just like the halfway theorist, its largely present causal indeterminacy (without at the same time holding it to be anything but fully real). Again, since the halfway theorist acknowledges the causal determinacy of some of the future he too must explain why we do not have non-inferential, precognitive knowledge of the future of at least those causally determinate events. Hence we must go on to investigate other considerations which may help us decide whether non-full theories are able to offer more acceptable ontologies of the future, remembering always that our interest is primarily to see whether we need to deny the reality of the future (by denying that it is subject to the law of bivalence) in order to avoid fatalism.

VI

It has been proposed that an ontologically revealing asymmetry between past and future is discoverable if we pay attention to the fact that predictions must be logically general in form whereas retrodictions can be singular. The future is a realm of possibilities and, therefore, contains no identifiable individuals that can be referred to by the subject expression of a prediction. I merely note that halfway theorists usually do not make clear what conditions must hold if designating expressions which purport to refer to future particulars are to succeed in referring under their theory.

The generality of predictions thesis has been stated in both an unrestricted and a restricted version. For present purposes I shall take it that a singular statement is one whose subject expression is used to identify an individual.[15]

The generality of predictions thesis in its unrestricted version asserts that *no* statement about the future can be a singular statement.[16] What, however, should we say about the frequently advanced counter example which refers in the subject term to a presently existing individual and predicts something he will accomplish in the future? For example, 'President Nixon will fly to Mars'.

It is obvious that this statement satisfies the proposed criterion for singularity. Mayo contends that although we have 'got' the present President Nixon we have not 'got' the future President Nixon, hence this statement, which is really about a future event in the history of President Nixon and not about the presently existing individual, fails to refer. But Gale and Thalberg, in the article cited, point out, albeit in a different way, that this confuses the reference of the subject term of the prediction and the future event reported by the statement. We have got the former *individual* but we have not got the latter *event*. If a doctor says to his patient, 'Brown, you will die within six months' — we proceed to comfort the present Brown for we have no doubt as to whom the doctor referred, though we fervently hope the event reported will not occur.

It might be replied that we really are referring to a future not a present individual in the Nixon and Brown cases, because only certain future extensions of these men will count as being self-identical with them. However, for anyone making spatio-temporal continuity a necessary criterion of this-worldly identity attributions, a logical guarantee of self-identity is provided. Anyone adopting such a position would conclude that if this criterion were met, the same man as predicted to accomplish a certain feat does so. All this apart, the possibility of there being a doubt or a puzzle about self-identity can only be raised if the prediction *refers* to a presently existing individual.

Thirdly, we are entitled to ask about the status of past-tensed assertions for we seem no longer to have the individual in question any more than we have a future individual if we take an approach like Mayo's. This challenge places the onus of proof on Mayo who would have to show us how we have got the past individual but not the future one, on pain of obliterating the desired asymmetry.

Clearly the thesis needs modification if it is to support non-full theories about the future. It will have been observed that the sort of counter example to the unrestricted thesis that has been considered, made reference to *presently existing individuals*. A limited or restricted version such as that proposed by Prior or by Gale and Thalberg evades such counter examples. Gale and Thalberg write:

> Any prediction referring to a future individual must be general although some retrodictions referring to past individuals are singular. (p. 202)

That predictions about presently non-existent individuals do not identify individuals (the thesis stated) is not to be confused (according to its advocates) with the false claim that we cannot describe and pinpoint future individuals. It is clear then that the restricted version hinges on driving a wedge between definite descriptions and singular *identifying* expressions. Gale and Thalberg try to justify this wedge by appeal to ordinary language as the only valid source of our concept of identification.

They suggest that there are two relevant senses in which one can identify an individual: (1) by demonstratively picking it out and (2) by naming it. Since, according to these authors, one can give a unique definite description and still fail to pick out the person to whom it refers (e.g. in a police line-up) and pick out something without being able to describe it (e.g. a lost item), identifying must be distinguished from describing. (I frankly am sceptical about some of these claims but will concede them for sake of argument.) Furthermore, since one cannot demonstratively identify future (or past) individuals (except where there may be photographs of some past individuals) the naming sense must occupy us more.

The case for asymmetry hinges then on the claim that we cannot identify future individuals by naming them, because they do not have names. We can *make up* a name for a future individual but to name a future individual would require the *presence* of the individual at a naming ritual. Once, however, a name has been bestowed upon an individual it can be used with the logical force of a proper name in statements referring to any time, even times prior to that at which the naming ritual took place. Proper names are *given to* bearers whereas a description *fits* a certain bearer because it has the described property (there cannot be a proper name with no bearer but there can be descriptions which fit nothing). While these are all plausible claims one could reasonably dispute them. For instance, one could contend that names have already been given to next year's hurricanes not just made up for them. But I do not want to place any reliance on the availability of alternative views to the one being considered.

However, what happens to the asymmetry thus established if we imagine that naming rituals are abolished? That is, what if there were no names for things but only ones made up for things (possibly having definite descriptions)? At this point advocates of the restricted thesis are apt to fall back on the asymmetries mentioned previously like the lack of a future analogue for traces and memory. This manoeuvre suggests that the thesis in the end really rests upon these logical asymmetries and not conversely. Moreover, it seems that it is not even the case that they are independent evidences of asymmetry. Furthermore, it may be doubted that there is a wedge between definite descriptions and singular identifying expressions. Finally, it may be doubted whether the asymmetry of causality requires explanation. It may merely reflect linguistic convention or just be grounded in facts about the causal structure of the world and of human knowing. The restricted and more plausible version of the generality of predictions thesis is, therefore, far too inconclusive a basis for accepting non-full theories of the future in order to avoid fatalism.

VII

So far I have been concerned with the question of the alleged explanatory advantages of non-full theories against the full future theory. It has been argued recently that outright refutation of the non-full theories is possible if one deploys the following two arguments:

(i) The halfway theorist says that some predictions are as yet neither true nor false. But some causal laws are true now for their present truth is demanded to ensure that some future events are causally determined and thus that predictions of their occurrence are true now. The halfway theorist withholds truth from particular predictions until sufficient conditions for their truth obtain (i.e. until all possibility of falsification has passed). But it may be asked in virtue of what facts are these supposed causal laws true as of now, or, why should we not withhold truth from every putative law-statement until all possibility of the occurrence of counter-cases to it has passed (i.e. forever in the case of supposed laws containing no specified time-limit)?[17]

(ii) In the four-dimensional space-time manifold proposed by Einsteinian Relativity theory simultaneity is relative to co-ordinate systems and so is futurity. Roughly, what is present for you may be future for me, and *vice versa*, if we are using different co-ordinate systems. So my predictions are about events in your present or past and are thus either true or false (this is incompatible with the view of pre-Einsteinian non-full theories that there is an absolute future). On a realist rather than an instrumentalist view of relativity the non-full theories formulated in pre-relativistic ways are unacceptable.[18]

It is Fitzgerald's contention that the halfway theorist could go one of four ways concerning the first argument and none is acceptable. Firstly, he may deny that genuine laws are required for the reality of certain future regions, in short that a particularistic rather than a universalistic theory of causation will do the trick. But this anaemic type of law is implausible.

Secondly, the position could be taken that genuine laws are required for the reality of the future but that the truth and law-status of these laws is an *a priori* fact. This logical entailment theory of causality is implausible.

Thirdly, it might be admitted that laws are required for the reality of future particulars, and that they are not *a priori* truths, but it might be added that the world's past and present features alone suffice to impart to them their genuine nomological status. But how can past and present features be a sufficient condition for the non-existence of future counterinstances to the law statements? If there are no such genuine laws nothing in the future is causally necessitated by present and past and the position collapses into the empty future theory. Alternatively one might resort to the implausible particularistic view of causality.

Fourthly, it might be said that it is just a brute fact that certain regions of the future are real and others unreal. That is, it just happens to be a fact about the future that there are no counterinstances to certain lawlike statements which also have no present or past countercases. Moreover every real future particular is related to present or past particulars by one of those laws. It should be noted that buying the brute inexplicability view precludes one from offering explanations as to why certain particulars *are* real and others unreal (as against why we might *believe* this latter claim). Now again we find that the burden must be borne by the further claim that positing this bruteness enables us to better explain facts about the passage and unidirectionality of time, causality, memory and our lack (comparatively) of knowledge about the future. However, we have found reason to be sceptical about the non-full theories' capacity to explain these facts.

But, according to Fitzgerald, we can scrub the competitors to the full future theory once and for all by pointing to their incompatibility with relativity theory. Unfortunately, Fitzgerald's claim is too sweeping. Storrs McCall has argued in 'Temporal Flux' (art. cit., p. 280) that if one is to make non-full theories take account of relativity theory then the first thing one must do is erase from the Minkowski diagram all those events which do not correspond to propositions currently true for a given observer. If this step is taken the force of Fitzgerald's important argument is somewhat blunted since it is no longer the case that an event E_1 which has come within the absolute past of an observer O_1 must inevitably one day come within the absolute past of O_2, assuming that the two observers are not receding from one another at the speed of light. This is so because the proposition

'That E_1 *occurs* is true for O_1'

is not at the time either true or false for O_2 (on pain of acknowledging the timelessness of truth and of the full future theory which it entails).

Happily, this debate about the compatibility of this observer-oriented picture of the universe with relativity theory can be sidestepped, because I think it can be shown that the step taken early in the chapter — that of denying the operation of the law of bivalence as regards propositions about the future — is unnecessary for avoiding fatalism.

VIII

Firstly, I wish to deny that the truth or otherwise of the full future theory bears on the question of whether we live in an effort-throttling fatalistic world. To say that it is timelessly true that a certain event will occur or not, is not even to say, or logically imply, that the occurrence of that event is causally determined.[19]

When we recognise that the doctrine of the space-time manifold does not even imply the weaker doctrine of determinism we are less stirred by the claim that it implies fatalism. The doctrine of determinism asserts that the laws of nature connect earlier and later spatial cross-sections of the manifold in a determinate way. Indeterminism, being a denial of this sort of connectedness, is equally compatible with the manifold.[20]

It is clear that my position flatly contradicts that of philosophers (such as Reichenbach) who argue that the coming into being of events is implied by the indeterminism of quantum physics. But more significant than that for present purposes is that since arguments for fatalism depend for much of their force on the alleged consequences of the full future theory, the absence of these consequences removes whatever teeth arguments from fatalism might seem to possess. A believer in the full future theory need not, therefore, resort to denying the applicability of the law of bivalence to certain propositions about the future.

Previously, when I introduced McCall's suggestion about denying the law of bivalence, I conceded for the sake of argument, that no one could perform any action a past (or present) necessary condition of which is lacking. It may plausibly be contended, however, that there is no more contradiction in saying that one may have the power so to act that past situations would be other than in fact they are, than there is in saying that one has the power so to act that future situations would be other than in fact they are.[21] It will be recalled that no problem was found with this latter claim for it was pointed out that even though we do not so act that future situations are other than they are, it does not follow from this that we lack the power so to act that they would be other than they are.

Consider the following situation. Suppose that at t_1 I decide to make a phone call at t_2 rather than make myself a milk-shake. Suppose further that conditions are 'normal' at t_1 and t_2 in that there are present no defeating conditions (such as being coerced at gun-point, being hypnotised and so on) and suppose too that I have the ability (know-how and resources), to make either the call or the milk-shake. Suppose, finally, that under the circumstances which prevail at t_1, my decision is empirically sufficient for my making the phone call at t_2 (the world is governed by empirical laws to that effect).

Clearly, it is in my power to make the milk-shake at t_2, since I know how to do so, have the resources and the conditions for the exercise of this ability are normal. If I were to exercise this power then I would not, at t_1, have decided to make the phone call at t_2 or else the circumstances at t_1 would have been different. Hence my power to make a milk-shake at t_2 is a power so to act that an earlier situation would be other than in fact it is. It is the power to perform an act such that if it were performed then either I would not at t_1 have decided to make the phone-call at t_2 or else the circumstances at t_1 would have been different.

But it might be objected firstly that I just do not have the power to do anything but make the call at t_2. But this forces us to accept the claim that, under normal conditions, my own decision renders me powerless to do anything but what I do. This need not be accepted for there is nothing in the claim above which commits us to thinking that we can 'alter' the earlier by the later or that what was once true is now false. This way of putting it may be misleading unless we distinguish between saying something is timelessly true and saying of an act that it is true *before* I perform it that I will perform it. This latter involves the identifying of two distinct times because it misleadingly suggests that it is a statement about the earlier time when it is a statement which is made true not by what happens at the earlier but at the later time. And that fact suggests strongly that the statement is *at least* in part about the later time. Making sense of a statement such as 'It was true at t_1 that E would occur at t_2', is at the very least not straightforward, but not, I think, impossible. (Further attention will be devoted to that very task in Chapter 12, Section III.)

Secondly, it might more plausibly be objected that since, under the circumstances, my decision to phone is empirically sufficient for my phoning, it is not in my power to change my mind and make a milk-shake instead. But although it (logically) cannot both be that my decision, under the circumstances, is empirically sufficient for my doing what I decide to do and also that I change my mind and do not do it, it does not follow that it is not in my power to change my mind and make the milk-shake instead. To maintain the contrary would be to suppose that some sort of indeterminism is *essential* to human freedom on grounds that if ever, under normal conditions, my own decision is empirically sufficient for my doing what I do, then my own decision compels me to do what I do. There will be more about these matters in Chapters 8 to 11.

A third objection might be raised, however: 'Once the decision is made you could not exercise the power to change your mind and make the milk-shake. Since a power which could not be exercised is not a real power you would have no such power at all.' While it is true that a power which could not be exercised is not a power, one can justifiably deny that the power could not be exercised on the ground that all that follows from the case is that under the circumstances I *would* not exercise the power. The objector might persist: 'But even if you wanted to do something else, how could you?' Suppose it is true that if I wanted to do something else then I would change my mind and do it. In that case *I will not want* to do something else. It is quite obvious that the territory just traversed is not one in which only fatalism needs to be considered. There are obvious connections with the question of the compatibility of determinism and freedom to be considered in later chapters.

However, at this point it is my purpose only to point out that the above account, if correct (and it seems to me to be at the very least, plausible), provides a second ground for refusing to succumb to the temptation of fatalism or of denying the operation of the law of bivalence over some future propositions as a means of resisting the temptation.

4 Determinism

I am not going to argue for the truth of determinism. In this chapter I shall be undertaking less epoch-making tasks. I propose to do three things.

Firstly, I shall set out just what content the doctrine of determinism will be given in the remainder of the book. This will involve consideration of certain other ways in which the content of the doctrine could be spelled out. I make no bones of the fact that my discussion of determinism *as a doctrine*, is silent on many related questions. An adequate analysis of the doctrine is something which philosophers of science and those skilled in the metaphysical problems of causation, in particular, must furnish.[1] Fortunately, though, I can safely bypass the technical difficulties associated with the doctrine of determinism, because a workable notion, reasonably adequate for application to the area of human freedom and action, is available without an excursion into the philosophy of science, or, analyses of causation.

Secondly, I shall suggest, without directly arguing for, the status that the doctrine of determinism will be accorded in my discussions of determinism and freedom.

Thirdly, I will consider some objections that are often levelled at the construction I place on the doctrine. I have indicated that I will not be arguing directly for that construction. My attempt to counter the objections just referred to will constitute, nevertheless, an indirect (but very limited) defence of that construction.

I

I suggested in the previous chapter that the doctrine of determinism is the claim that there is a functional connection or law of nature which links earlier and later spatial cross-sections of the space-time manifold in a determinate way. At that stage it was unnecessary to take time out in defence of this construction of the doctrine. Nevertheless, I must now offer such a defence for several reasons. Firstly, there is a good deal of semantic unclarity associated with the doctrine especially in its application to the question of freedom.

Secondly, it is important to discuss the relation between determinism and freedom in connection with an account of those concepts that does not block *a priori*, consideration of the commonly proposed alternatives in the debate regarding their relations. The account, in other words, must get at the heart of these notions as they are understood by adherents of the traditionally opposed positions. Any account which begs the question in favour of one or other of the opponents, or veils the real issues separating the opponents, will not permit progress to be made in considering how the doctrine of determinism bears on the issue of freedom of action and decision. I will endeavour to show that the construction I have placed on the doctrine does throw into clear relief the issues dividing the various proponents.

Many formulations of the doctrine of determinism are constructed in terms of the possibility of knowing, predicting, or explaining all that happens. The most popular alternative to the one I have offered comes from this category — it is the view that what is determined is what can in principle be predicted. Predictability, of course, goes beyond mere correct assertions (or guesses or hunches) for it must be information-based. A position often taken is that:

(1) 'Event e is determined'

and (2) 'Event e is rationally predictable'

are synonymous.

There are, however, several difficulties with this formulation. Firstly, it seems perfectly sensible to imagine a case in which the event, e, has as its cause a simultaneously occurring event, f, and in which f is undetermined. In such a case e (while determined) is not rationally predictable. A predictability theorist might say that such a case *cannot* arise according to the doctrine of determinism. This, of course, requires dropping the notion of synonymy in favour of logical equivalence of the generalised forms of (1) and (2).

Further, it has been argued that for some types of cause it is physically impossible to find out whether the cause c_1 occurred, from which we could predict an effect e_1, until e_1 has itself occurred. Popper[2] has argued that even if classical mechanics were true it would not be (contrary to all appearances) a deterministic theory for this reason. But such impossibility of rational prediction seems irrelevant to any consideration of the truth or otherwise of the doctrine of determinism.

Thirdly, and most significantly, the whole notion of predictability is eliminable for the following reason. The basis upon which knowledge, prediction or explanation of some event must rest if it is to sustain a definition of determinism, is the lawful character of the event or the existence of a sufficient (causal) condition of the event. This lawfulness or sufficiency is obviously independent of what it is humanly possible to predict (know or explain). But, even predictability in principle[3] presupposes the concept of determinism or concepts which could themselves be used to define determinism. What I have said concerning the relation of predictability and determinism is, I think, sufficient for present purposes. There is, however, a good deal to be said about the relations of predictability and determinism *and* human freedom. Consideration of these matters must be postponed until Chapter 8. In that chapter I will consider in detail a number of arguments which rely on the alleged impossibility in principle of predicting free human actions as a means of grounding human freedom.

The view that the doctrine of determinism asserts that 'every event has a cause' (alternatively called the law of causation and similar to the principle of sufficient reason on some accounts of that principle), is much nearer to the one I have given. It might well be asked which, if either, is preferable. Let us consider some objections to the view that the doctrine of determinism is captured by the claim that every event has a cause.

First, an objection to using the language of events is sometimes made along the following lines.[4] Suppose it is determined that Jones catches the train to work on Thursday (i.e. there is a law governing this consequence). The proposition that 'Jones catches an eight-carriage train with a one-eyed guard which leaves his station at 8.04 a.m. and so on' is extensionally equivalent with 'Jones catches the train to work on Thursday'. However, there may be no law which governs the facts about the train Jones catches to such a degree of specificity, and in the absence of such a law it is false that it is determined that 'Jones catches an eight-carriage train. . . .'. This latter consideration is not in my view especially persuasive, for one need only say that under some description there will be a law, but not necessarily a law for every description.

There is a second objection. It is that the definition of determinism in terms of events is less convincing than one not employing the notion, because such 'non-events' as states surely come within the scope of determinism. Since the definition in terms of events, which we might construe as changes of state, makes changes mandatory, such 'unchanges' are excluded. But the contention is that they should not be excluded. The way to bring these unchanges within the scope of a deterministic theory is simply to drop talk of events in favour of states. This enables us to account for both states and events since events, being changes of state, consist in passing through a series of states with only two members and are entirely described when the pair of states is described.

Now Donald Davidson[5] has spiritedly defended the claim that we *need* an ontology of events if we are going to make sense of much of our common talk about causation. He urges the special importance that this has for explaining singular causal statements. On his view singular causal statements entail no law but they do entail that there is a law. He is aware that one cannot do justice to all our causal talk, though, just by appeal to events even if the concept of event is widened. His way out of this difficulty involves distinguishing causal explanations, which typically, he says, relate statements not events, and the analysis of causal relations which crucially involves events.

I am not competent to say just how wide is the gulf, if gulf there be, between the two proposed definitions. What I shall say is, therefore, tentative. It seems to me that Davidson is right to stress the need for event-talk if we wish to properly account for our causal vocabulary. Nevertheless, there does seem to be some justification when one is endeavouring to come up with a suitable definition of a *technical* concept, for a refusal to allow considerations of vocabulary to be decisive, even if neither account rests on considerations of vocabulary *alone*.

Without wishing to minimise the differences between the two definitions it is obvious that the really crucial idea of causal law is present in both. Davidson rightly points out that the relation between causal laws and singular causal statements (which will involve events) is not straightforward. But he does recognise the importance of causal laws — we know there must be one even though we may not know what it is. My claim is that it is useful to make the notion of causal law plain in the definition of determinism. I do not want to make the strong claim that the view suggested here is importantly superior to another account such as 'every event has a cause'.

There is just one more consideration I shall advance on this matter. Traditionally determinism has been taken to produce a unique situation. Any theory which is deterministic relative to statistical properties only, will be too weak, for it loses this sense of uniqueness. In other words, the sufficiency of the determining conditions must play a part in any appropriate definition. With this in mind I would claim that the formulation suggested is to be preferred to one referring only to 'cause'. For if one uses the notion of cause it must be always borne in mind that there has been a departure from the ordinary sense of the term 'cause', causal propositions rarely being specified in the guise of sufficient conditions. I think that an account making plain reference to laws conveys this deep-seated commitment to the idea of sufficient conditions.

In this book my interest in the doctrine of determinism is exhausted by its application to human action and decision. I suggest, then, that for present purposes, the definition of determinism given in the previous chapter be modified in the following way. The claim that a certain action (or decision) at time t is determined, is the claim that:

There is a causal law linking pertinent information about

the agent and his environment at an earlier spatial cross-section of the manifold than t, and the action at t, in a determinate way.

I will conclude this section with some brief remarks about this modified definition. First, the definition given does not commit a determinist to the view that the causal laws governing human behaviour must be psychological, or, that they must be physiological, must be chemical or must be physical. All that is claimed is that there is some set of causal laws.

Secondly, the information will be completely specifiable independently of t (and most often prior to t). Furthermore, the definition entails that any individual would perform the same action under relevantly identical conditions. This, of course, immediately sets up a tension with those accounts of freedom which depend on denying the truth of determinism.

Finally, it will be apparent that the definition stresses the nomological aspect of the doctrine of determinism. The omission, though, of the notion of nomic necessity may perhaps seem strange. There is, I wish to contend, an important reason for not including that notion.

I have already stressed the point that, if at all possible, discussion of the doctrine of determinism should be steered clear of other controversial questions. One related dispute (because of the frequent construction of definitions of determinism in causal language) is that between a regularity and a necessitarian view of 'cause'. Since I think that most, if not all, parties to the dispute over determinism and freedom would still dispute the question on the definition given, I think it best to use it rather than one which makes determinism hinge on a necessitarian analysis of causation. To take the latter course would rule out all those who supported a regularity thesis of causation, from defending a compatibilist position. Furthermore, adopting the definition proposed enables one to avoid becoming embroiled in a discussion of the sense of necessity (which is agreed to be a non-logical sense) supported by necessitarian analysts.

II

Thus far my concern has been with spelling out the claim made by the general doctrine of determinism. A good many questions have, however, been raised regarding the status of this extremely general or universal thesis. The doctrine has often been thought not subject to disconfirmation — the failure to find laws in a certain domain can be explained by a determinist in such a way as to render it never necessary to describe an event as uncaused.[6] And it has also been thought to defy outright confirmation.

A good many philosophers therefore regard the doctrine of determinism as significant only in an instrumentalist not a realist way. Thus it has been suggested that the doctrine is a maxim governing the conduct of scientific inquiry, that it is a statement of the goals of science or that it is a postulate. It does seem, though, that even if one took the doctrine as merely giving a bit of advice, this would not exhaustively characterise it, since it would seem that if it gives advice it does so by making a claim. Compare the dual nature of 'The treasure is located in the southern half of the island', which might give advice in certain circumstances but only by making an assertion.

Now, I wish to take the doctrine as an empirical one. I do not propose to spend much time defending this construction, but at least two points need to be made. First, it seems clear that taking the doctrine in the way I have suggested is more natural. I do not wish to minimise the problems, but the worries about the falsifiability or verifiability of determinism do not seem to warrant taking this natural interest out of the doctrine. One could, for example, admit that determinism is unfalsifiable but not be thereby committed to its untestability or vacuousness. It might be possible, for instance, to say that it is an empirical claim because empirical claims are all and only those claims which are either verifiable or falsifiable. That the doctrine is not *conclusively* able to be either verified or falsified may, furthermore, not severely disadvantage the doctrine, for it is always possible, but not always reasonable, to ask of other universal empirical generalisations whether they are *really* true.

Secondly, and for my part, much more importantly, I will

take the doctrine as an empirically significant claim because its importance in relation to human action and decisions is tied up with its having such empirical significance. The sort of worry that those concerned with the effect of determinism on human freedom have had in mind, would not come into the picture if the less natural constructions be the only legitimate ones. Since I propose to show that even if determinism is an empirically true doctrine, men may still act and decide freely, taking the doctrine as I have indicated I will, ensures that it is no 'paper tiger' that I am up against. Nevertheless, it will be a subsidiary contention of mine that since worries about human freedom stem for the most part from the belief that the world is determined or may be determined, it is quite another matter whether belief in freedom would be jeopardised should the world prove to be thoroughly indeterministic. It will be my claim that it is perfectly sensible to believe that actions can be free even though undetermined.

III

As I indicated at the start of the chapter it is necessary to give some attention to certain objections levelled at the claim that the world is, or may be, deterministic. This is a convenient point at which to turn to these matters.

There are undoubtedly some philosophers who consider that it is a waste of time and effort considering the putative impact of the truth of determinism on human freedom. They take such a line because they believe for a variety of reasons, that determinism is known to be untrue. I shall consider three such objections — one which stems from the achievements of modern science, the other two from *a priori* arguments against the truth of the doctrine as I have detailed it.

Quantum theory is a very well substantiated scientific theory which accounts for a whole host of physical and chemical phenomena. The laws of quantum theory are statistical, unlike those of the doctrine of determinism which are universal. Thus given a light source emitting photons, an intercepting screen with a slit in it, and a plate beyond the screen, the laws of quantum theory predict only to a certain degree of probability whereabouts on the plate a photon emitted at a given instant will arrive.

The evidence, furthermore, suggests that free subatomic particles such as photons travel along continuous paths in such a way as to make it in principle impossible for observers to measure both the position and the momentum of a particle at the same time, to an accuracy greater than h/4π, where h is Planck's constant. We can measure the position of a particle only at the cost of interfering with its momentum, and measuring its momentum involves altering its position. On the dominant interpretation of this evidence, it is claimed that because we cannot talk with certainty of the simultaneous position and momentum of a particle, we cannot talk of its having a causally determined path.

Now I am not competent to challenge the evidence or the interpretation just given, and, even if I were, it would have to be conceded that within the present conceptual scheme of subatomic physics, the theory presents a serious challenge to a doctrine of determinism extended to the subatomic level. I do not, however, believe that the so-called 'Heisenberg results' show that particles *cannot* be causally determined in their paths. This is not to suggest (as against, say, von Neumann) that deterministic postulates could be added to existing quantum theory without contradiction. My point rather is that what the Heisenberg Principle of Uncertainty entitles one to say is that the view that elementary particles have causally determined paths is not empirically grounded. But, then, not everything that is the case is empirically verifiable.

Furthermore, one does not have to challenge the evidence or the Heisenberg interpretation, to be justified in claiming that it has to be *shown* that even if there is a breakdown in causal explanation at subatomic levels, that this rules out universal determinism at a macroscopic level. Some believe there is evidence that it does.[7] But, going one stage further, it has to be shown that microscopic indeterminacy has any more than marginal influence, if it has any at all, on human decisions and actions. To claim that a microscopic particle 'jump', which is possibly random, guarantees man's freedom is just not on. For human freedom would depend then on the fortuitous concurrence of the right kind of subatomic event (presumably a neurophysiological one) and of the human choice. The only way the quantum jump could be held to be of consequence for human *freedom* would be if the mind or the self could *select* the crucial subatomic event appropriate for its choice. Even leaving aside the dubious strength of talk about 'the self' (to which I will return in Chapters 9 and 10), such a view seems ruled out by the very evidence on which it is supposed to be reliant. But even if I am wrong about all these matters, I can nevertheless contend that it is worth arguing against the most dangerous possible opponent, even if the possible is not actual.

It has recently been argued[8] that if determinism is true, we can have no reasonable assurance that any of our various criteria of truth or warranted assertability are cogent. If there is to be a distinction knowledgeably applicable by us, between justifiable belief and baseless opinion, we must be in a position to assess our judgements independently of 'foreign influences', felt or unfelt. To do this we must act in recognition that our judgements are consonant with criteria that we do not just happen to have, but for which we can offer justification itself free from irrelevant, or not assurably relevant, causal conditions.

It is agreed on all sides, I think, that there is a difference between simply happening to be right about the merits of a position and being able rationally to defend one's belief about being right. Now according to proponents of the argument outlined, if determinism is true it must be self-defeating, for any effort of the latter kind (rational defence) could at best just *happen* to be worthwhile. Each of us thinks what he does and that is all there is to it. Which of us thinks *truly* is a question which is and must remain unanswerable. The argument does not say no one could or even does think truly, but that no one could know he does or confidently believe he does.

Now I think it is clear that to speak of one's beliefs just fortuitously happening to be right if determinism is true, because they are just simply the ones we happen to have been dished up, begs the question against a 'compatibilist' account of determinism and freedom. (Jordan's talk of 'foreign influences' seems to be a bird of the same feather.) The suggestion might well be true, but it needs to be argued for, just as 'hard determinism' might be the proper belief to hold concerning freedom, but needs to be argued for. However, I shall waive this important point.

The first thing I should like to mention is that there is a need to tread warily over the idea of our 'making up our own minds' about the strength of reasons and the force of warrants. I shall not claim that if our minds aren't causally 'made up' they must be randomly and hence not freely 'made up'.[9] What I would claim, though, is that my beliefs are only reasonable in Jordan's sense, if they yield a correct account of the world and, as David Wiggins[10] has pointed out, the world dictates the terms, not me. With perception and memory claims what I truly perceive and remember *must* be the outcome of a causal mechanism from that which is perceived or remembered to the effect, namely, my perceiving or remembering. (It should be acknowledged that on Wiggins' view 'the will' is not so tied and thus unlike these other mental notions.) While things may be less straightforward with 'knowing', as the ongoing debate about causal theories of knowing testifies, it still seems clear that whatever it is we know, must be operative in producing, and, must help account for, our knowledge.[11] One might also add that the working and efficacy of the various causes producing belief or knowledge will not be assessed just in virtue of their role as causes.

Secondly, let us accept Jordan's claim that we must proceed on the presumption that determinism is false. Let it be said, though, that determinism may still possibly be true — I think Jordan would accept this. Now it would seem that one might proceed even on this presumption to build up an overwhelmingly strong inductive case for the truth of determinism. What I have in mind is a situation similar to that of an asymptotic convergence. I would think that at the least this would produce a worry concerning pragmatic inconsistency, and conceivably lead to the abandonment of the presumption that determinism is false.

Thirdly, and finally, what Jordan's argument establishes, if, for the sake of argument, we allow that it is sound, is that we could never know that determinism is true. Leaving aside the immediately preceding worry, this would still not require me to give up the task of looking at the bearing the truth of determinism has on freedom, because for all we know, determinism might be true.

I turn now to the third of the arguments I want to consider. For some time J. R. Lucas has been propounding the view that the falsity of determinism follows from Gödel's theorem, which states that in any consistent system strong enough to produce simple arithmetic, there are formulae that cannot be proved within the system, but which we can see to be true.[1][2]

Lucas argues as follows. Each human being's reasoning, if he can really, as the determinists allege, be completely described in physical terms, may be viewed as a proof sequence in some logistic calculus. The conclusions which, according to the physical determinist, a particular man can produce as true, will, therefore, correspond to the theorems that can be proved in the corresponding logistic calculus.

We now construct a Gödelian formula in this logistic calculus, say L, which cannot itself be proved-in-the-logistic-calculus-L. Accordingly, says Lucas, the particular human being, who is, on the determinist account, represented by the logistic calculus L, cannot produce such a formula as being true. But the particular person *can* see that it is true. Any rational being could follow Gödel's argument and convince himself that the Gödelian formula, although unproveable-in-the-logistic-calculus-L, was nevertheless — in fact for that very reason — true.

It follows, says Lucas, that a human being cannot be described completely in terms of physical variables, all of whose values are completely determined by the conjunction of their values at some earlier time.

One might put the same argument in a slightly different way. According to Lucas, Gödel's theorem demonstrates that attempts to construct a computer which can do everything a man can do must fail, and therefore, any determinist theory which purports to explain in physical terms the intelligent activity of a rational being must be false. Lucas has himself put his contention in this alternative form.

First, while Lucas takes his argument to falsify *determinism* and thus remove what he regards as the only credible reason for disbelief in human freedom, his argument is an attack on *mechanism*. It seems a reasonable request to ask what he considers is the relation between the two theses. I would have thought that he would opt for the mechanist thesis entailing the determinist. The only line I can get on what he would say, though, suggests the contrary, for he has claimed that a machine whose instructions are indefinite would be no longer deterministic but would be mechanistic.[13] It seems to me that this is a strange view for the following reason. While I find the thesis of mechanism obscure, it does not seem legitimate to conflate it with the belief that there are causal laws *of some kind or another* linking earlier and later spatial cross-sections of the space-time manifold in a determinate way. However, I shall waive the point.

A second point concerns Lucas' apparent belief that the soundness of his argument rescues human freedom. Even if his argument goes through, he has to show that the fact that minds are not machines ensures that men are free. Perhaps minds aren't machines and men are free, but some positive argument is surely in order to show that the former fact, if fact it be, entails the latter fact.

But is his argument sound? Hilary Putnam[14] convincingly argued some years ago that Gödel's theorem has none of the implications imputed to it by Lucas (and others). Let T be a Turing machine which 'represents' me in the sense that T can prove just the mathematical statements I can prove. Then the argument is that I can discover a proposition that T cannot prove, and moreover I can prove (or, follow a proof of) this proposition. This allegedly refutes the assumption that T 'represents' me, hence I am not a Turing machine, a physical system.

Putnam correctly claims that the argument fallaciously misapplies Gödel's theorem. For,

given an arbitrary machine T, all I can do is find a proposition U such that I can prove:

(3) If T is consistent, U is true, where U is undecidable by T if T is in fact consistent. However, T can perfectly

well prove (3) too! And the statement U, which T *cannot*
prove (assuming consistency), I cannot prove either (unless
I can prove that T is consistent, which is unlikely if T is
very complicated)! (p. 142)

While I believe this argument 'fixes' Lucas for all present
purposes, I can imagine him saying that *practical* limitations
aren't sufficiently decisive against his logical argument.
Indeed in *The Freedom of the Will* (p. 138) he says that any
system not floored by the Gödel question is *eo ipso* not a
Turing machine within the meaning of the act! Now were
he to respond thus, it could be pointed out in reply that
Putnam is arguing that unless we can prove our own
consistency (assuming this to be a sensible notion), we can't
prove the Gödelian sentence. We could *guess* it, of course,
(after guessing our own consistency), but Lucas hasn't shown
that a machine couldn't guess its own consistency, too, and
so could equally well guess the truth of the empirical
sentences at issue.

But an even stronger objection seems available. It is
uninterestingly true that one Turing machine is capable of
proving *another* machine's Gödel statement (for a human
being could share that ability with the machine whose Gödel
statement is not in question). Presumably, therefore, if Lucas
were right, what distinguishes a man from a machine is the
possibility of the former, but not the latter, proving *his own*
Gödel statement, assuming the 'consistency' of both the man
and the machine. Lucas explicitly affirms that rational men
are 'consistent' in the sense at issue. Now I cannot for the life
of me make sense of what it would be for a human mind to
prove its own Gödel statement. Since Lucas makes this a
logically necessary and sufficient condition of being a
rational human being it would certainly need to be a
coherent suggestion. Let's allow that it is. What seems to
follow is that a man does have a Gödel statement. But once
this is admitted I think it follows that a human being is 'a
concrete instantiation of a formal system'. If this is the case
we seem to have arrived at what Lucas sets out to deny.

IV

In this chapter I have set out the status and content of the doctrine of determinism as it will be used in the book. It is important to bear in mind that I have not shown the doctrine to be true. Rather, I have merely asserted that the doctrine may intelligibly be taken as a true empirical claim of great and, perhaps, universal generality. While I have supported a realist as against an instrumentalist view of the doctrine — chiefly because no interesting consequences arise for freedom on an instrumentalist account — I do not *know* whether the doctrine does truly map the nature of our world.

In the next seven chapters I shall consider certain responses which those concerned with the problem of freedom and determinism have made to the following argument. If human decisions and actions are determined, then for all such decisions and actions, there are antecedently sufficient causal conditions. If there are sufficient conditions for any decision or action, then such decisions and actions are necessitated by those conditions. But, if decisions and actions are necessitated, no one could decide or act differently from the way he does. As we have seen, however, it is required *inter alia* of morally responsible decisions and actions that an agent must be able to act or decide differently from the way he does. Thus it follows from the truth of determinism that men never decide or act freely and cannot, therefore, be regarded as morally responsible beings. Finally, the doctrine of determinism holds true for human decisions and actions.

Quite apart from the fact that this argument, if sound, has important consequences for certain social practices such as punishment, it has immense significance for our conception of man *as* a morally responsible being, and *a fortiori* for our conception of ourselves as persons.

The responses which I shall discuss are widely divergent. I shall begin by considering the suggestion that the truth of determinism is irrelevant to human actions because the language of actions is logically irreducible to the language of antecedently sufficient causal conditions.

In Chapter 6 I turn to another view which I regard as an attempt to avoid, if not evade, the problem of deciding the soundness of the argument set out above. Briefly, on this view questions of whether a person was responsible for this or that action (or decision) are *prior to* questions of freedom. Thus, we don't have to decide whether freedom is compatible with the truth of determinism but just discover whether this, that or the other plea will pass.

I shall reject both of these attempts to avoid consideration of what, I believe, and shall argue, is a substantive problem. From attempts to avoid the problem I shall move to those approaches under which the problem is thought genuine. In Chapters 7, 8, 9 and 10, I will consider what are termed 'incompatibilist' positions. The first of these is 'hard determinism'. Hard determinists believe the argument set out earlier is sound. In the chapter devoted to consideration of hard determinism I shall seek to render the stance of the hard determinist less plausible. In the nature of the case, though, I shall have to leave the discussion very much up in the air at the end of the chapter, because the strongest contention against the hard determinist position is that freedom of decision and action *are* compatible with determinism. My defence of that claim must wait until Chapter 11. Thus my argument against the hard determinist position spans Chapters 7 and 11.

The intervening chapters will be devoted to a consideration of three incompatibilist stances which all agree that the argument previously reproduced is valid. But the argument is thought to be unsound on the ground that men know themselves to act freely and hence know the doctrine of determinism to be false. I shall consider three distinct ways in which this general thesis is defended. First, in Chapter 8, I shall discuss and reject the claim that epistemological considerations about the predictability of human decisions and actions show that they cannot be determined.

Second, in Chapter 9, I shall take up the claims of traditional libertarians (the general term for incompatibilists who believe men are free agents). These 'contra-causal' libertarians shall be defended against certain commonly levelled objections but, nevertheless, it will be argued that the contra-causal libertarian account is not very plausible.

Third, in Chapter 10, a recently revived version of libertarianism — 'agent-causation' libertarianism — will be discussed and found wanting, although I shall suggest that it is a more plausible version of libertarianism.

As with my attack on hard determinism, some of my argument against the libertarian positions noted, comes in Chapter 11 where I shall argue for the compatibility of freedom and determinism.

While I believe determinism and freedom are compatible, it will be a subsidiary aim of mine to show that if our world proves to be non-deterministic at the macroscopic level of human decisions and actions, it would still be reasonable to believe in human freedom. The basis of my claim will be that the standard reason for believing the above claim false, namely that if decisions and actions aren't determined they will be random and unfree, is unsound.

5 'Two-domainism' and Freedom

Consider the following remarks by A. I. Melden who in his
Free Action (London, 1961), argues that there is a

> logical incoherence involved in the supposition that
> actions, desires, intentions, etc., stand in causal relations,
> either in the Humean sense or in any sense in which the
> term 'causal' is employed in the natural sciences...
> determinism, if it employs this sense of cause, is not false
> but radically confused. So it is with indeterminism and
> libertarianism which grant to determinism the intel-
> ligibility of employing the causal model... Given this fatal
> blunder, actions degenerate into mere bodily happenings.
> (p. 201)[1]

It is evident that the underlying claim here (and elsewhere
in the book) is not a version of libertarianism, the doctrine
that, as a matter of contingent fact, deterministic accounts of
action cannot be provided for at least some actions. Rather it
is the stronger claim, which I will label (D) for convenience:

(D) It is conceptually, or, in principle, impossible to
provide deterministic explanations of *action*.

In this chapter I propose to do three things. Firstly, I will
consider some supporting arguments for (D). There is by now
a formidable array of counter arguments against this support.
Some of what I have to say here (Sections II and III below)
has already been said elsewhere. The justifications for
rehearsing these counters along with others in a compre-
hensive way, is that support for (D) is still widespread in the
literature and further that there seems little point in throwing
away ladders. This procedure, if successful, will in itself go a
long way toward restoring confidence in the alternative view

that it is possible to provide deterministic analyses of action. But even if this part of the strategy proved successful it would still remain open that some additional and more successful arguments might be advanced in support of (D). The second part of the strategy will, therefore, involve consideration of some positive arguments in favour of the plausibility of providing deterministic analyses of action. Finally, I will try to show that a successful defence of (D) would not show that the doctrine of determinism can have no bearing on human freedom. That is, that the doctrine of determinism may or may not be false, but certainly isn't radically confused, insofar as it is appropriate to decisions and actions.

In speaking of 'two-domainists' and of their 'opponents' (causal theorists), I do not intend to suggest that there are two monolithic blocks of opinion. Rather there are clear methodological and substantive characteristics common to the bodies of opinion in which I am interested in this chapter. Characteristically, the two-domainists distinguish between persons as physiological organisms and as beings who act (agents). Persons as agents are creatures to whom it is essential that teleological concepts apply and these concepts are not reducible, either logically or empirically, to physicalistic discourse and modes of explanation. The methods of explanation and the concepts employed in these two domains are incompatible. Two-domainists generally proceed by conceptual analysis rather than by appeal to scientific investigations. Their opponents, however, stress the essential identity in method and modes of explanation between the physical sciences and the social.

Before proceeding to consider in detail the crucial differences in approach and opinion between these two groups, I wish to sketch a number of points on which they are agreed. It is generally agreed among parties to the controversy about action that there is an intuitive distinction to be made between cases of genuine action and mere happenings. The availability of such a distinction does not preclude the existence of borderline cases which pose difficulties in classification. The disagreement which remains, concerns the nature of the characteristics possessed by all those things which, on intuitive grounds, unhesitatingly qualify as actions, but which are missing in mere happenings.

There is, furthermore, an additional area of agreement concerning this pre-analytic distinction. Both the two-domainists and their opponents agree in rejecting several attempts at characterising the distinction. Firstly, it is agreed that action cannot be distinguished from mere happenings by equating action with bodily behaviour *simpliciter*[2] or, secondly, with bodily behaviour plus a non-causally related concurrent mental event. In neither case is there a sufficient condition for action. As regards the former, persons undergo twitches and nervous spasms, can have their limbs moved by machines or other persons, can perhaps be said to act by refraining from bodily movement or by omitting to make some movement. An appeal to some such idea as 'negative behaviour' in these latter instances would involve one in the difficulty of explicating that idea as well and might require us to say (absurdly) that people are *always* acting. As regards the second characterisation, it is likewise not the case that the occurrence of the behaviour and the mental event (such as a pro-attitude) is logically sufficient for the performance of the action. A person might have the strongest relevant pro-attitude toward kicking a certain doctor in the shin, and actually do so as a consequence of the doctor's tapping the person's knee during a medical examination. (The kick results from a reflex movement of the patient's foot. Such a reflex movement, even accompanied by the mental state, is not sufficient to characterise action as against a mere happening.)

The third characterisation which 'two-domainists' and their opponents are united in rejecting is the volitional theory. Granted that neither of the characterisations considered above picks out actions, it might be contended that what is essential to the contrast between actions and mere happenings is the *voluntary*[3] nature of action. Advocates of the volitional theory have contended this and claimed that a bit of behaviour is voluntary, if, and only if, it is *caused* by the occurrence of a special sort of event, namely, a *volition*. Thus the defining feature of an action is that it is a voluntary event and what makes an event voluntary is that it is caused by a person's act of will or volition.

I regard the rejection of the volitional theory as an area of agreement in a qualified way. Even though opponents of two-domainism have not been as adamant in their rejection of the volitional theory, they have been loath to accept it, albeit for different reasons. Two-domainists object to it in principle. Causal theorists in general wish to eliminate volitions in favour of wants and beliefs. While I think the following analysis deficient (a point I discuss in Chapter 11, Section III), I am aware that some have been sympathetic to the volitional theory perhaps because they would say that 'A did x (intentionally)' entails 'A tried to do x', where the 'trying' caused the doing of x.

With this qualification in mind I shall now consider a twofold attack which has been waged against the volitional theory. It has, firstly, been attacked on empirical grounds. The contention here is that people sometimes act without any introspectable antecedent deliberation, choice or effort. I am not particularly happy with some arguments offered in support of this contention even though I think the contention itself is very likely well-directed. Thus, when Richard Taylor[4] argues in *Action and Purpose* (Englewood Cliffs, N.J., 1966) that if I experience something then I will be immediately aware of it and if I am not so aware of it that I haven't experienced it, he is unconvincing. It is at least plausible that a person can experience something without being immediately aware, or aware at all, that he is experiencing it. Volitions might be more like unrecognised desires than like pains. The conflicting testimony from introspective evidence certainly ensures that the empirical attack is not of 'knock-down' force.[5]

The second part of the attack consists in Ryle's claim that the volitional theory leads to an infinite regress and a vicious one at that. Suppose that there are volitions which cause bodily and mental behaviour. Then either these volitions are caused or they are not. If they are themselves caused the question arises concerning the cause of the volition's cause and so on *ad infinitum*. If volitions are, however, not themselves caused but are uncaused causes, it seems they are just things that persons make happen. But this won't do for they were introduced in order to avoid saying that in acting we just make something happen. Thus, either the problem has just been shunted back one step (and hence the analysis is inadequate), or a new mystery just as perplexing as the notion of acting has been introduced.

The conclusion of the objection is that if volitions are the causes of (voluntary) actions then either a vicious regress results, or, no advance is made in the analysis of human action.

But there are well-known reasons for rejecting the dilemma by breaking the first horn (the regress). A non-vicious regress can be shown to result from supposing that every volition is caused. What distinguishes action from mere behaviour, if one takes this line, is that the causal chain associated with acting includes a volition, whereas the causal chain associated with mere behaviour does not. In short, even if every event, including volitions, is caused, this is still no reason for claiming that a person would have to do an infinite number of things in acting voluntarily. Provided the causal chain incorporates the volition the behaviour is voluntary action. This is an appropriate place to point out that since wants are not acts, the regress objection does not even get off the ground if volitions are replaced by wants.

I have already noted in passing that a distinction should be drawn between voluntary action (in the sense used by adherents to the volitional theory) and free action. It will become clear that it is free action that needs to be considered in relation to determinism, though voluntariness is a necessary condition of freedom of action. The volitional theory, whether or not it is adequate, should be viewed as an attempt to account for the distinction between (voluntary) action and mere happenings — not as an attempt to give the final word on the problem of freedom and determinism.

We have now exhausted the agreements and can look at the substantial disagreements between two-domainists and causal theorists. Two-domainists contend that what is essential to human action cannot be discovered by revising the volitional theory (or its like), for it is so radically misconceived as to lead one into a philosophical *cul-de-sac*. We 'understand' human action by appeal to the logical connections that such action has with the complex of desires, intentions, reasons, conventions and rules that are inextricably involved in social life. The understanding which deterministic or causal explanation can offer is only relevant to bodily behaviour or movement, not action. The attempt by the volitional theory (or any causal theory) to replace the former by the latter is a conceptual error, doomed to failure in an *a priori* way. The volitional theory relies on the mistaken notion that motives, desires, intentions and so on are interior events, processes or states of the person. The having of intentions (and other *teleological* features) is what differentiates actions. But this is by no means to revive the volitional theory with its talk of present mental causes, because intentions and so on are neither present, nor mental,[6] nor are they the causes of action.

Causal theorists on the other hand deny that the volitional theory must be abandoned as wrong-headed even though they agree that it is itself mistaken.

II

I will now formulate some of the claims made by two-domainists and denied by causal theorists. These claims and their supporting arguments constitute the bulk of the defence of principle (D). Attacks on them are, therefore, attacks on supporting evidence for (D) and in turn on (D) itself.

Charles Taylor[7] has written:

> The element of 'purposiveness' in a given system, the inherent tendency toward a certain end, which is conveyed by saying that the events happen 'for the sake of' the end, cannot be identified as a special entity which directs the behaviour from within, but consists rather in the fact that in beings with a purpose an event's being required for a given end is a sufficient condition of its occurrence.

The sentiment here and elsewhere is that:
I. The form of a teleological explanation of behaviour (one in terms of purposes, or, in the case of human beings, intentions) is not logically reducible to the form of a causal explanation.

At the same location Taylor argues that the distinctively teleological aspect of action comes out in the following. Assume an agent A and assume that B is a piece of his behaviour to be explained. Then if A has the goal G, and the state S of A and the environment E of A is such that G is achieved only if B occurs, then B occurs.

It has been pointed out that this does not seem to be correct if only for the reason that it is not the fact that G occurs only if B occurs which makes A do B, but rather the fact that A believes that G occurs only if B occurs.[8]

Furthermore, what A does is not merely a function of his goals but of which goals he wants to satisfy most in the situation. If we bear that in mind we need to revise the formulation given above and substitute for it something like this: If in environment E and in state S, G is the goal most desired by A and A believes that doing B is the only way to get S, then A does B. But it is immediately obvious that this formulation could be accepted by a 'causal theorist', which indeed is characteristic of those adopted by causal theorists. It might be objected, though, that this revised formulation is not applicable to those systems to which we cannot justifiably ascribe beliefs and pro-attitudes which, nevertheless, appear to be teleological. Even if it were not plausible to suggest that we could reduce *apparently* teleological to non-teleological explanations, that is, to ones making no mention of purposes, the objection could bring little comfort to quite a few of the two-domainists. Some of them claim that teleological concepts apply to non-humans (perhaps excepting the higher animals) only analogically. Peters,[9] S. Hampshire[10] and P. Winch[11] all stress that intentional action is the province of those animals which can express intentions linguistically or which can follow rules. This seems far less plausible than the possibility of reducing the apparently teleological to non-teleological explanations.

Perhaps two-domainists might well concede under such pressure that the revised formulation is compatible with its being the premise of an ordinary causal explanation. This would not require their acceding to the further claim that the substance of the formulation is compatible with its being the premise of an ordinary causal explanation.

III

In line with this last remark it has been claimed that:

II. The intentions and desires which bring about behaviour are not its causal antecedents. They may be *reasons* for actions but not causes.

This particular thesis has been defended by a number of crucial supporting arguments. Indeed the bulk of the two-domainist case rests on the seven arguments which I shall consider in this section. The counter-attack against several of these arguments is formidable and I will draw on that attack to contend that reasons for actions *can be* causes.

Some examples of the opposing positions follow briefly. Melden has written in *Free Action*:

> I have contended not only that the intention cannot function as a Humean cause of the action of raising the arm, on the ground that if it did it could not possibly explain the action in the sense in which actions are explained by intentions, but also that the intention cannot be identified with any of the items that cross the agent's mind during the incident. (p. 93)

Charles Taylor extends the claim when he says in *The Explanation of Behaviour*:

> We could not say that the intention was the causal antecedent of the behaviour. For the two are not contingently connected in the normal way. We are not explaining the behaviour by the 'law', other things being equal, intending X is followed by doing X, for this is part of what we mean by 'intending X', that, in the absence of interfering factors, it is followed by doing X. (p. 33)

On the other hand Donald Davidson[1][2] has argued that the following are both necessary conditions for defining the relation of reasons to the actions they explain:

C_1. R is a primary reason why an agent performed the action A under the description d only if R consists of a pro-attitude of the agent toward actions with a certain property, and a belief of the agent that A, under the description d, has that property.

C_2. A primary reason for an action is its cause.

Before looking at the seven arguments it may be helpful to attend to some *prima facie* evidence about the sort of explanation we are giving when we explain what an agent does by referring to his reasons (pro-attitudes and beliefs). It seems plausible to claim that such explanations are *prima facie* causal explanations. First, idioms which are used elsewhere of causal relationships are often used in speaking of an agent's reason for action.

Second, by altering what a person wants or believes, or by getting him to adopt new wants or beliefs, it is often possible to influence his action and behaviour. Consider the case of a robber who convinces his victim that he should hand over his wallet rather than suffer physical violence. I would claim that such behaviour is voluntary action though it is not free action. A number of writers on causation have suggested that causal relations are often marked out by the fact that some factors can be controlled by manipulating others. William Dray, for instance, claims in *Laws and Explanation in History* (Oxford, 1957) that we cannot consistently say 'x does not cause y though by manipulating x we can control y' (p. 94).

Third, as Gean has pointed out in the paper previously cited, statements of an agent's reasons seem capable of supporting counterfactuals such as 'If he had not known (or believed, or wanted etc.) that x, *ceteris paribus*, he would not have done y'. The ability to support counterfactuals parallels standard causal explanations.

Even though a *prima facie* case can be made out along the lines considered, we cannot regard the relationship between (primary) reasons and the actions they explain as causal, unless it is possible to defeat the arguments now to be scrutinised.

II.1　It is argued that the factors appealed to in the claim that a (primary) reason for an action is its cause, namely beliefs and pro-attitudes, are not *events* and therefore cannot be causes (since they are not of the right logical type).

One preliminary point. There is an ambiguity connected with speaking of believing and wanting. We may be speaking of what is believed or wanted. In this sense there is no question that these are not causes. But we may be speaking of the believing or wanting. Causal theorists are interested in this latter sense. Strictly then, the question is whether in the latter sense we are dealing with the causes of a person's voluntary actions.

Let us first allow that only events may be properly spoken of as causes. Even so the argument is unconvincing. We could with Davidson (in 'Actions, Reasons and Causes') point out that:

> States and dispositions are not events, but the onslaught of a state or disposition is. A desire to hurt your feelings may spring up at the moment you anger me; I may start wanting to eat a melon just when I see one; and beliefs may begin at the moment we notice, perceive, learn or remember something. (p. 694)

That is, we may say that wants and beliefs are not themselves events, but the coming into such a state (coming to have it) is an event and thus a change of antecedent conditions. As Davidson claims, very often (maybe even typically) we are not in possession of knowledge of the event though we are sure there was one. Our ignorance of the event or sequence of events does not make us prepared to conclude that there was no such event.

We could on the other hand take a somewhat different tack while still assuming that only events can be causes. We might urge that the having of wants and beliefs constitutes part of the antecedent causal conditions and thus part of the causally determining set of factors associated with action.

But a second objection could be mounted to this argument by challenging the contention that only events can be causes. We frequently refer to states, standing conditions and even the failure of events to occur, as causes. Why could not the having of intentions, for instance, be considered part of the causal conditions or causal factors? This seems reasonable when it is recognised that the having of an intention consists in having (primary) reasons for action which become the reasons why the action is done just in case it gets done. Describing a person's intentions requires making reference to the desires and beliefs actually effective in him (as causal factors).

The first argument seems unsuccessful.

II.2 It is also argued that explanations in terms of (primary) reasons cannot be causal because there is a *logical* connection between the factors of wants and beliefs and the action to be explained. Since a causal relationship is a *contingent* one, explanations in terms of (primary) reasons cannot be causal.

This is one variant of the so-called 'argument from distinct existences'.

Melden argues in *Free Action*:

If the relation were causal, the wanting to do would be, indeed it must be, describable independently of any reference to the doing. But it is logically essential to the wanting that it is the wanting to do something of the required sort with the thing one has. Hence the relation between the wanting to do and the doing cannot be a causal one. (p. 128)

M. F. Cohen[13] claims,

. . . the motive *and* belief taken together determine in an *a priori* fashion what action can be said to follow from the desire. Hence the connection between the motive explanation and the statement of the action which it explains is not empirical but analytic, and the motive explanation fails to satisfy the contingency principle of empirical causality. (p. 331)

It might be well to point out that this argument does not really depend on a Humean analysis of causation as is often stated but upon a *contingent* analysis of causation.

There are some very serious worries about this argument. Firstly, we may surely characterise a cause in such a way that it is logically and not merely contingently connected with its effect. As Medlin[14] has pointed out there is, for example, a logical link between a child and its parents in that a person could not be a parent unless it had had a child. Yet no one is going to deny that there is a causal relation between parent and child.

Secondly, there is an oddity in the idea that causal relations are empirical rather than logical. Davidson[15] has noted that such a claim surely could not mean that every true causal statement is empirical. For suppose it is true that 'A caused B', it follows then that the cause of B = A and by substitution we have the analytic statement 'the cause of B caused B'. The truth of a causal proposition in other words is dependent on *what* events are described, the analytic or synthetic status of the proposition on *how* the events are described.

Nevertheless, it might well be maintained, as Davidson himself observes, that a reason explains an action only when the descriptions are appropriately fixed, and the appropriate descriptions are not logically independent. Clearly there would be a logical connection between reason and action if we supposed that to say a man wanted to do x *meant* that he would perform any action he believed would achieve x. But this would trivialise the ability of (primary) reasons to explain actions. There is no logical *or* factual difficulty in supposing that a person might, for example, want to eat, know that his wife has put the food he sees on the table there for him to eat and yet not eat. Nor will it do to say that for one to want to do something *means* that he will at least try to do it unless he wants to do something else more. As a definition of 'wanting' such a proposal would be circular. Wanting requires at most a dispositional analysis involving the idea of the thing wanted. (And 'central state materialists' have contended that such an analysis will depend in turn on talk of *states*.)

Even if one admitted a logical connection between the *concepts* of, say, wanting and doing, one could justifiably contend that the possibility of causal explanations of actions requires only that the *events* in question are contingently connected. If it is objected that wantings are not events and

so cannot be causes of actions we have just come full circle
back to argument I.

Even though the 'argument from distinct existences' seems
to me to fail there is perhaps a modicum of truth contained
within it. Many philosophers have thought that it must be
possible truly to characterise the cause in such a way that,
under that description, it is only contingently connected with
its effect.[16] But, even if this is so, it by no means serves to
establish II.2.

> II.3   A closely related argument is the following. A
> statement of what the agent wants and believes does
> not explain by telling us *how he comes to act* as he
> does, but instead it explains by enabling us more
> fully to characterise the act; it tells us *what kind of
> act* is done. But if this is so we do not have two
> logically separate factors (the cause and the effect)
> but only one under two different descriptions.

Thus, in *Free Action*, Melden asserts:

> In any simple causal explanation of one event by reference
> to another, it is not the identity or the character of the
> effect that is at issue, but the conditions in which it
> occurs — how it came to be . . . . As the alleged cause of
> the action, it cannot serve further to characterise the
> action. As motive it must — for it tells us what in fact the
> person was doing. (p. 88)

I shall allow for the sake of argument that there is a type
of explanation which consists in saying what (kind of) act the
agent is performing. Melden's own example of a driver who
signals by raising his arm, illustrates this type of explanation.
In answer to the question 'Why did he put his arm out like
that?' we might reply, 'To signal a turn'. His raising his arm
is, in the circumstances, signalling. It is clear that this sort of
explanation is not causal explanation. But, even so, several
objections can be levelled at this argument.[17]

Firstly, Melden's example is so well-chosen as to hide the
fact that there are probably only a few special cases which fit

the pattern outlined. There seem to be other cases in which
stating one's reasons does *not* enable anyone to say more
fully what kind of action one's action is (e.g. picking up my
umbrella as I go out in order to avoid getting wet because I
believe it will rain). Secondly, even if we settle the question
about what sort of action an agent has performed we have
not thereby ruled out questions about why an agent has done
such a thing. We can, for instance, ask why an agent signalled
his turn. Just saying that his act was an act of signalling tells
us nothing about *why* he signalled. Thirdly, saying that a man
is signalling a turn by means of extending his arm, probably
depends on the possibility of explanation by reasons. If he
did not want to signal or did not know (believe) that
extending one's arm was the means of signalling, it is
plausible to doubt that he signals at all.

Hence, if explanation in terms of primary reasons is not
reducible to mere specification of the kind of act being
performed, then no ground has been offered for claiming the
presence of a logical (and non-causal) relation between 'he
raised his arm' and 'he wanted to . . . and believed. . .'

II.4 It has been charged that explanations in terms of
      (primary) reasons cannot be causal since they fail to
      imply generalisations to the effect that in relevantly
      similar circumstances, the same result will occur.
      That is, the covering-law analysis of explanation
      adopted in the physical sciences is said to be
      inappropriate in the social sciences.

Hart and Honoré allege in *Causation in the Law* (Oxford,
1959) that:

The statement that one person did something because, for
example, another threatened him, carries no implication or
covert assertion that if the circumstances were repeated
the same action would follow. (p. 52)

Covering-law theorists assert that a satisfactory explanation meets the formal condition that the explanandum is
logically deducible from the explanans, where the explanans

incorporates a general law and a statement of initial conditions and from these initial conditions the explanandum follows invariably (or usually) in accordance with the law. I have included the weaker sense here because some covering-law theorists allow non-deductive probability relations between explanans and explanandum.

Again, Davidson has pointed out that ignorance of the sort of laws required by covering-law theorists does not in fact inhibit valid causal explanation. Provided we know directly which factor(s) caused an event, we have adequate evidence for the existence of a causal law covering the case. He goes on to point out that we are usually far more certain of a singular causal connection than we are of any causal law governing the case. Consider:

(a) 'A caused B' entails some particular law involving the predicates used in the descriptions 'A' and 'B'

(b) 'A caused B' entails that there exists a causal law instantiated by some true descriptions of A and B.

Each of these formulations sustains causal explanations in terms of laws. But only the second, (b), fits most causal explanations and it fits explanations in terms of a man's (primary) reason equally well.

Perhaps an example will help clarify the point I want to make. I drop a vase from a tall building and assert that dropping it caused it to break. In so asserting I imply that given similar circumstances, the same result would occur. But if I were to drop an exactly similar vase under relevantly similar circumstances and it failed to break, what then? Assuming causal statements *do* imply generalisations I could only say that there was some difference in the two cases. Why couldn't this much be true of explanations of human behaviour? Why couldn't it be the case that if the relevant psychological and physiological facts are not duplicated for an agent, then *ceteris paribus* that accounts for a difference in his behaviour? Especially since human beings are much more idiosyncratic things than vases.

II.5 It is argued that the kind of knowledge one has of one's own reasons in acting is incompatible with the existence of a causal relation between reasons and action. The privileged position one has in knowing one's intentions does not come by induction or observation and these are the ways in which one comes to know about causal relations. Furthermore (and this ties in with argument II.4. above) because of the agent's conclusive knowledge of his own reasons, the way in which we support or refute reason-explanations shows that they do not imply generalisations. The only relevant generalisations are ones constructed out of instances in which we recognise that the agent was acting for a reason and this was known independently of such generalisations.

Four things can be said in reply. Firstly, even though an agent's testimony is normally conclusive, it is also possible for his testimony to be mistaken without this leading to doubt about his sincerity or memory. A person may be deceived about his own motives. The fact that a person may be deceived does not show that first person reports are not normally 'conclusive', but it does show that we cannot analyse reason-explanations or the generalisations which may be used to support them, in terms of first-person reports.

Secondly, even if it be granted:

(a)   That the agent's testimony is conclusive in the required sense,

and

(b)   that the only relevant generalisations are ones constructed out of instances in which we recognise that the agent was acting for a reason and this was known independently of such generalisations,

this still would not show that explanations in terms of reasons cannot be causal. Davidson[18], for instance, points out that it may only show that in the case of knowled[ge of] one's reasons, we know that a causal relation exist[s on the] basis of one instance. In such cases we can be sa[id] that generalisations to the effect that in rele[vant] circumstances the same result will occur, are tr[ue] of one instance.

Thirdly, there appear to be cases of straightforward causation in which one person is in a better position to know the cause of something's happening than is anyone else, and in which his honest testimony is as conclusive as that of the agent in giving his reasons for action. Some writers have appealed to cases which are inconclusive because they involve the idea of 'mental causation'. A better illustration might be found where, say, a student says 'Dropping that chemical into the liquid made it explode' when he didn't know the nature of the interacting chemicals but simply observed the two things come into contact and immediately explode.

Fourthly, there are cases in which we cannot ever rely upon the agent's statement of his reasons at all, namely when we are concerned with higher animals not able to use language to tell us what wants and beliefs moved them to act as they did. One would need to argue for the existence of some differentiating factor between higher animals and humans to prevent this conclusion's being extended to human action. Some 'two-domainists' are not loath to do this, though!

II.6   In support of thesis II, it is argued that the logic of the causal relation is different from that of the reason-action relation. The causal relation is transitive, but the latter is either intransitive or non-transitive.

This argument seems to be quite widespread but has not been criticised by causal theorists to my knowledge. I will cite only one example and refer to several others. Alan White in *The Philosophy of Action* (Oxford, 1968) writes:

. . . if my curiosity to see what would happen can be said to have caused me to press a button and pressing a button used the death of some people in a room, then my sity might be said to have caused their death; but curiosity to see what happened was my reason for the button, it was not my reason for killing the 17)[19]

However, this argument trades on a misconception. Those who use it seem to have been misled into thinking that there is an entailment relation between the (primary) reason being the *cause* of the action under any description of the action and its being a *reason* for the action under any description. Clearly, however, opponents of the two-domainists need not claim there is an entailment. On the contrary they claim that something is a (primary) reason for a certain act only under a particular description of the action. A description, namely, relating pro-attitude and belief in such a way as to constitute a sufficient condition of the action's occurrence. Thus, in a case such as that of White's, the agent had no reason for the action of killing the people.[20]

II.7   Finally, it is claimed that reason-giving explanations have a special function. They justify an action or show its appropriateness in the circumstances. Teleological explanations, in other words, reveal the rationality of what an agent does or intends to do. Thus discourse about reasons belongs to the language of evaluation not to the objective, value-free description of natural events. Hence, reasons cannot be causes.

But even if the premise, that the special function of reasons is to provide a rationale for action, is true, it certainly does not follow that reasons cannot be causes. Although being a cause may not be sufficient for something to be a reason, its being a cause does not preclude it from being a reason either. Thus if it is the case that

(1)   x has a (primary) reason for doing some action;
(2)   x does that action *because* of the reason,

the question comes back again to the force of the 'because'. This argument does not seem to me to be able to rule out the possibility that only the causal relation renders the 'because' intelligible.

I conclude, therefore, that none of the seven arguments I have considered, has the force credited to it by two-domainists and hence that neither individually nor collectively do they establish a logical inconsistency or obscurity in the view that teleological explanations of action are causal explanations. We have seen to date that neither the form, nor the substance, of teleological explanations preclude their being causal explanations. Perhaps this seems a relatively weak point at which to arrive. Not so, however, for two-domainists seek to deny the *possibility* I have to date defended. Whether that possibility is actualised does not enter into consideration of the truth of principle (D).

IV

Now even though the major part of the attack on (D) and defence of the possibility of a deterministic account of action has been rehearsed, there are yet a couple more claims with which I must deal.

Not only have two-domainists argued that action is to be explained non-causally; they have sometimes claimed action is exempt from causal categories altogether. Thus

III. Action (intentional behaviour) cannot be given a causal explanation at all because no supposed explanation of an action can be correct which is incompatible with the claim that it was brought about by an intention.

Charles Taylor writes in *The Explanation of Behaviour*:

If a given piece of behaviour is rightly classified as an action, then we cannot account for it by some causal antecedent, where the law linking antecedent (E) to behaviour (B) is not itself conditional on some law or rule governing the intention or purpose. For if the law linking E to B were not dependent on some law linking E and the intention, I, to do B, then E—B would hold whether or not E—I held. But then B would occur on E whether the corresponding intention was present or not. And then, even when it is present, it cannot be said to bring about the behaviour so long as this is done by E. Thus to account for B in terms of E would be to offer a rival account, to disqualify B as an action. (pp. 34—5)

On Taylor's view, if B is an action, the most that can be hoped for in the way of a causal explanation is a linkage E—I—B where E is a cause of I. But since I, by II above, cannot be a cause of B (only a reason), then though B is explained by I it is not causally explained. Hence actions cannot be causally explained.

We have already seen that II has not been established, so this thesis, which is dependent on the truth of thesis II, is in bother. Furthermore, there is to my mind, very grave doubt about the sense of the claim that I non-causally *brings about* B. If I could understand what that might mean I concede that there may well be no incompatibility or contradiction in the claim that E causally brings about I (and hence B) while I non-causally brings B about, too. I confess that I do not, however, understand.

This argument is allied with

IV. Actions are not reducible to bodily movements *simpliciter*, from which one can infer that actions are not the same as bodily movements *simpliciter*.

It has been held that two-domainists are guilty of a contradiction in claiming that actions cannot be caused but that movements can, since they acknowledge that movements are sometimes identical with actions.[21] At least one other writer has attempted to absolve two-domainists of this charge.[22] I will endeavour to show that there is a contradiction; that even if there were no real contradiction there would still be other problems; finally, that if two-domainists care to adopt a different way of speaking they can avoid the contradiction. I will try to show these three things in turn.

Melden writes in *Free Action*:

... although the bodily happening needs to be distinguished from the action of raising the arm, the former, in *appropriate circumstances*, is the very same event as the latter. (p. 74, my italics)

When Melden here speaks of 'appropriate circumstances' I think he is referring to the social institutions and practices that, according to him, determine what action any given movement is.[23] These 'rules' are quite independent of the causes of the movement (which are, say, brain states for argument's sake).

I think all can agree that it is perfectly possible for a bodily movement which brings about a certain result to be the very same thing as an action which is directed to that result. What Melden seems to be claiming though is that the same movements might constitute distinct actions (depending on context, rules being followed and so on).

But this won't help avoid the contradiction. For if there is any degree of seriousness in talk about *identity* then what goes for x goes for y if x and y are really identical. Thus if causal talk goes for bodily movements it does so for actions. Furthermore, it seems pretty likely that it will also be apposite for institutions and practices.

Before attempting to indicate a way out of the above contradiction, it should be pointed out that if, in fact, two-domainists are not guilty of a genuine contradiction in the claim under consideration, some of them may be guilty of vicious circularity. I suspect that for at least some of the two-domainists, an action is performed only if a rule is followed. But the notion of rule-following must surely be understood in terms of action. To obey a rule is to *act* in a prescribed way. Any explication of action in terms of 'rule-following behaviour' would thus be viciously circular. Furthermore it may well be false that actions can only be performed if rules are followed. Not only can one act deliberately contrary to established practices, traditions and rules, but it seems plausible to say that one can act in new, innovating ways which are not rule-governed.[24]

To return to the putative contradiction. It seems to me that if two-domainists were to drop talk of identity in favour of some such notion as 'constituting', the point about the role of institutions in relation to *some* actions could be retained without succumbing to a contradiction. The bodily movement could be the outcome of antecedently sufficient causal factors but be constitutive of an action only under a certain (different) description which referred to the institutions, rules and so on.

V

I want briefly to make one point in this section. Whatever way two-domainists jump on the foregoing matter it seems that they must face the spectre of determinism. Consider a bodily movement, BM. Either there are antecedently suffici-ent (causal) conditions for the occurrence of BM or there are not. If there are, then given the causal conditions BM occurs. Suppose now that BM occurs under such circum-stances that it is an action. If it is the case that the presence of antecedently sufficient conditions necessitates a particular movement in such a way that the movement cannot occur freely, saying that that movement occurs under certain rules, customs, practices and so on cannot affect the *necessity* of the outcome. Appeal to these rules and so on *may* avoid contradiction but it cannot, as far as I can see, allow one to sidestep the issue of the compatibility of freedom and determinism. These rules can only classify or categorise action, if they can do anything at all. Adherence to argument IV (filled in as sympathetically as above) is a natural fruit of the rest of the two-domainist case. It appears, however, to undermine it!

VI

I have argued against various theses which are supposed to ground principle (D), that is, the principle that:

It is conceptually or, in principle, impossible to provide deterministic explanations of *action*.

Not one of these theses (or their supporting arguments) appears to have come off unscathed. I have concentrated on arguments rather than on the methodology which leads to these arguments. In fact, even though I have conceded a good deal for the sake of argument, this methodological founda-tion may well be even more shaky than some of the arguments.[25] However, for my purposes, the arguments themselves are sufficiently shaky to allow me justifiably to conclude that recent work in the philosophy of action, rather than showing the problem of freedom and determinism is a pseudo-problem, strengthens the claim that since voluntary action is best understood as occurring when the causal chain associated with behaviour includes the (primary) reason, voluntary action is a necessary condition of free action. And if the most plausible understanding of voluntary action emerges from considering such action as the outcome of certain causal antecedents rather than of others, this augurs well for the compatibilist position regarding freedom and determinism. However, it only 'augurs well', that is, it is in line with, but by no means establishes that position. The scheme is obviously equally acceptable to the 'hard determinists', whose position is considered in Chapters 7 and 11.

My main concern at the moment though is to stress that a satisfactory philosophy of action is very much groundwork in relation to the problem of freedom and determinism. That problem still remains despite the attempt by two-domainists to evade it. Perhaps, though, the problem can still be evaded. In the next chapter I shall look at a more promising attempt to sidestep the problem.

6 'Aristotle's View' and Freedom

A position sometimes adopted in discussions of freedom is one dubbed and, I believe, espoused by J. L. Austin — he referred to it as 'Aristotle's view'.[1] Briefly this is the position that questions of whether a person is responsible for this or that action are prior to questions of freedom. Thus, to discover whether someone acted freely or responsibly — these two predicates are not always clearly distinguished — we must discover whether this, that or the other plea will pass. These pleas are usually considered under the legal heads of duress, provocation, accident, mistake and insanity. Because this position appeals to the notion of defeasibility[2] it is sometimes referred to in connection with that term.

I propose to argue that this position, which has sometimes constituted an attempt to evade the problem of freedom and determinism, is untenable. I should point out that I will be assimilating Austin's not altogether clear position to the defeasibility position. I do recognise that Austin's discussion is far more conservative than, say, Hart's in that he does not concern himself with Hart's notion of ascriptive discourse, according to which the language of action is primarily used only when ascribing responsibility to a certain person's behaviour, nor with Hart's central contention that the concept of an action is both ascriptive and defeasible. (In his Preface to *Punishment and Responsibility* (Oxford, 1968) Hart himself subsequently disowned these main contentions of his earlier paper.) But it is responsibility rather than the nature of action-talk and defeasibility rather than ascriptivism with which I am here concerned, and, to that extent, the assimilation of the two positions seems justified.

I

In 'A Plea for Excuses' Austin observes that there are many situations in which a person accused of doing an action A protests the accuracy or fairness of saying that he did A on the grounds that he is to be excused, since what happened was inadvertent, accidental, done by mistake, or somesuch. Should the person really have an excuse, then it will either no longer be possible simply to say that he did it (because he did not do anything, or, did some other action), or it will be misleading simply to say that he did it.

Later in the same paper, Austin claims that the study of excuses will throw light on the problem of freedom. He urges that there is

> . . . little doubt that to say we acted freely (in the philosopher's use. . .) is only to say that we acted not-unfreely. (p. 6)

Further, he claims that:

> . . . in examining all the ways in which each action may not be free i.e. all cases in which it will not do to say simply 'X did A', we may hope to dispose of the problem of freedom. (p. 6)

He has usually been understood as suggesting here that there is a conceptual link between the concept of freedom and particular excuses such that the only way to explicate the concept of freedom is negatively by reference to the absence of the particular excuses. Even so, he seems to have been unsure about what he wished to claim for he goes on to ask whether it is not responsibility rather than freedom which is to be cleared up by studying and enumerating the particular excuses. His answer evinces his uncertainty:

> . . . But in fact 'responsibility' too seems not really apt in all cases: I do not evade responsibility when I plead clumsiness or tactlessness, nor, often, when I plead that I did it unwillingly or reluctantly, and still less if in the circumstances I plead that I had no choice. . . . It may be then, that at least two key terms, Freedom and Responsibility, are needed: the relation between them is not clear, and it may be hoped that the investigation of excuses will contribute towards its clarification. (p. 7)

It does seem that Austin was unsure to which, if either, of the following two alternatives he was committed.[3]

(F) That the concept of freedom can be explained negatively by reference to the absence of particular excuses, so that 'He did A freely' means (roughly anyway) 'His A'ing was not accidental, not a mistake, not done under duress and so on.'

(R) That the concept of responsibility can be explained negatively by reference to the absence of particular excuses, so that 'He is responsible for doing A' means (roughly anyway) 'His A'ing was not accidental, not a mistake and so on.'

Bronaugh, Nowell-Smith, (and perhaps Austin) *seem* to come down in support of (F) rather than (R). Nevertheless the confusion to which I alluded previously makes me chary of being confident that it is (F) rather than (R) that they really wish to defend. Hart's position was even more uncertain. It does seem that he would have supported both (F) and (R) for he wanted to claim both that the concept of human action, and that of responsibility, is defeasible. The two claims being linked to each other because sentences of the form 'X did A' are used to ascribe responsibility. I will contend that neither (F) nor (R) is defensible, and hence that the problem of freedom and determinism cannot be side-stepped by giving support to either (F) or (R).

II

A free action, on the defeasibility or Aristotelian view, is one in which none of the excuses, for example, accident, mistake or insanity is present. But when we examine our system of excuses we find that not all accidents excuse, not all mistakes excuse. For instance we do not excuse a father who, intending to shoot an apple from the top of his son's head, misses and instead shoots his son. That the shooting was accidental does not excuse the father, for the act was reckless. The problem arises then of how we are to distinguish those cases of mistakes, accidents and insanity, say, that do excuse from those that do not.

One way in which defeasibility theorists who wish to defend (F) might try to solve this problem is by saying that where the law allows that a certain instance of accident, mistake, insanity and so on, excuses, such instances are excusable. Thus 'freedom', on such an account, would not be the absence of all accidents, mistakes and so on, but would nevertheless be analysable defeasibly as the absence of legal accidents, legal mistakes, legal insanity and so on discoverable in the relevant statutes and common law judgements.

A couple of points need to be made in relation to this reply.[4] First off, as a description of the legal situation as we have it, this just seems false. The issue of locating the burden of proof seems to be a matter of legal policy alone and one can conceive of acceptable legal systems in which the burdens of proof (as we now know them) were switched. So nothing fundamental seems to be at stake and that rather takes the gloss off the counter being considered.

Secondly, and far more importantly, the problem about excuses is not just the problem about what excuses *are* permitted, which isn't always a straightforward matter, but also of what excuses *ought* to be permitted. What the legal system enshrines, no matter how clearly it is spelled out, surely cannot be the last word. We do (and ought to) criticise particular legal systems from time to time. Now, if notions such as 'he could not have acted otherwise' are, as defeasibility theorists contend, just a summary of the particular excuses that the legal system does permit, these mere summaries couldn't be used to criticise the particular permitted excuses. We are left with an insoluble problem if we accept that these terms are only a summary of the excuses allowed by the system, yet insist, as we do, on using these terms to help us pick out the system and then, in turn, to criticise and reform it.

The defeasibility theorist, may, however, not wish to resolve the problem of excuses by pointing to what the legal system permits. He might say that it would be possible to give a defeasibility analysis of 'he could have helped it', for example, by reference to the absence of excuses that *ought* to be allowed. That is, 'can' or 'free' would be analysed in terms of the absence of those accidents and mistakes that ought to be excused, of those cases of insanity that ought to be excused and so on.

Now one should not forget that, according to the defeasibility theory, terms such as 'free' cannot be defined by means of necessary and sufficient conditions. It follows from this claim that 'unfree' cannot be so defined either. This is significant, because if freedom is alleged to involve the absence of excuses that *ought* to be allowed (as against those that are, in fact, allowed) such a rationale provides a *general* criterion of excuses. Yet clearly if you have a general rationale of excuses, then you have a general criterion for distinguishing those actions that ought to be excused from those that ought not and this seems inconsistent with the defeasibility theory.

Even so, perhaps the defeasibility theorists may say that although we may adopt a general *criterion* for distinguishing actions that ought to be free from those that ought not, the meaning of 'free' is still defeasible. What the criterion of 'free' is, will depend on our moral standards. On the other hand the meaning will be absence of accidents that ought to be excused, of mistakes that ought to be excused and so on.

Let us allow for the moment that drawing this distinction avoids the embarrassing inconsistency[5] and, furthermore, furnishes an explanation of the criticism and evaluation of our legal system of excuses. At that rate though 'freedom' and 'unfreedom' would still only be summary-terms, they will provide a summary of the excuses that *ought* to be allowed and this summary could then be used to evaluate the summary of excuses that our system *presently* allows.

The problems with this attractive way out are twofold. Firstly, we can justifiably ask why the meaning of 'free', for instance, is to be understood in the way sketched. I know no reason for accepting the claim that the meaning of the term 'free' is 'absence of accidents, mistakes (and so on) that ought to be excused'. The onus seems to rest squarely on the defeasibility theorist, and (to my knowledge) has not been taken up.

Secondly, and more significantly, under the defeasibility theory, the system of excuses is arrived at independently of terms like 'can'.[6] Yet in our present practice (the chosen battlefield for defeasibility theorists), 'can' helps us decide which cases of accidents, mistakes, duress, insanity and so on *ought* to be excused. But, on the defeasibility analysis, we must *first* find out which accidents, mistakes, or what have you, ought to excuse, for this in turn determines whether or not such accidents, mistakes and so on could be avoided.

Despite the evident attraction of this way out for defeasibility theorists, the two preceding objections seem to me decisively to preclude its use.

I have been considering the defeasibility theory as the claim that 'free' means 'not E_1, not E_2, not E_3', where E_1, E_2, E_3 are names of different specified excuses (forming an enumerable set). I have alluded to but not pressed home an important worry about this construction of the defeasibility theory. If there is an enumerable set of excuses that excuse, presumably there is something in virtue of which they (and not other candidates) do excuse, and which can be used to explain the meaning of 'free'. But if this is so, it should be possible to explain the meaning of 'free' by reference to the absence of that feature common to E_1, E_2 E_3. It is difficult to see how the possibility of an account of 'free' as 'not E_1, not E_2, not E_3' can rule out the possibility of an account in terms of the absence of the common factor in E_1, E_2, E_3. Yet, unless it can be shown that the latter sort of account is impossible if the former is possible, then it cannot be maintained that the only way to explain the meaning of 'free' is by reference to an enumerable set of excuses.

Thus, the drawing of a distinction between the meaning and the criterion of 'free' as a way out of the inconsistency involved in admitting a general rationale of excuses on the defeasibility theory, fails.

III

Perhaps, though, I have been too stringent in construing (F) as requiring an enumerable set of excuses. Maybe one should take the claim made by (F) to involve the different proposal that 'free' means 'not accidental, not a mistake, not inadvertent. . . and not excusable in any other way'. That is, 'free' means 'not-excusable' in the event of an action's being performed.

Now this construction of (F) runs up against the fact that not all excuses excuse completely and thus that one can have an excuse for one's action but still be said to have done it freely, and of the fact that not all excuses excuse by establishing that an action was not free. These seem to me to be fatal obstacles.[7]

Firstly, sometimes an excuse excuses only to a limited extent as occurs when there is a plea in mitigation. In such cases it is often plausible to see the excuse not as a denial that there was a performance of a free act. Hart[8] has maintained that such pleas in mitigation are not properly classed as excuses, on the ground that excuses must exclude conviction and punishment *completely*. This just seems to be a stipulative definition. The sort of considerations which in practice are used to differentiate complete excuses from factors which merely mitigate the gravity of an offence do not, however, seem to be different in kind but only in degree. There seems every reason, therefore, to resist the stipulation made by Hart.

Secondly, not all excuses excuse by establishing that an action was not free. To defend oneself against an accusation by pleading that one was under duress is to defend oneself very differently from the way in which one defends oneself by pleading that one's act was done by mistake. In the latter case there is an implicit denial of intentionality but not of freedom.

It seems then that (F) is a false thesis on either of the two constructions I have considered.

IV

It is time now to consider the second thesis, (R), which is perhaps a more plausible suggestion, for it is reasonable to suppose that the kinds of excuses which preclude responsibility are very various, and, that just as excuses sometimes excuse completely and sometimes only partially, so sometimes we do hold people either completely or partially responsible.

In 'The Ascription of Responsibility and Rights', Hart claimed that certain legal concepts like 'trespass' and 'contract' cannot be defined by specifying the necessary and sufficient conditions for their correct application. These concepts, like those of human action and of responsibility, he alleged were defeasible in that while positive conditions for their application may be satisfied on a given occasion, they may still not have application on that occasion if one of a number of defences succeeds. According to Hart, the only satisfactory way to explain defeasible concepts is by reference to the defences, which if successful, deny the application of these defeasible concepts.

Certainly whether or not someone has a defence is relevant most times to whether he is responsible. However, the real question is whether it follows from this that 'responsibility' can be defined defeasibly and cannot be defined positively in general terms. One preliminary issue needs to be broached at this point. What is the sense of 'responsibility' at issue here?

First, there are cases in which a person is held to be *legally* responsible for some act even though he had a defence which would normally enable him to evade responsibility. If this is correct then there is some doubt whether a defeasibility analysis of even legal responsibility can be given, let alone of moral responsibility.[9] In cases in which liability is strict, the normal defences are inadmissible. It is, therefore, difficult to see how a defeasible definition of legal responsibility is possible in such cases, since the presence or absence of a defence does not make the difference between being and not being legally responsible. The only way out here for the defeasibility theorist is to argue that the existence of strict liability offences results in people being punished for things for which, *according to usual legal criteria*, they are not responsible. This, at the very least, reduces the force of the objection.[10] At the same time, however, it confines the defeasibility thesis in such a way as to minimise its significance in connection with the problem of freedom and determinism.

Second, if the crucial concept of responsibility were definable defeasibly then it should follow that if something is a defence on one occasion it is a defence on all occasions. For, if there were a defence, D, which excused on some occasions but not on others, then it would not follow from the fact that a person had such a defence that he was not responsible for what he did. Yet earlier in this chapter I have argued that certain defences excuse only on occasions. Thus, for example, the defence of mistake (and perhaps of duress) varies in its success, and one of the important considerations in assessing its success is how much care the agent could have been expected to take in order to avoid such a mistake.

Thirdly, as Holdcroft points out, if the concept of responsibility were only definable defeasibly, all we could say in response to the question 'Why is the fact that A has defence D a reason for not holding him responsible for what he did?' would be 'Because that's how the concept of responsibility is defined'. This seems to be an unsatisfactory answer, though, for if it is not possible to give a general characterisation of the notion of a defence then disputes about defences and responsibility would not be resolvable even in principle. On the other hand, if as the foregoing comments suggest, the notion of a defence can be, and should be, characterised in a general way, why not the concept of responsibility? Furthermore, even if it were allowed that both defeasible and general definitions could be furnished there seems no obvious reason for claiming that the latter is parasitic on or logically secondary to the former.

V

In this final section I want to look closely at an articulate account of the underlying thinking of defeasibility theorists which leads them to believe they can dispose of the problem of freedom. I do not claim that the views to be considered in this section would find complete support among defeasibility theorists. I do think, however, that these views capture the spirit and mood of this attempt to avoid the problem of freedom and determinism.

Defeasibility theorists minimise the role of 'can'. Indeed Bronaugh says that 'he could not help it' is not a reason for excusing people, because we first decide to excuse and then say that such people as we excuse could not help doing what they did. Similarly, we first decide to punish certain people and then add that such people could have helped what they did.[11] Hence we cannot give as our reason for excusing people, the fact that they could not help what they are doing — rather we first decide whether to excuse and *then* if we decide to excuse, say that they could not have helped it. The following argument has been used to support such a view:

> Considering any factual condition which is frequently deemed to excuse, it can be meaningfully asserted of an agent in the condition that he had a choice *and* that he did not have a choice. Since both, it will be found could be meaningfully said, the decision as to whether one asserts 'there was a choice' or denies it can be shown to be a decision about what one is morally ready to excuse in the light of the conditions. If this is true, then it is impossible to decide whether there was a choice until it is known whether an excuse exists.[12]

Now it is true that at least sometimes when we are able to say 'he could not have acted otherwise', we could also say 'he could have acted otherwise'. Take the case of duress — A threatens to kill B unless he commits treason. Here, since he could have chosen to die instead, there seems to be a sense in which he could have helped it and a sense in which he could not. In discussing 'two-domainism' I asserted my preference for talking of such actions as voluntary but unfree.

The same sort of approach could be taken with many cases of provocation, accident, mistake, insanity and so on. Whether we can help accidents and mistakes that could have been prevented, varies with how much care could be expected of us (or how much more care where the care we took was incapable of preventing the accident or mistake).

But is Bronaugh right in thinking that it is *always* the case that we could have helped what we did? He considers the following counter-example. A person is suddenly, without his knowledge, injected with a drug which makes him violent. Before it wears off he runs wild injuring several people. The question arises as to whether this is a case where the agent just could *not* have helped doing what he did. Assume that it is a case in which it is implausible to say he both could and could not help it. Why, then, cannot we excuse this person on the grounds that he could not help what he was doing? Bronaugh's answer to this question is that this is not a genuine case of an excusing condition because the person was not *doing* anything. He was not acting, the injuries were produced by the drug not by him, hence no question of excuses comes up.

The argument here seems to be something like the following. Whenever there is an act there must be a choice, therefore we must always be able to help what we *do*. Thus, even where it is possible to say 'he could not have helped it' this cannot be the reason for excusing a person. On the contrary, we first decide whether to excuse him, and then, accordingly, say he could have helped it, or he could not.

There are a number of points which I wish to make in this connection.[13] First of all, even if we allow for the sake of argument that actions must involve choice, it is still reasonable to ask why talk of excuses is relevant only to actions and not to bodily movements. Where a driver allows himself to fall asleep at the wheel we might *as well* say that he was culpable for his bodily movements. Likewise, with omissions, where there has been neither an action nor a bodily movement, we sometimes acknowledge that we could have helped them and sometimes that we could not. Perhaps Bronaugh would say that omissions are acts, though. If not, he seems quite wrong in arguing that talk of excuses is relevant only when we are acting. Further, he seems to be incorrect in saying that in cases like the drugging one, talk of 'he could have helped it' is irrelevant. One reason why it is relevant is that the person could not help the harm he caused.

Secondly, even if an action always involves choice, it does not follow that the agent who has done the act and violated the law could have conformed to the law. 'He could have acted otherwise' does not entail 'He could have conformed to the law'. Surely no one would so interpret 'action' that unless you could conform to the law, you have not acted when you break it!

Thirdly, even if Bronaugh were right in believing that whenever talk of excuses is relevant, the agent could have helped violating the law, it would still be relevant to find out whether the agent could have conformed to the law easily, or with difficulty. Responsibility is often a matter of degree, as I have already indicated in Chapter 2.

Fourthly, and more importantly, in our current system, 'he could have helped it' plays a role far beyond that allowed by Bronaugh and like-minded writers, because in their system if certain people ought not to be excused then it follows in a strict way that these people could have avoided what they did. As things stand, 'can' is one of the determinants of our system of excuses, while the 'can' in Bronaugh's view, for instance, is wholly derivative from the system of excuses. This shows how wide of the mark is the claim that the system defended by defeasibility theorists is the same as our system.

Fifthly, and most importantly, the sort of philosophy of action embodied in the thinking lying at the base of the defeasibility theory is indefensible. I have argued at length in the preceding chapter for a causal analysis which I consider is a more defensible position, and rest my case on its strength.

I suggest, therefore, that the attempt by those defeasibility theorists who believe their claims enable one to sidestep the problem of freedom and determinism, is a failure. It fails because the thesis itself, whether construed as one about freedom or as one about responsibility, is demonstrably false and, furthermore, it fails because the sort of thinking underlying it fails to furnish a satisfactory account of our system of excuses or of our concept of action.

Investigation of the two attempts to skirt around the problem of freedom and determinism hasn't revealed any ground for believing that aim is achievable. I turn, therefore, to the first of the accounts which seeks a direct confrontation with the problem as stated earlier in the essay.

7 'Hard Determinism' and Freedom

According to advocates of the position known as 'hard determinism', moral responsibility presupposes that we categorically could have decided or acted otherwise, but since our decisions are caused (or in an alternative version, are the products of hereditary and environmental factors), it follows that we are not free in this sense. Certain moral consequences are said to flow from this view, for example, that we are never justified in *morally* blaming anyone, though we may be justified in making use of non-moral blame. Alternatively, it is said to imply that we are never justified in maintaining that anyone *deserves* or *merits* blame, though blame (moral or non-moral) may be *justified* by its utilitarian effects. (I have already made some reference to these matters in Chapter 2.)

In this regard, the attitude of the hard determinist is very like that of the fatalist, for each considers whatever happens is unavoidable. Nevertheless, the parallel attitudes are arrived at from different considerations. The hard determinist maintains that moral responsibility is incompatible with the fact that our actions and decisions are parts of causal sequences (ancestorially caused). Many philosophers claim that the difference between hard determinism and fatalism is that the former does not claim that events will occur independently of their causes, whereas the latter does. This, however, is a mistaken view of fatalism. The philosophically formidable versions of fatalism (such as I considered earlier) do not claim that all things will turn out as they will no matter what a man does, nor do they deny causal efficacy to human actions (or, for that matter, to any sort of events). The two doctrines must be otherwise distinguished. I think this is best done in the light of the considerations adduced in support. Fatalism is alleged to be supported by considerations of a formal or logical kind alone. These considerations are such that it is hard to imagine any intelligible world not

91

being characterised by them. The hard determinist position, on the other hand, is supported allegedly by empirical considerations coupled with a proper understanding of 'freedom' and of 'moral responsibility'. In this case the empirical considerations *need* not even be thought of as requisite for rendering intelligible our world (as against other possible ones). They might well, of course, be thought to do just that, especially if the doctrine of determinism is taken as a near-relative of the principle of sufficient reason. The one doctrine may be true, therefore, even though the other is false.

In this chapter I shall attempt to cast doubt on the thesis of hard determinism. I will begin by considering the views of its two most important recent advocates. I will offer some critical comments on each of them. Then I will proceed to consider the claim in a more general way. My main thrust against hard determinism comes, however, in Chapter 11 where I argue that human freedom *is* compatible with the truth of determinism.

I

Let us begin by considering the view that if we take 'moral responsibility' in its *proper* sense then the doctrine of determinism implies that we are not morally responsible. Such a position has been defended by Paul Edwards.[1] He does not deny that determinism is compatible with freedom of action, if we mean that free actions are those that may be influenced through the use of blame. He does not even deny that we may sometimes use the expression 'moral responsibility' in such a way that it requires freedom in this sense only. However, he maintains this is an improper sense. The question then is why determinism excludes 'moral responsibility' in the proper sense.

According to Edwards, in order that we should be justified in holding someone morally responsible, he must have had it in his power to act otherwise. To have had such power, he must have *chosen his own character*. But the doctrine of determinism implies that a person's character is formed by hereditary and environmental factors not of that person's own making or choosing (p. 123).[2]

Now even if hereditary and environmental factors are the antecedently sufficient causal conditions for a person's character, it does not directly follow that a person lacks the power to do otherwise. This cannot be just assumed on pain of begging the question against the view that determinism is compatible with possession of such a power. The assumption stands in need of further argument. This is not to say that there cannot be such arguments, only that Edwards does not offer any. Secondly, even if it made sense to demand of every free, responsible agent that he chose his own character (which, in light of the fact that it would seem to presuppose one already be what one is to become, seems quite unrealistic), *and* one conceded that the truth of determinism made the demand impossible of fulfilment, it still would not follow directly that a person would be less powerless (more powerful) had he chosen his own character. This last point arises from consideration of the fact that power to choose one's character would be utterly irrelevant in a situation in which one just lacked the required power to do some act that would be the right thing to do in the given situation. Thirdly, even allowing that no one can choose his own character, it does not follow that one is responsible for what he does or that no one is in any significant sense free, *unless* it be true that one would only be responsible or free if one chose one's own character. There are grounds for resisting such a suggestion which I will go over in Section II below.

Edward's attempt to show that we have not chosen our own character (and hence can never be held morally responsible) is beside the point. What he needs (and what he has not given) is an argument for the claim that moral responsibility is annihilated or reduced just in the cases in which decisions or actions are part of causal sequences.

II

Whereas Edwards tried to reach his conclusions by arguing from the putative consequences of the doctrine of determinism, other philosophers[3] have tried to reach similar conclusions from premises referring to psychological factors. Indeed, Hospers specifically disavows determinism on the ground that it is non-disconfirmable. Even so, he does on occasion appeal to deterministic considerations, for he remarks that we excuse persons from responsibility on production of a deterministic account of the development of their character traits.[4] Furthermore, for Hospers, the ability to overcome early environment — for example, by the exertion of effort — is also determined by other aspects of the early environment, or, just purely fortuitous! This applies equally to the 'neurotic' and the 'normal'.

Hospers distinguishes between what he calls an 'upper' and a 'deeper' level of moral discourse. If we conduct our discussion on the upper level, we are *justified* in considering people free insofar as they would have acted otherwise if they had wanted to, and in making use of moral blame insofar as this helps to make them do what they ought to do. But to talk about *deserving* moral blame requires shifting to the other level of discourse. For we would deserve blame for our wrongdoings only if we had been 'responsible for the character out of which those actions spring' (p. 120). But we are not responsible in this sense, for our characters are formed by hereditary and environmental factors.

Most of the points made against Edwards apply also to Hospers. There are some additional criticisms which can be directed at Hospers. Firstly, like many hard determinists, he makes spectacular generalisations from the actions of neurotic and generally less than fully competent persons to the actions of (more) normal and (more) fully competent ones. I shall return to this in Section III, and in Chapter 11, but the move seems to stand in need of some supporting arguments that might justify it. His only constructive suggestion in this direction is that the differences are not marks of greater freedom but simply of luck.

Secondly, allowing with Hospers for the moment that some people are 'lucky' enough not to be neurotic and also to be capable of 'making the effort',[5] it follows that no matter how they came by such a power that they possess it. It would seem reasonable to say that having such power makes them free agents (who can thus rightfully bear and receive moral deserts of blame and praise). That being so, not being lucky enough to have the power would serve as an abnormal or excusing condition. In addition to contrasting

the neurotic and the (lucky) normal, Hospers distinguishes
lucky and unlucky neurotics, the former of whom can be
cured. They can be cured because they are fortunate enough
to be able to 'exert the effort' and 'try to be cured'.
Presumably such persons *are* responsible for their being or
not being morally responsible (supposing this latter to be the
result of the therapy voluntarily undergone).

Now, the arguments about neurotics presuppose that it
makes sense to talk about responsibility for character as well
as for conduct, in that one could choose his own character.
But in the final section of his paper, Hospers claims that it is
meaningless to talk of responsibility for one's own character.
It has been pointed out against Hospers, that if moral
responsibility is a vacuous concept, so, too, is moral
innocence and hence one cannot plead (as Hospers does) for
the moral innocents on pain of inconsistency.[6] There is,
furthermore, a pragmatic inconsistency in holding that others
are unjustified in blaming the innocent (as Hospers and
Edwards claim) when one blames people for blaming the
innocent. On the hard determinist account offered by them,
no one is to be blamed for anything, including holding views
opposed to that of hard determinism.

Furthermore, if the sort of arguments offered by Hospers
depend, as they seem to do, on empirical considerations, the
most that they could prove would be that it is probable that
we aren't free in the required sense.[7] In that case if it is an
empirical premise that we have not caused or chosen our
character, or that it is caused by early childhood experiences,
it can only function in a sound argument if an empirical
relation could be established between some childhood experiences and an adult's lack of power to do otherwise.
Hospers does not really do more than make some sweeping
claims about such putative relations. In the next section their
plausibility will be considered.

III

I mentioned previously that Hospers and other hard determinists make spectacular generalisations from the actions of
neurotic and generally less than fully competent persons to
the actions of normal and fully competent ones. The issue

must now be taken up again and related to the question of the putative empirical relations between the causes of people's characters and the actions such people engage in.

Hard determinists have acknowledged the oddity of speaking as though childhood influences *cause* (or even partially cause) adult actions. Thus it is more usual to find them saying that early conditioning causes character, and adult actions 'flow from' or 'grow out of' such character.

Just what could this vague expression 'grows out of' (or such others used elsewhere as 'expresses', 'flows from') mean? Hospers (p. 130) seems to suggest that it is not intended as a pseudonym for 'causes' — but rather as a way of expressing the unavoidability he attributes to the actions of neurotics who are also unlucky. From this one must suppose that the hard determinist is claiming that if the person did not have the character he does have, he would not act as he does act and, further, that since he is not responsible for his character, he does not deserve to be blamed for any of his actions.

But this seems to beg the question. For suppose that Fred would not have bashed Jill if he did not have a brutal nature. Saying that Fred has a brutal nature or character seems to require a *dispositional* cashing-out in such a way as to support the claim that Fred (often, more often than not, frequently) acts brutally. Hence to say that he is not responsible for his brutal nature can only mean that he is not responsible for his brutal acts (including bashing Jill) and thus begs the question. I hasten to add, though, if one ignores Hospers' disavowal of any commitment to determinism, that this charge loses much of its force if, as 'central state materialists' claim, dispositions are really causal states. On such an account it is much easier to draw a line between 'acts' and 'natures'.

There is a further point about these causes of neurotic behaviour which are said to be beyond the agent's control. It is that one should distinguish carefully between specific neurotic acts and general patterns of neurotic behaviour. As Harvey Mullane[5] has suggested it is only the *general* pattern of behaviour which can legitimately be taken as caused by unconscious processes over which the agent has no control.

Specific acts no doubt reflect the person's neuroticism, but it seems more than unrealistic to claim that one can demonstrate that they are a necessary effect of his psychological disturbance. The most that seems justifiably open to anyone to claim is that the neurotic's act was less 'free' than that of his non-neurotic counterparts. But talk of such degrees of freedom can only be congenial to the compatibilist or libertarian, not the hard determinist.

I want to move on now to some other general criticisms. There are three such criticisms I wish to investigate. But, as will emerge, none is decisive as against hard determinism.

It seems that the thesis of hard determinism purports to be a special case of the general principle that if some untoward event E occurs in consequence of some other event (state of affairs etc.) C, and a given person is not responsible for C, then he is not responsible for E. The general principle seems unexceptionable. The point of appealing to it is to show that some particular case is to be distinguished from other cases in which people are held responsible for the consequences of their actions. Hard determinism borrows its plausibility from this distinguishing principle but it is then proclaimed that the principle is pointless because the distinction it is used to draw does not exist. In similar vein the hard determinist urges that we abandon the distinction between human action (with its attendant notion of responsibility) and mere happenings. What has seemed to some to emerge from such considerations is that hard determinism does have great force when viewed as pointing to the fact that *some prima facie* actions are mere happenings and that *some* cases we might not exempt under the general principle mentioned previously should be exempt. But when taken as the claim that not merely some but *all* such situations need to be reviewed, it may very well be self-stultifying.[9] Nevertheless I reluctantly concede that a hard determinist could reply that what I have called a general principle of responsibility is just that, but is known to be so on *a priori* grounds. Hard determinists could thus claim that it is an *a priori* axiom, but add that it has, in fact, never been satisfied. The objection seems likely to produce only an impasse about whether it *has* been.

It has been contended that worries arise for the notion of

personal identity under the hard determinist thesis.[10] If it is not possible to hold people responsible for their actions (so to speak), on the ground that they did not choose or make the circumstances and so on which moulded their characters, it might be questioned where one is to locate the helpless victim upon whom such a character has been 'foisted'. I do not think one should repose much confidence in this attack on hard determinism, largely because one cannot be confident that a hard determinist *needs* to say people are anything more than bundles of traits.[11]

The third and final worry alluded to above may well be thought to show more about my dogmatic belief in freedom than about anything else. Later on, in Chapter 11, when I try to take the matter further I will endeavour to furnish greater support for the position taken here. For the present I want to draw attention to the fact that neither Freud, nor any of the hard determinists who have appealed to his work, has shown that we must obliterate the distinction between our *wanting* to do some act and our *craving* to do it where our craving is such that it must be satisfied no matter what the force of the reasons for and against doing the act. It seems clear to me that we are not always in this craving position, and that making the distinction between wanting and craving shows that it is a radical and doubtful thesis to accept that we are *ever and always* non-agents and non-deciders who are pulled about by circumstances beyond our control. This seems to reinforce a claim which has already been broached, namely the difficulty in construing hard determinism as an 'across-the-board' thesis, rather than as just an important reminder to be taken into account *on occasion* in considering the presence of extenuating circumstances.

Thus I contend that it has not been established that we are never free to act (because of ancestral causes or factors of heredity and environment) and, therefore, that it has not been established that we are never justified in imputing moral blame, nor that some agents on some occasions do not deserve such blame. Nevertheless, without arguments to show that all causes cannot just be assimilated in the manner of the hard determinist, I acknowledge the incompleteness of my argument as it stands. Before attempting to remedy that, I want, however, to consider arguments which seek to establish that human beings can be *known* to be free and hence, that determinism must be false. As the preceding remark indicates, proponents of these arguments agree that determinism is incompatible with freedom. They disagree with the hard determinist contention that human freedom must be an illusion. It will become evident that I have more sympathy with these 'libertarians' in their belief in human freedom. Nevertheless, I shall argue that libertarian positions have not to date been very convincingly defended. At the same time I shall contend that the libertarian position might well be shown to be true (if the world happens to be indeterministic at the level of human decisions and actions).

8 Epistemic Indeterminism and Freedom

It has become a popular move to attach the freedom of an agent to epistemic uncertainty about what he will do. Some adherents of this move are unhappy with the traditional doctrine of ontological indeterminism, at least in relation to macro-level physical events, because it entails an unacceptable and mysterious gap in causality. Nevertheless, they believe that special difficulties of a purely conceptual sort arise in the realm of action which are unparalleled in the realm of physical phenomena. These difficulties are supposed to give rise to an indirect argument against the claim that actions are determined. It must be emphasised that in attacking the argument, I am offering no proof of the claim that actions *are* determined. As I argued in Chapter 5, the basic features of human action are quite compatible with the contention that actions are determined. In this chapter my concern is still with the tenability not the truth of the thesis that actions are determined, but the considerations I discuss are quite distinct from those looked at in Chapter 5.

The indirect argument with which I am concerned takes the following form:

If actions are determined, then it is in principle possible to predict them with certainty.
It is not in principle possible for actions to be predicted with certainty.
Therefore, actions are not determined.

In this chapter I will be more concerned with the truth of the second premise, though I believe that both premises are false. For the sake of argument I will sometimes take the first as true even though I have already argued against its truth when I criticised the contention of certain writers who not only assume that determinism entails predictability but even

100

define the doctrine as the thesis that every event is predictable in principle.

In general, supporters of the argument under review back their second premise by contrasting the predictability of human behaviour with that of physical events. I shall claim that the second premise as it functions in the argument is false, on the ground that there are no essential differences between actions and physical events with respect to the problem of prediction.

I

It will have been noticed that the argument outlined above leaves inexplicit the sense of 'possibility of prediction'. It will be helpful briefly to characterise four species of 'possibility', which are relevant to the notion of 'possibility of prediction', before moving on to consider the argument for epistemic indeterminism.[1] The four species are 'logical possibility', 'logical compossibility', 'physical possibility' and 'causal compossibility'.

An event is logically possible if, and only if, any proposition expressing it is not self-contradictory, and logically impossible if, and only if, such a proposition is self-contradictory. Thus my broad-jumping twenty feet at time t is a logically possible event, but my drawing a rectangular circle at t is not.

A set of two or more events is logically compossible if, and only if, the conjunction of any set of propositions which express all the members of the set is logically consistent. A set is logically incompossible (not logically compossible) if, and only if, each of the events is logically possible but the conjunction of some set of propositions expressing all the members of the set is logically inconsistent. For example, x's being a man from 11 a.m. to 12 noon is logically incompossible with x's turning into a man at 12 noon.

An event is physically possible, if, and only if, no proposition expressing it is inconsistent with any proposition expressing a law of nature and physically impossible if, and only if, any proposition expressing it is inconsistent with some proposition or propositions expressing laws of nature. For example, even if a tachyon can travel faster than the speed of light, a man's travelling faster than the speed of light is physically impossible. Some events are physically impossible for certain kinds of entities though not for others. 'Bodily lifting "The White House" ' is an event such that it is physically impossible for beings with the physical constitution of humans.

For any set of events, each of which is logically possible and physically possible, and which jointly constitute a logically compossible set, the set is a causally compossible one if, and only if, there are no propositions expressing laws of nature such that the conjunction of these propositions with propositions expressing the events which go to make up the set, is logically inconsistent. Each member of the set is causally compossible with, or relative to, the other members. A set of events is causally incompossible if, and only if, there are some laws of nature such that the conjunction of propositions expressing those laws with propositions expressing the member events is logically inconsistent. Thus, if the negation of a given member of a set is causally necessitated by the other members of the set, then the set is causally incompossible. It should be noted that the question of the causal compossibility of predictions of action cannot arise unless the other three species of possibility are satisified.

II

Suppose that we take the case of an invention such as that of the corkscrew.[2] Cranston argues that in the intended sense of 'prediction' no one could have thought of the corkscrew prior to its inventor doing so and hence no one could have predicted the invention of the corkscrew. In order to make the prediction, one would have to think of the corkscrew before the inventor and *ex hypothesi* one could not. This is a case of putative logical incompossibility for it amounts to the claim that the three events: the inventor's thinking of the corkscrew at time t, no one else's ever thinking of the corkscrew prior to t, and someone predicting the inventor's inventing the corkscrew, are logically incompossible. Now it might be urged that some of these constitute states of affairs, or, perhaps, negations of events rather than events. This is likely true but for the sake of argument it is not necessary to press the point, for the claim being made is sufficiently clear for my purposes.

I propose to argue the following two claims against this putative example of logical incompossibility. Firstly, that the example fails to establish any special status for human behaviour, and secondly, that it fails to show that the human phenomena involved are undetermined.[3]

The example fails to establish a special status for human behaviour, and secondly, that it fails to show that the human be produced for physical phenomena. Consider the following analogous case. Given the construction previously placed on 'logical incompossibility', the event of a hailstone storm damaging an orchard *by surprise* is logically incompossible with the event's being predicted. It is logically incompossible for hailstorms damaging orchards by surprise to be predicted, because were anyone to predict these events then *ex hypothesi* they could no longer be described as 'hailstorms damaging orchards by surprise'.

Secondly, and more importantly, the example of the invention of the corkscrew fails to show that the human phenomena involved are undetermined. Let us lead into this claim by considering the hailstorm case again for a moment. The hailstorm case, which has the same logical structure, does not bear on the determinism issue. Although it is logically incompossible for anyone to predict the event which is the hailstorm's damaging the orchard by surprise, this in no way inclines the meteorologist to suppose that this event is undetermined. Similarly, the logical incompossibilities fail to show that inventions are undetermined because they do not demonstrate that these events are not governed by laws of nature for the notion of a law of nature is in no way involved in the concept of logical incompossibility. Thus these logical incompossibilities do not demonstrate the absence of laws and antecedent conditions capable of determining inventions.

The critical error in Cranston's claim is the assumption that if an event is determined under a given description, then it must be possible to predict it under *that* description. Suppose that the inventor's (I's) thinking of the corkscrew at t is deducible from laws and antecedent conditions. Suppose further that the fact that no one ever thinks of the corkscrew before t is also deducible from laws and antecedent conditions. Then the event consisting in I's *inventing* the corkscrew at t would be determined, but it still would be logically incompossible for it to have been predicted under that description. What this shows is not that inventions are undetermined actions, but that the alleged entailment between determinism and predictability is not an entailment. At any rate, the fact that an event is determined under a given description does not entail that it is *logically compossible* for it to be predicted under that description. It is also an error, as Goldman points out, to think that determinism entails the possibility of retrodicting or explaining every event under any description. Suppose that L thinks of the corkscrew at t and that no one ever thinks of the corkscrew after t. Suppose, moreover, that both of these events are deducible from laws and antecedent conditions. Call 'thinking of x for the last time', 'postventing x'. Clearly we may say of L that he postvented the corkscrew and that this action of his is determined. However, it is logically incompossible for anyone to *retrodict* L's postventing the corkscrew for to do so he would himself have to think of the corkscrew and, *ex hypothesi*, L thought of it for the *last* time at t.

III

I want now to consider an influential attempt to pose a problem for predicting not actions but decisions.[4] Ginet argues that decisions cannot be caused because:

(a) It is conceptually impossible for a person to know what a decision of his is going to be before he makes it;

and

(b) If it were conceptually possible for a decision to be caused, then it would be conceptually possible for a person to know what a decision of his was going to be before making it.

In support of (b) he cites two conditions which are jointly sufficient for knowing a decision before making it (under the assumption that the decision is caused). First, that the decider knows, before his decision, the causal law whose consequent describes his action. Second, that the decider knows, before his decision, the existence of all the factors described by the antecedent of the causal law.

Piecing together Ginet's argument, the following outline emerges and captures his strategy. He contends that:

(1) In making a decision one comes to know what one is going to (try to) do.
Thus (a) one cannot know before (or while) making a decision what the decision will be.

(2) Causal laws and causally relevant facts are in principle knowable by anyone at any time.
Thus (b) if agent A is caused to make a decision at time t, it is in principle possible for anyone, including A, to know at t or at any time before t that A will so decide at t.

(3) Therefore, decisions cannot be caused.

(4) Therefore, 'if there are decisions, they are (necessarily) not part of the causal order. . .'.

There is a great deal wrong with this argument. Nevertheless, my procedure will be to grant as much as possible to Ginet and then show that the argument still does not establish its conclusions. Having done that, I will then point out that the concessions granted to Ginet need not, in fact, be made. Let us begin then by conceding Ginet (1) and (a) from above.

Suppose now that Harry, at t, decides to take a wife. Had Harry predicted that he would make this decision — and had this prediction involved *knowledge* — he could not have decided later to do the act in question, namely, take a wife. For if, before t, he had known that he would decide to do it, he would have known then that he would take a wife, or try to take a wife. But if, before t, he had known that he would take a wife (or try to take a wife), then he could not, at t, have *passed into* a state of knowing that he would take a wife. On Ginet's account, Harry could not have predicted that he would make this decision.

Several of Ginet's critics[5] have pointed out that it is possible that Harry might make his prediction, forget it and fail to remember or relearn it in the interval between making his prediction and making his decision. In order to avoid this difficulty we must say that Harry not only knows, before t, that he will decide to take a wife, but also *continues* to know this up until t and hence cannot at t, decide to take a wife. The following three events then are logically incompossible — Harry's deciding at t, to take a wife; Harry's predicting (i.e. knowing) that he will decide to take a wife; and Harry's continuing to know this until t. I have thus conceded (1) and (a) from the outline of Ginet's argument set out above. What of (2), (b), (3) and (4)? That is, does the admission of the preceding logical incompossibility establish that decisions are undetermined?

I see no reason for denying the possibility that a person's passing into a state of knowing, or intending, to do a certain act is deducible from laws and antecedent conditions. But although this event would be determined (under the given description) it would not be logically compossible for that person to have both predicted it (under that description), and continued to know it, until t. Hence a decision-type incompossibility does not show that the phenomenon of making decisions is undetermined.

I want briefly to return to the concessions made above to Ginet's argument. He claimed (and I conceded for the sake of argument) that in making a decision one comes to know what one is going to (try to) do. This claim is false in at least some relevant cases.[6] Considering those acts one does upon or because of a decision, Ginet maintains that the only possible way to know what they will be is to know what the decision is or will be. He further maintains that the only way to know this is to have already made the decision.

Against these claims I would suggest first that it seems obvious that others can sometimes know what someone else will (try to) do before he makes the appropriate decision. But if they can know this, then it seems that he can know it, too, just in those cases where he is told! A lawyer might well tell a client that he knows the client will carry out the terms of a will prior to the client even being cognisant of its contents. It seems feasible to say that this is sufficient to warrant a claim by the client that he himself knows that he will (decide to) fulfil the conditions of the will *before* he decides to do so. It

might be objected that when the client decides to fulfil the
conditions of the will, the description under which he makes
the decision is not that under which he knew he would
decide. It does not seem to me that this need be so but I will
not delay to debate the point,[7] rather I will furnish several
more examples as counters to Ginet's claims.

Secondly, knowing what one will do, or even why one will
so act, does not require, or provide a substitute for, a
decision. The will must still be moved or move. A person
tempted to do something that he knows he should not do can
know that even though he will fight the temptation, he will
finally give in and decide to do it. The struggle precedes the
decision, but it comes or continues after the knowledge.[8]

Thirdly, one could know that one will end up doing
something in virtue of one's inductive knowledge and yet not
have the slightest intention at the time of deciding to do it.
Suppose that a terrorist is, against his will, being 're-educated'
and suppose further that he knows that, owing to the
methods employed, all who are re-educated subsequently
decide never to take terrorist action again. Why couldn't such
a person justifiably claim to know on such inductive evidence
about others, that he will, subsequently to being re-educated
decide never to act as a terrorist again, even though being as
yet unreformed, he does not have the slightest intention of
making such a decision?

This example shows that we can have inductive knowledge
of our own future actions, knowledge which is not based on
having already made a decision or formed an intention to
perform the future action. Stuart Hampshire,[9] by contrast,
has recently claimed:

> I cannot intelligibly justify a claim to certain knowledge of
> what I shall voluntarily do on a specific occasion by an
> inductive argument; if I do really know what I shall do,
> voluntarily and entirely of my own free will, on a specific
> occasion, I must know this in virtue of a firm intention to
> act in a certain way.

But I think the terrorist example shows this contention of his
is false, provided that the re-education process doesn't
destroy the subject's freedom.

The three counter-examples I have offered seem also to falsify item (1) in Ginet's original argument. But falsifying (1) leaves (a) without support. Furthermore, I have already pointed out that Ginet's own formulations of (1) and (a) need strengthening in order to overcome the objection that someone might make a prediction, forget it and fail to remember or relearn it in the interval between making the prediction and making the decision. If we do not afford Ginet this help, he must revise both (a) and the subsequent items in his argument. It would take us too far afield to hound him in this way, but the revisions which seem open to him fail to pull the argument through[10] and certainly cannot show that human actions are undetermined.

IV

Is it *physically possible* to make scientific predictions of human actions? I propose to consider this question only briefly since it is the notion of causal compossibility (to which it leads) that is more significant for my purposes.

It might be argued that it is physically impossible for human beings (or any finite entities operating within the causal order of the universe) to make scientific predictions of actions, because human beings cannot learn enough about antecedent conditions to deduce what will be done. We need not restrict our discussion in the way Popper[11] does to predictions made by classical mechanical calculating machines. Even if there are limitations on the predictive capacities of such machines it doesn't follow that the same limitations arise for other beings capable of making predictions. Nor need we think (as he does) in terms of the physical impossibility of a *single being* making scientific predictions of *all* events. For it is perfectly compatible with establishing such an impossibility that every event can still be predicted by some being or other.

Even so the argument needs toughening up a bit to make it more formidable. Scientific predictions, it might be claimed, require knowledge of *infinitely* many facts, but it is physically impossible for a finite being(s) to know infinitely many facts. The infinity requirement has been added in here (once again following Goldman) because it seems that in order to *deduce* that even a specified finite system will yield a given result, one must know that no interference from outside the system occurs, and knowing this *may* involve knowing *all* states of the world at any one time. (Even this demand may not be the same as one for knowledge of infinitely many facts, but I shall not enter into a dispute over the point.)

Nevertheless, the argument is of questionable force. Firstly, it isn't clear that the deduction of actions from antecedent conditions and laws, requires knowledge of infinitely many facts. Secondly, even if the argument goes through, it seems to prove *too much*. For if the knowledge of infinitely many facts is required in order to make scientific predictions of actions, the same would be true for scientific predictions of physical events. The argument, in other words, fails to establish any special immunity from prediction for human action. Finally, even if it is physically impossible for any finite being to make scientific predictions of actions this would still not prove that actions are undetermined. It is always crucial, it seems to me, to keep ontic and epistemic considerations separate as far as is possible in discussing human freedom.

It should not be thought that it has been shown it is physically possible for some beings scientifically to predict actions, or that it is not. There may well be sound arguments to one or other of these conclusions. However, since the question of the causal compossibility of predicting actions has loomed larger than that of the physical possibility of doing so, and since the former depends on the latter possibility, I will proceed as if it is physically possible to predict actions.

V

I have contended that determinism does not entail that it is physically possible to make scientific predictions of events, including free human actions. Hence, neither does determinism entail that there are causally compossible worlds in which scientific predictions of actions occur. However, since we are assuming that scientific predictions are physically possible, it would be an important negative result if it could be shown that one cannot construct causally compossible worlds in which scientific predictions are made of free actions. This would not prove that free actions are undetermined, but it would suggest a disparity between actions and physical phenomena. For, assuming that scientific predictions are physically possible, it does seem that there could be causally compossible worlds in which scientific predictions are made of physical events.

Much the same can be said of the issue of constructing causally compossible worlds in which scientific predictions are made of free actions *and* in which the agent learns beforehand of the prediction. Determinism does not entail that there must be such causally compossible worlds. But were no such worlds able to be constructed, one might well claim a disparity between free actions and physical phenomena.

Consider then the following possible objections. Firstly, it might be said that the difference between physical phenomena and actions is that predictions of actions can defeat themselves; but predictions of physical events cannot.

In order to show why this objection fails and also to set the scene for some later considerations let us first consider the problem confronting an election predictor. Assume that he knows what the precise results of an imminent election are going to be provided he makes no public prediction of the result. Because if he publishes a prediction, some of the voters, having found out what the results will be, may change their votes and thereby falsify his prediction. How, then, can a pollster make a genuinely scientific and accurate prediction of an election? Can he take into account the effect his prediction will produce? It seems that he can, as long as he knows the propensity of the voters to *change* their voting intention in accordance with their expectations of the outcome.

Let us suppose that our pollster has ascertained that, two days before the election, sixty per cent of the electorate plans to vote for candidate A and forty per cent for B. He also knows that, unless he publishes his prediction, the percentages will be the same on election day. Suppose further that he knows that there is a certain 'band-waggon' effect obtaining in the voting community — that is, the effect when persons are more likely to vote for a candidate when they expect him to win.[12] That this band-waggon effect holds in the community could be discovered either by studying previous election phenomena or perhaps by deducing it from 'higher-level' generalisations found to be true of the community.

What emerges from the pollster example is that all the antecedent conditions relevant to the outcome cannot be known until it is known what prediction (if any) the pollster will make. His prediction (or failure of prediction) is itself an important antecedent condition. However, one of the crucial determinants of the outcome — the original voting intention of the electorate — is given independently of the pollster's prediction. Thus, while holding that factor constant, the pollster calculates what the outcome of the election *would be, if* he were to make certain predictions.

If someone wishes to predict a single person's behaviour and yet allow him to learn of the prediction, the predictor must employ the same sort of strategy as the pollster. He must take into account what the agent's reaction will be to the prediction. There are several kinds of circumstance in which, having made the appropriate calculations, he will be able to make a correct prediction. These are where:

(i)   the agent learns of the prediction but does not want to falsify it;

(ii) upon hearing the prediction, the agent decides to falsify it. But later, when the time of the action approaches, he acquires overriding reasons for doing after all what was predicted;

(iii) having decided to refute the prediction, the agent performs the action conforming with it because he doesn't realise that he is conforming with it;

(iv) at the time of the action the agent lacks either the ability or the opportunity to do anything but conform with the prediction though he may have believed that he would be able to falsify it.

In any of these four kinds of circumstances, the predictor would be able to calculate that his prediction, together with numerous other antecedent conditions, would causally suffice for the agent's performance of the predicted action. In the first three types of circumstance the agent performs the predicted action *freely*. The possibility of a scientific prediction does not require that the agent be unable to act in a manner different from that predicted. All that is required is that the agent will not *in fact* act in a certain way (i.e. contrary to the prediction).

Now let us return to the objection that the difference between physical phenomena and action is that predictions of actions can defeat themselves; but predictions of physical events cannot. This seems false for one can construct cases in which the causal effect of a putative prediction of a physical event falsifies that prediction. Take the following possible case. Mary boasts that a certain flower arrangement of hers will withstand disarrangement throughout the remainder of the evening. She bases her claim on scientific calculations she has made regarding the direction and velocity of wind currents in the room at the time and on their maximum effects, on estimates of the character of her guests and so on. However, in her agitation to get one up on the other women present, she makes her boast in a high-pitched voice. She strikes a note sufficient to shatter the vase containing her arrangement. This neglected factor suffices to disturb the arrangement and thus falsifies her boastful prediction! This first objection fails.

But it might be urged, secondly, that predictions of physical events can refute themselves because the predictor may fail to take into account the effect of his own prediction. But were he, according to this objection, to take this effect into account, he would make a correct prediction. On the other hand, the objection continues, there are conditions connected with the prediction of action in which, no matter what prediction the predictor makes, his prediction will be falsified. Here there is no question of inaccurate calculation or of insufficient information for, according to this objection, *whatever* he predicts will be incorrect. Finally, it would be claimed that this situation arises only in connection with human action, not physical events.

Now to try to meet this objection. Suppose that I wish to predict what action you will perform at a specified future time, but that I shan't try to change or affect your behaviour except by making my prediction. Suppose further that the following conditions obtain. At this moment you want to falsify any prediction that I shall make of your action. Moreover, you will still have this desire at the specified time of the action and it will override any conflicting desires then present. Right now you intend to do action A, but you are prepared to do ~A if I predict that you will perform A. At the specified time you have the ability and opportunity to do ~A. Finally, conditions are such that, if I make a prediction in English in your presence, you will understand it, remember it throughout the time interval, and will be able to tell whether any of your actions will conform to it or not. Given the satisfaction of all these conditions, *whatever* I predict will be falsified. That is, no prediction of mine is causally compossible with the occurrence of the event I predict.

Notice that this example does not establish that it is causally incompossible *simpliciter* for me to make a correct scientific prediction of your action, but only that I cannot do it in a certain manner. If I were to predict it otherwise than in that manner, by, say, writing it down and depositing the prediction in a bank vault, the effect on your action would not occur. Thus it is causally compossible to make the prediction under conditions other than those stipulated. But specification of the manner of prediction seems to be a fairly general requirement for predictions, not just for predictions of action.

But what significance is there in the fact that it is causally incompossible, in some circumstances, for a correct prediction of an action to be made in some specified manner? First, it has no significance as far as the truth of determinism is concerned. Indeed, the very construction of the case in which no prediction was possible *presupposed* the existence of laws of nature which, together with a given prediction, would result in a certain action. This seems to support the thesis that actions are determined, rather than defeat it. The only reason one might have for thinking the contrary is the assumption that determinism entails predictability and I have already argued that such an assumption is false. Secondly, the case produced above may not reflect a peculiarity of human action, since parallel examples can be established for physical phenomena.

Alvin Goldman[13] has devised a case which provides such a parallel. Imagine a certain physical apparatus placed in front of a piano keyboard. A bar extends from the apparatus and is positioned above a certain key. (He considers only white keys.) If the apparatus is not disturbed, the bar will strike that key at a certain time. Now let us suppose that the apparatus is sensitive to sound, and, in particular, can discriminate between sounds of varying pitches. If the apparatus picks up a certain sound, the position of the bar will move to the right and proceed to strike the key immediately to the right of the original one, if there is such a key. Specifically, if the sound has the same pitch as that of the key over which the bar is poised, the bar will move. If the monitored sound has any other pitch, the bar will remain in its position and proceed to strike that key.

Now suppose that someone wishes to make predictions of the behaviour of the apparatus. He wishes to predict what key the bar will strike. As with the case of human action, a restriction is placed on the *manner* in which he can make his prediction. The prediction must be expressed according to a specific set of conventions or symbols. To predict that the bar will strike middle C, for example, the predictor must emit a sound with the pitch of middle C and so on. Furthermore, the emission of the sound must be made contiguously with the apparatus. Given these restrictions it will be causally incompossible for the predictor to make a correct prediction. If he predicts that the bar will strike middle C the bar will only hit middle C if it is poised above it and if it is so poised his prediction must be falsified for the bar will proceed on to, and strike, D. If he predicts any other behaviour he will still not prove to be right.[14]

All that the foregoing discussion shows is that under *some* conditions it is not causally compossible to predict a man's action in a way which allows him to learn of the prediction.

This does not rule out the possibility that there are *other* conditions, in which such predictions would be causally compossible. The existence of such conditions suffices to establish the possibility (in principle) of scientific predictions of free actions about which the agent hears or reads. Furthermore, there are cases in which one could predict accurately simply by not divulging the content of the prediction.

VI

I have contended that determinism does not entail the possibility of prediction in any relevant sense and I have further claimed that those who have tried to establish a disparity between actions and physical phenomena hinging on these various species of possibility of prediction have failed to do so.

It remains to make one final comment about this whole approach in attaching the freedom of an agent to epistemic uncertainty about what he will do. I wish to claim that it is not even a necessary condition, still less a necessary and sufficient condition for my being able to take different courses of action that it should be uncertain which I shall take — whether it be uncertain to others or to myself.

Thus it is no good, to cite Hampshire's position, making our freedom reside in the opportunity which knowledge would give us to 'acquiesce in an action and thus make it ours'. This would be a genuine freedom only if there were a real alternative to our doing exactly the thing we did do in exactly the manner in which we did it. This is an altogether different issue.

What I have endeavoured to show then is that free human action is quite compatible with the contention that such actions are determined and susceptible of prediction. Discomfort with the idea that determinism and susceptibility to prediction deprive men of the essential characteristics of freedom — choice, decision, deliberation and so on — is unwarranted.

9 Contra-causal Libertarianism and Freedom

The libertarian believes that the concept of freedom is incompatible with the concept of determinism. Since libertarians contend that men do sometimes have the freedom to act in alternative ways, they argue that at least some human actions are not subject to deterministic laws. The operation of causal laws in domains other than perhaps the quantum, is not, of course, denied. In this chapter and the next I propose to investigate the claims of two kinds of libertarianism. In the present chapter I discuss the more traditional view of libertarian or self-caused freedom as consisting in decisions and actions which are the causal outcomes of certain inner acts (themselves thought to be separable from and antecedent to such actions, but *not* in turn caused by prior causes). Libertarianism is not to be confused with 'two-domainism' for it is thought to be contingently, not conceptually, true.

The most prominent version of the libertarian thesis of contra-causal freedom is 'moral libertarianism', which has been energetically defended in recent philosophy by C. A. Campbell[1] but can probably be found at least as far back as Kant.

I

According to moral libertarians, the crucial question is not whether there is some sense in which we are free, but whether we are free in the sense required in order that we shall deem it proper to attribute *moral* praise or blame to agents. Put another way, the question is whether determinism (or indeterminism) is logically compatible with moral responsibility.

In order to answer this question it is necessary, according to moral libertarians, to analyse 'the moral consciousness'. Analysis of this consciousness reveals firstly, that the critical issue is whether our choices and decisions (our 'inner acts')

116

are free or not, because even if external circumstances prevent a morally wrong act, we may still be morally responsible for having decided to do the act, and on the other hand, we are not responsible for an action unless it is the upshot of an inner act. Secondly, the analysis of our moral consciousness reveals that in order that we shall be proper objects of moral praise or blame, our decisions must be free in the sense that the following conditions are fulfilled:

(i) the sole cause (author) of the decision is the agent ('the self') and not the agent's formed character, for this character is the consequence of hereditary and environmental factors;

(ii) the agent could categorically have decided otherwise than he in fact did. That is, he possessed the power to choose a different alternative action, even though all antecedent conditions remained unchanged — he could have not only done otherwise, but could have chosen otherwise.

I mentioned previously that libertarians argue that only some human actions are contra-causally free. According to moral libertarians it is moral choices, in particular, that display human freedom. The notion of a moral choice is crucial to an understanding of moral libertarianism, so a few words of explanation are warranted. An exponent of moral libertarianism contends that a situation of moral choice arises when a decision must be made between following one's strongest desire and doing what one believes ought to be done. The force of the 'ought' here is that it marks out a duty. Typically, it is urged that we place ourselves imaginatively in this position so as to enable a sincere report of what we would then say. This appeal to introspection of one's moral consciousness, it is then argued, shows that it is impossible for us to disbelieve the following two things:

(i) That just as we are we could take either course (following our strongest desire or doing our duty), by either making or not making the effort of will required to do our duty;

(ii)   that unless we believed ourselves free in this absolute (or categorical) sense to take either course of action, we could not hold ourselves morally responsible for our actions.

According to moral libertarians, any determinist doubt of the two propositions just noted, comes from treating a moral choice as a phenomenon for an *external* observer to describe. Adoption of the external observer's approach seems to leave scope for only two possibilities, determinism or randomness. But the self does not adopt the external observer's approach and knows the action is neither causally determined nor random. If the determinist will not accede to the internal observer's approach (the appeal to introspection), he just cuts himself off from the only way in which the issue can be settled, and, therefore, begs the question.

In contrast to the situation *apropos* such moral choices, that for all other choices (non-moral ones) is radically different. (I should add that J. Mabbott concedes that it would be an open question whether there were any free choices were there no moral choices.) At any given time we have a set of dispositions which may be called our 'formed character', according to the moral libertarian. When we make choices and decisions, this character manifests itself in the fact that our preference, or strongest desire, will be in favour of one course of action. Our character, and hence our strongest desire, is determined by heredity and past experience. In non-moral choices, therefore, we must follow our strongest desire. In moral choices, on the other hand we experience our strongest desire (what we most want to do) as being in conflict with our duty.

The following succinct statement of the foregoing claims is Campbell's and is taken from his paper 'In Defence of Free Will':

... the agent himself in the situation of moral temptation does not, and indeed could not, regard his formed character as having any influence whatever upon his act of decision as such. For the very nature of that decision, as it presents itself to him, is as to whether he will or will not permit his formed character to dictate his action. In other words the agent distinguishes sharply between the self which makes the decision, and the self which, as formed character, determines not the decision but the situation within which the decision takes place. Rightly or wrongly, the agent believes that through his act of decision he can oppose and transcend his own formed character in the interest of duty. . . the agent *cannot* regard his formed character as in any sense a determinant of the act of decision as such. (pp. 43f, Campbell's italics)

One final point should perhaps be made in this brief exposition of moral libertarianism. It concerns the theory of moral worth underlying many accounts of moral libertarianism. Since the central notion of a moral choice is tied to those cases in which obligation and strongest desire conflict, it is no surprise that an action is often said to have no distinctively moral worth unless the agent more strongly desires to do something else. This view of moral worth appears to follow inexorably on certain accounts of moral libertarianism. An action has moral merit or demerit if, and only if, the agent was responsible for it. He is morally responsible if, and only if, he could have done and chosen otherwise. He could have done and chosen otherwise if, and only if, the alternatives were undetermined. The only undetermined alternatives are those concerned with his either making the effort of will to do his duty or just allowing his desiring nature (his formed character) to have its way. Therefore, only when strongest desire conflicts with duty — when the moral action is not what the agent most wants to do — does the issue of distinctive moral worth arise. Many advocates of this view see it as having affinities with the Kantian. But Kant could be taken as saying that while an action done *from* the strongest desire has no moral worth, a man can perform a morally worthy action which *accords* with his strongest desire. In the latter circumstance the action might be done from some other motive such as respect for the moral law but happen to be the one which he most desired to do. That he most desired to do it was not, therefore, his motive. The moral libertarian would be well advised to avoid the eccentric position often held (and outlined above), and instead adopt the view I have just sketched (regardless of its faithfulness to Kant's thought).

II

Throughout the next few sections I wish to subject the theory of moral libertarianism to close scrutiny. Some of the issues discussed are, nevertheless, germane to all varieties of libertarianism and hence some of the criticisms I shall make of moral libertarianism apply more widely.

The first issue I shall take up concerns the notion of 'contra-causality'. It is often maintained in critical discussions of libertarianism, especially by those I call 'hard compatibilists', who believe it is necessary for an act to be determined if it is to be free, that in denying that some events (free actions) are totally caused, libertarians are thereby committed to the absurd claim that free actions are just random or chance occurrences.[2] For the notion of moral responsibility, which according to libertarians is only satisfied by the reality of contra-causal freedom, would be reduced to absurdity if it coincided with mere random or (more accurately) accidental occurrence. At this stage my main interest is in the fairness of this charge, because libertarians claim that an event's being undetermined is not the same as its being accidental. Even though I shall be quite critical of the theory of libertarianism I propose to defend libertarians against this charge.

It must be stressed from the outset that there are several varieties of 'indeterminism'. When libertarians in general, and moral libertarians in particular, assert that the concept of (moral) libertarianism presupposes contra-causality or indeterminism, attention must be given to the cash value of such a claim in relation to the three views that are all called 'indeterminism'.

One view, the view of indeterminism which I shall suggest is held more by the critics than the supporters of libertarianism, is that events are *totally uncaused*. This sort of indeterminism amounts to chaos. A second view states that there is *an element* of non-causation in most, if not all, events. Advocates of this second view characteristically appeal to the so-called 'indeterminacy principle', to which I have already referred in Chapter 4, in support of their contention. The third view is sometimes termed 'philosophical indeterminism' and is to be distinguished from each of the earlier views. On this account it is not denied that determinism holds for most events, nor is 'freedom' defined in terms of 'chance' or 'spontaneity' as it sometimes is on the other two. A free action, according to philosophical indeterminists, is a self-caused action, not a spontaneous or fortuitous one. Indeterminism of this third sort is the *contradictory*, not the *contrary*, of the deterministic thesis. Thus the libertarian denies only the presence of a *sufficient* condition. Room is left for the admission that most events perhaps are totally determined and for the further admission that all events are perhaps affected to some degree by antecedent conditions (after all, free acts on this view are made in particular causal contexts).

Critics of libertarianism, who charge it with identifying free action with random action, do not usually take care in sifting out the notion of indeterminism defended by libertarians. They assume, therefore, that if actions are undetermined they must be the result of blind chance or accident, neither of which is likely to throw up serious candidates for free action. Indeed very often indeterminism is *defined* as blind chance.[3] But if there are distinct senses of indeterminism, there is very little plausibility in the claim that blind chance (as it is ordinarily conceived) is entailed by, much less definable in terms of, indeterminism. The ordinary conception of blind chance resides in the first not the third sort of indeterminism distinguished above. (Quite apart from the fact that such oft-used illustrations of blind chance as the result of the spinning of a roulette or chocolate wheel ought not to be appealed to, since the motions involved are all probably totally caused, the libertarian could justifiably resist their introduction into the discussion simply because they are inanimate objects.)

Perhaps an example will help drive home the distinction I am urging. Suppose a man's brain is so wired up that if an electron goes down the left side of a grid, he will get a sudden and overpowering desire to shout. If the electron's moving down the left side of that grid is causally undetermined, then if the electron does move down the left side of the grid and thereby causes the man to shout, it makes sense, perhaps, to say that it was a mere accident that he shouted. But how different is such an action from one that is supposed to be of the intentional, duty-fulfilling, desire-resisting sort envisaged by the moral libertarian?

It might be objected, though, that the description of free action offered by the contra-causal libertarian, namely as one depending on self-causation, is implicitly incoherent, since if one attempts to fill in the details of such an account of choice and decision, one either ends up assuming causal determination or pure chance to be the operative factor. The reply I would suggest to this line of objection is that the burden of proof seems to rest squarely on the shoulders of those who suggest that the description, *despite appearances*, is implicitly incoherent.

I hope that what I have urged to date will carry sufficient conviction to at least allay the suspicion that 'contra-causality' comes to nothing more than randomness. Thus I will concede that Campbell's identification of contra-causality with self-determination holds up. On his account, then, a self-determined act is one caused by the self and is not just an occurrence of pure chance. The self supposedly acts in opposition to certain causal factors — those of desire or formed character — but still does so in the context of causal order not of chaos. Nevertheless, critics of libertarianism at this point counter by asserting that if 'self-determined' is to mean 'determined by the self', it is necessary to give some account of the self.[4] Indeed Campbell concedes that this new objection is generally felt by those unsympathetic to libertarianism to be the most conclusive objection to the theory.[5] The objection comes to this: can any intelligible meaning be attached to the claim that an act, which is not an expression of the self's character, is yet the self's act? According to moral libertarians, and here they diverge in opinion from those other libertarians who make no appeal to talk of selves, doubt about the intelligibility of this claim stems from adoption of the external rather than the introspective viewpoint. I turn to consider the issue of introspection as the source of knowledge of our freedom in the next section of the chapter. For the moment, therefore, I will try to bypass considerations relating to it, but one should notice that many libertarians believe there is more to human life than a scientific, empirical or external viewpoint can capture. Perhaps this lies behind the general commitment of moral libertarians, if not other libertarians, to the dualist view of mind. A second factor is suggested by Campbell's claim that the self comprehends man's character. He goes on to argue that since the self is aware of its evaluation of the character, it cannot be derived from or caused by the character. But that an individual can decide whether or not to evaluate all his decisions, does not ensure that this decision is not caused by some feature of his past.

Obviously the self is not an event caused by other events. It is the cause of certain acts or events. But the question arises concerning the cause of the self. The following argument may be put forward.[6] If the self is not caused by some event, then it is either uncaused or self-caused. Obviously, if the self is uncaused, moral libertarianism reduces to one of the views of indeterminism so strenuously denied previously. The other alternative is that the self is self-caused. But what might it mean to say that anything is self-caused? A necessary condition of a cause is that it exists prior in time to an effect. If the self were self-caused, then it would exist prior to its own existence and this is manifestly impossible.

I think this argument is unsuccessful, because it does not seem to be the case that it is a necessary condition of a cause that it exist prior in time to an effect. The notion of a cause which occurs simultaneously with its effect is nowadays widely thought to be respectable. By coupling this consideration with the further claim that since the self is not an event it is improper to ask for its cause, the libertarian could avoid the force of the preceding argument. Alternatively, the libertarian might wish to appeal to the notion of immanent causation in the manner of agency theorists.[7] This idea of immanent causation is discussed in the next chapter. At the moment I shall confine my attention to the problems surrounding selves. Some of the remarks that I make will retain their force for agency theories too.

Undoubtedly it is with the anticipated appeal by empiricists to Occam's razor in mind, that belief in transempirical entities tends to be walled around by an appeal to a self-determinist variety of indeterminism (or, as in agency theory, to immanent causation). This permits the transempirical entity to manifest itself in the empirical domain, albeit in a way which some empiricists will still insist is random.

Nevertheless, it might seem possible to argue in such a way as to avoid the Occamist objections. In some realist accounts of the philosophy of science, theoretical terms within a theory are taken as referring positively to entities believed to exist just because they account for certain phenomena of ordinary experience in an economic and enlightening way. It might be contended that this is the very sort of role which the concept of a self plays and that this fact constitutes good grounds for including the self in our ontic schedules.

But drawing upon the notion of a transempirical self *does not* seem to yield any more economic or enlightening explanation of human phenomena which appeal to an empirical self cannot also provide. For example, there is no need to postulate the existence of a transempirical self in order to explain how we can decide about our decisions or evaluate our character in a situation of moral temptation, for these are perfectly open to empirical investigation. This seems a good deal more reasonable than the maintenance of an *a priori* belief that in some respect an empirical account of the brain in neurophysiological terms, say, will stop short of complete determinism. Perhaps the final account will stop short, but it will do so, I should guess, for *empirical* reasons.

I will wind up my criticism of the appeal to a transempirical self by suggesting some *prima facie* odd consequences of its use by libertarians. To begin with, it is, I suggest, distinctly odd to say that a person is morally responsible for an act of his if it was grounded in his transempirical self, but without responsibility if it was caused by his desire to do the act. Furthermore, even if the self is allowed to be the originator of a particular act, what is the source of the libertarian refusal to countenance the possibility that the self originates it with such a strength that the agent is unable to act otherwise? Surely not a desire to beg the question! Finally, even if it is improper (as I previously conceded for the sake of argument) to ask what is the cause of the self, it doesn't follow that there is an impropriety in asking what are the various causes of the self doing now this, now that and so on.

It seems, therefore, that some critics of libertarianism have been unfair in charging libertarians with identifying the freedom of moral responsibility with randomness, because they have ridden rough-shod over the various forms of indeterminism. Libertarians overcome the charge by pointing out that their concept of self-determination, while contra-causal, is not identifiable with blind chance. So far so good. The initial objection is, however, only overcome by recourse to the idea of self-determination — an idea which itself is perhaps problematic, but is, at least, intelligible. Unfortunately commitment to self-determination involves commitment to either a transempirical self, or, to agency as an irreducible philosophical category. I have argued that belief in transempirical selves is less reasonable than belief in empirical selves and that there are some odd consequences of the use to which libertarians put their belief in transempirical selves. I shall take up the alternative claim about agency in the next chapter.

It is time now to see whether these criticisms ultimately fail because they rely on the external rather than the internal viewpoint. We must, that is, carefully scrutinise the role of introspection in the theory of moral libertarianism.

III

In considering the role of introspection within moral libertarianism, the central question is whether introspection reveals on certain occasions that the self makes decisions not fully determined by antecedent states and whether in such contexts of choice the self is faced with genuine alternatives which resist interpretation in compatibilist (determinist) ways. In Section I, I quoted a passage from Campbell which made a stronger claim than that introspecting agents do *in fact* reach such conclusions about the self. There Campbell maintains that the introspecting agent *cannot* but come to those conclusions about the self. I will concentrate on the weaker *de facto* claim, because if it fails it is hard to see how the stronger could still succeed. Nevertheless, I shall point out that Campbell, at least, seems to switch horses at times.

It has been objected that an undetermined freedom is not the sort of thing which we could observe by introspection, and that the libertarian must, therefore, be in some way interpreting the experience of choice which he stresses.[8] To this criticism Campbell has replied that he did not claim to introspect a contra-causal activity but rather 'a *belief* — seemingly ineradicable — that one is contra-causally active'.[9] Presumably what this unusual manner of speaking comes to is that when we introspect in a situation of moral choice we do not introspect an experience that then has to be interpreted, but, rather, a belief to the effect that the only cause of the decision or choice is the introspecting agent. Introspecting such a belief must however mean more than merely that if I ask myself whether I believe a proposition which positively asserts my contra-causal freedom, I find I do. If that were all that was meant the notion would be trivial, for we could introspect anything whatever that we believed to be true.[10] The onus of proof seems to be on Campbell and other moral libertarians, at this stage to show what more is meant. I shall assume that they can shoulder this onus in order that I may go on to consider the role of introspection with a mite more confidence in its respectability and not be prevented from considering further objections.

Suppose a timid man under hypnosis is convinced on the occasion of his being hypnotised that he is free. Obviously, though, he is deceived. Since the experience of introspecting his freedom in this case is not significantly different from the experience in other cases when he is not, in fact, deceived, the experiences in either situation must be discounted as irrelevant to the question of freedom.

The reply which the moral libertarian would no doubt offer to this sceptical line would be that in other areas (such as in connection with physical objects, other minds, past events) even though experiences can be deceptive, they nevertheless do provide adequate counter-evidence to the sceptical position. Thus, arguing that because an experience may be deceptive it does not provide adequate evidence for accepting a hypothesis, is not *generally* tenable, and, hence, need not be adopted in relation to introspecting one's belief in contra-causal freedom.[11]

It is equally likely that the objector will reply by arguing that the case of freedom cannot be assimilated to the other cases (physical objects, other minds and past events). He will claim this on the ground that beliefs derived from introspection in these other areas are independently checkable, whereas that in the area of freedom is not. I do not find this reply very convincing for it hinges, I think, on withdrawing the across-the-board scepticism in the other cases but not in the area of freedom, by having recourse to the notion of independent evidence, when that evidence, too, would be discounted by the serious sceptic. But perhaps there *is* something different about the case of freedom. I will suggest an objection which is based on such a difference and which, I think, has force.

There is far more disagreement among serious men (the source of wisdom for most libertarians) about the introspection of a belief in *contra-causal* freedom, than there is concerning the introspection of beliefs about other minds, physical objects and past events. Now, moral libertarians have not been unaware of the disagreement about the results of a non-trivial appeal to introspection. Indeed, I wish to claim that their awareness of this point tends to result in an illegitimate switching of horses. Instead of relying on the weaker *de facto* appeal, a stronger conceptually-oriented appeal tends to be substituted and this points, in my view, to a serious confusion.

Thus, Campbell[12] says the philosopher should ask himself whether, in a situation of moral choice,

> ... (he) can *help* believing ... that his moral decision is *not* necessitated by his character as so far formed (how *could* it be, when the very essence of the decision is, for the agent, whether or not to *oppose* his character as so far formed, in its manifestation as 'strongest desire'?).

The force of this passage is clearly intended to be conceptual, because if one agreed with Campbell concerning formed character, strongest desire and so on, one would contradict oneself if one said that character determined moral choice. But in the discussion of an objection that *others* may disagree with his introspections, which follows immediately after the passage quoted, Campbell argues that his own findings are confirmed by many others who seriously attempt the required experiment. This reply either begs the question about the seriousness of the introspective experiment or, more probably, evinces the confusion I have pointed to — namely that between the merely *de facto* and the conceptual.[13] If the introspective appeal is to be unfalsifiable it can't be genuine, if it is genuine and falsifiable, men can disagree about the results of their introspections, and they do just that.

Even were there no such inconsistency as I have alluded to, it would seem to me that it is thinkable that the context of decision, as presented in introspection, should be subject to causal determination. Indeed, in Chapter 5 I argued that this was not only thinkable, but that the most plausible understanding of voluntary action emerges from considering such action as the outcome of some causal antecedents rather than others. It might be said that from the point of view of our concept of moral responsibility, being subject to causal determination would be tantamount to coercion. But that remark, I think, points up the need for philosophical (rather than introspective) reflection.[14] Inspection of one's own current activity of conscious origination could hardly be held to yield a determinate conception of moral responsibility. But, if that be so, then we have to use other means in order to decide the content of the concept of moral responsibility. This seems to me to furnish an additional reason for denying that the introspecting agent will *in introspecting* find himself free in a contra-causal sense.

IV

In this section I shall critically look at the theory of moral worth which I previously isolated,[15] and argue that it is deficient because of its inadequacy in dealing with the very thing to which it appeals for support — the judgements of serious men. This inadequacy casts grave doubt on the claim of the theory to capture the sense of freedom necessary and sufficient for moral responsibility.

First of all, moral libertarians seem to imply that a wrongdoer who did not think about how he ought to act cannot be morally responsible. That is a very strange consequence! No doubt the moral libertarian will reply to this charge by claiming that as long as the man's reasoning is taken to be determined, clearly there could be no question of properly blaming a man for not seeing he had a moral obligation. The moral libertarian does distinguish (as well he might) between serious and careless moral judgements. The former alone are to be given weight. But this perfectly reasonable point lays the moral libertarian open to an *ad hominem* objection. There are cases of self-righteousness, of callousness, of moral laziness and of plain insensitivity to moral considerations where serious-minded men blame others precisely because these others fail to realise that they should have been experiencing a moral conflict in place of their insensitivity or laziness or whatever. A further oddity may be noted in passing. Moral libertarians seem to postulate a very odd principle of causality, for it withdraws in the moment the agent thinks about his duty and reappears as soon as he forgets about it or fails to think about it because of any of the sorts of reasons considered above.

Secondly, moral libertarians defend a view of undetermined freedom which allows of no degrees, it is an either-or notion.

Thirdly, there seems every likelihood that duty and strongest desire will on occasion coincide. What might the moral libertarian say of such a situation? According to Campbell, when a man's duty and strongest desire coincide, he *cannot help* doing what is in fact his duty, and so deserves no moral praise for what he cannot help doing. But surely this is distinctly odd because a man's capacity is not removed by his not wanting to do anything other than what he did. If I have no inclination to be deceitful this surely does not mean that I cannot help being truthful.

Fourthly, moral libertarians have a problem with the important matter of moral training. The moral libertarian would presumably envisage the function of moral training as

helping people to do their duty from inclination. However, if
the training is successful, the acts it cultivates will be in the
anomalous category of being morally worthless. For where
moral training is completely successful it eliminates moral
worth and responsibility. This consequence of the theory's
view of moral worth, seems to me to reduce the plausibility
of moral libertarianism.

The theory's account of moral worth seems to me to be
quite unacceptable for the four reasons I have advanced.
Since that aspect of moral libertarianism is sometimes
advocated as if it were an inexorable consequence of the rest
of the theory, its unacceptability must influence one's
assessment of the rest of the theory. I did point out in
Section I, that moral libertarians *need* not adopt such a view
of moral worth (though they usually do).

V

A somewhat different version of libertarianism, from the
more familiar one I have considered, has recently been
advanced by R. L. Franklin.[16] According to Franklin there is
no necessity to postulate a special type of causal relation
between a self and its decision and a metaphysic of the self
that would make this possible. My criticisms of these very
features of moral libertarianism, therefore, accord with
Franklin's rejection of them. Franklin, furthermore, rejects
the view that the most likely candidate for an undetermined
decision is the decision to act on or contrary to our duty, just
as I have done. Nevertheless, Franklin is a libertarian for he
believes that it is *natural* to suppose our choices are
undetermined, though, in his view, the dispute between the
libertarian and the determinist reflects a deep division in
conceptions of man and the relation of man to the universe.

It seems to be a very reasonable request to ask for the cash
value of the notion of 'naturalness' to which Franklin
appeals. In his discussion of it (pp 53-9) he suggests that the
libertarian examines one set of phenomena — human
choice — and the determinist another — the process of
explanation, each with a view to showing that his account of
the phenomena fits, as it were, without strain, in a way that
the rival ones do not. Both opponents then are claiming to
provide natural accounts.

But since the determinist has no need of the concept of naturalness it hardly seems likely that Franklin has correctly stated what the determinist is trying to do. No one, in other words, could deny that a deterministic account of an occurrence is in some sense an explanation of it. Further-more, as I have already argued in several places, the determinist extends a legitimate model of explanation to the area of choice because it affords a more plausible account of why a particular alternative (rather than another) occurred, than does an indeterminist or self-determinist account. Hence, the issue does not turn on the concept of naturalness, but, rather, on the relative plausibilities of arguments offered by libertarians, determinists or whoever in support of the explanatory force of their position.

The really distinctive feature of Franklin's version of libertarianism comes in his contention that the most plausible candidate for an undetermined type of action, which moral responsibility presupposes, is the selective directing of atten-tion associated with choice. The choice need not just be a moral choice, though moral choice is *one* paradigm case of the selective directing of attention. According to Franklin, when we consciously decide to concentrate on or pursue some train of thought or aspect of an alternative, we are engaging in the undetermined selective directing of our attention.

Perhaps some reasons can be advanced to show that such acts are undetermined but Franklin offers no arguments to show that they are the best candidates. Indeed his discussion (pp. 71—9) of the selective directing of attention is strikingly cursory. Even though he considers his version of liber-tarianism is superior to that of moral libertarianism on this point, the only suggestion he appears to offer in support of his claim is that it accounts for more than just choices occasioned by a conflict between desire and duty.

Consider some difficult decision between A and B. It seems possible, firstly, to selectively direct my attention to aspects of A and B without thereby arriving at a decision to choose one rather than the other. The situation of strongly weighting one alternative on one count and weakly on others, and strongly weighting a different alternative on some other count and weakly on the rest, is very common. We often decide such matters of conflict by doing what we really want to do, or, on independent grounds, consider it more important or more expedient, perhaps, to do one rather than the other thing. In the latter case there seems as much or as little reason to believe that such value judgements are determined with some specificity as to believe that the directing of one's attention to A or B is determined. In this respect the situation is like that with moral libertarianism, for conceptions of duty as well as desires might well be believed determined.

It is perhaps a little unfair to single out a few, albeit central, features of Franklin's version of libertarianism since his is an extensive work and since he believes there (currently) are no 'knock-down' arguments one way or the other. Nevertheless I consider his position, as exemplified in these features I have isolated, is no more, nor any less, convincing than is the moral libertarian's.

There is one point which I would do well to make at this stage in order to allay a possible suspicion. It is a well known feature of libertarian accounts that part of their platform consists in an attack on the analyses of compatibilist accounts of freedom and determinism. It may well be thought suspicious that I have said not a word about it. However, my silence should not be construed as an attempt to evade the issue. Rather, for the sake of methodological elegance, I have chosen to consider the whole issue of compatibilism in a separate chapter. In the chapter after next I shall seek to defend a compatibilist position against both libertarian and hard determinist attacks. What I have to say there will serve to wipe the slate clean concerning this central claim of libertarians.

VI

In this final section I wish to stress a point which I have previously hinted at in Section II of this chapter. The point concerns the widespread conviction (for want of a happier term) that we are free. This conviction constitutes on my view a *prima facie* presumption in favour of either a compatibilist or a libertarian account, for each of these sets out to defend that conviction against arguments designed to show that the conviction is illusory.[17] I have, furthermore, contended that if the world should prove to be indeterministic at the level of human thought and behaviour, it would not follow that human decisions and actions would be random and unfree. Whether or not any adequate theory of libertarianism in such a world would closely resemble the moral libertarian position discussed in this chapter, is quite another matter. There are of course other versions of libertarianism. I have discussed one in this chapter. In the next chapter I shall give close scrutiny to another.

10 Agent-causation Libertarianism and Freedom

Certain contemporary philosophers[1], who tend to be wedded to the *a priori* principle that every event has some cause, but, nevertheless, are dissatisfied with a deterministically oriented theory of responsibility, have recently attempted to revive[2] a theory of agency as a means of providing a satisfactory basis for moral responsibility. These attempts stem from two preliminary assumptions about such responsibility, namely:

    (i)   that ascription of responsibility cannot be philosophically justified simply on the grounds that the agent could have done otherwise if he had wanted to; one must also know that there was a real possibility for him to want or choose to do otherwise (i.e., that his original choice was not the necessary effect of causal factors);

    (ii)   that if the agent is the ultimate and undetermined cause of an action, then it is philosophically justified to assign responsibility for that (intentional) action to the agent.

It is clear that these assumptions are characteristic of a libertarian conception of freedom and responsibility. Despite the general characterisation as libertarian, agent-causation views run parallel at certain crucial points with 'two-domainist' views. Some agent-causation theorists claim that all human actions are purposive and that reasons are not causes.[3] These are clear points of agreement with two-domainism. The disagreement (and it is a vital one) comes over the further claim to which agent-causation theorists would subscribe, namely, that even though reasons are not causes, actions may have causes *other than* reasons.

This last ploy enables agent-causation theorists to make their most ingenious point. I have suggested that they tend to be wedded to the *a priori* principle that every event has some cause and that actions may have causes (other than reasons). These two claims might well seem opposed to the two assumptions underlying agent-causation views of responsibility. The opposition, however, is only apparent. For agent-causation theorists go on to claim that the causes of actions are not other antecedent *events*, but, rather, *agents*. Furthermore, it is held that agents cause events to occur in a sense quite distinct from that in which events or states cause other events or states to occur. This indeed explains why there is some overlapping with the views of two-domainists, according to whom there cannot be a mental event (e.g., a desire and accompanying beliefs about the best means of realising the desire) which causes action. Chisholm[4] calls causation by agents 'immanent causation' and causation by events 'transeunt causation'. Actions are not physical events caused by either the inner acts of some transempirical self or by antecedent physical events, according to agent-causation theorists, but are caused or brought about by persons.

I

Two initial points of concern must be taken up here. Firstly, doubts may be voiced about the intelligibility of the concept of immanent causation. Secondly, it may be suspected that the theory does after all involve an ontological commitment to the existence of substantival, transempirical selves, whose existence I have already argued one is entitled to doubt.

First, then, let us consider the intelligibility of immanent causation. Chisholm[5] replies to the charge that the concept is unintelligible by asserting that the concept of transeunt causation is of equal intelligibility. Since, he says, the only difference between the relations is the difference between the first terms, immanent causation is not a different kind of causation because the term 'causation' is univocal. Any problems regarding causation, therefore, are shared. But this conclusion of Chisholm's hinges on an unexamined assumption, namely, that all analyses of causation which *require* the first term of a causal proposition to be an event or state are wrong. Now Richard Taylor has tried to fill in this gap by arguing for the truth of that very assumption or, at least, by arguing that one analysis of causation requiring the first term of a causal proposition to be an event, is in error. The analysis he criticizes (in *Action and Purpose*) is the Humean regularity theory. While I have a good deal of sympathy with this critique of an invariable sequence analysis and, further-more, with the notion of a person's possessing real causal power, what strictly has to be established is firstly, that such an analysis as the invariable sequence one is wrong *and*, secondly, that *any and every* event analysis is mistaken. Quite apart from the obvious incompleteness of Taylor's attack, one should also bear in mind the further fact that arguments of 'knock-down' force are not easily come by in the area of theories of causation.

But there are even more severe difficulties confronting the agent-causationist. If the agent-causationist is right there is a kind of causality which does not reduce to event-causality and which helps us understand the notion of agency (which Taylor thinks is not subject to further analysis). Donald Davidson[6] has pointed out that the idea of agent-causality faces a dilemma from which there is no acceptable escape. *Either* the causing by an agent of a primitive action (like pointing one's finger) is an event separable from the primitive action *or* it is not a discrete and separable event.

Yet if the causing by the agent is an event it will presumably have to be spelled out in terms of an internal act of will or the like. This is clearly unacceptable because the whole agent-causation programme repudiates the possibility of such a replacement since it drives one straight back to affirming ordinary event-causation as fundamental. If it be contended that the prior event is somehow not an action, then the agent-causation position amounts to explaining agency by appeal to the utterly obscure idea of a 'causing to happen' which is not a 'doing'. Chisholm does indeed con-tend in 'Freedom and Action' (p. 19) that many things an agent causes to happen, in the sense that they are events caused by things he does, are not events of which he is the agent, that is, are not doings. He claims that when a person points his finger, because he does not know just what necessary cerebral events and movements of muscles are needed for his performance, he cannot be said to be doing

something in making these brain events and muscle movements happen. But this is plainly false because one can surely
be doing something without knowing one is. I shall borrow
an illustration from Davidson. He points out correctly that a
man may be making ten carbon copies as he writes, and be
intending to do just that; but it does not follow that he
knows he is, simply because all he knows in fact is that he is
trying to make the copies.

I turn, therefore, to the second horn of the dilemma,
according to which, one is impaled if one supposes that
agent-causation does *not* introduce an event in addition to
the primitive action of pointing one's finger, because making
such a supposition makes the role of the concept of cause
quite vacuous. This follows from the fact that one says no
more in saying the agent caused the action than when one
speaks of him as the agent of the action. Agent-causation is
alleged to be distinctive in not being capable of expansion
into event causation and in not being subject to laws
connecting events with other events. But appeal to agent-
causation does not seem to yield any significant gain in
explanation of the relation between an agent and his act. In
Chapter 5 I argued that analysing intentions in terms of
ordinary event-event causality *does* illuminate the relation.

The upshot of all the preceding considerations is the denial
that agent-causation talk represents any significant gain over
the more traditional libertarian dependence on the transempirical self. Neither kind of talk, I suggest, answers to
anything in reality.[7] Nevertheless, I shall proceed as if there
was a more obvious justification for agent-causation theories
because there is much of interest to be investigated still.

II

In this section I wish critically to analyse the basic programme of agent-causation: the grounding of responsibility in
the conception of a metaphysically free agent. It is generally
agreed that any acceptable theory of responsibility must
account for both the fact that men are sometimes properly
held responsible and sometimes properly held not to be
responsible. It is only 'generally agreed' that this is so for
while fatalists and hard determinists, for example, could

perhaps be said to acknowledge the distinction, they regard the class of people properly held to be morally responsible as, in fact, empty. This lack of universal agreement is of no great worry here, for agent-causation theorists do accept the distinction and on that count the argument of this section has, at least, *ad hominem* force. What I propose to show is that agent-causation theories make it impossible to provide criteria for distinguishing between the two sorts of case.

According to Chisholm in 'Freedom and Action' (and Taylor seems to be committed to similar views):

> ... whenever a man does something A, then (by 'immanent causation') he makes a certain cerebral event happen, and this cerebral event (by 'transeunt causation') makes A happen. (p. 20)

In this manner allowance can be made for the fact that all actions involving physical movement are caused by identifiable physiological events, while maintaining that, *qua* actions, they are immanently caused by the person. Let it be allowed that it now becomes analytically true to say that the person is the cause of *all* his actions. Is a person responsible for *all* his actions? Along with nearly all others interested in the philosophy of action, agent-causation theorists would answer 'no' to this question. For there are at least *some* actions that a man may do for which he cannot properly be held responsible. Those actions done under conditions of coercion, compulsion and so on might well be genuine actions, being voluntarily and deliberately caused by the agent. Both Taylor and Chisholm are in full agreement with such a view. Thus Taylor[8] believes that an agent may be caused by some event to perform an action (i.e. he may be caused to cause an action). It is primarily on this ground that Taylor argues that the differences he explores between action discourse and discourse about natural events do not *disprove* determinism, since the fact that an agent is a first cause of action does not preclude his being caused to act as he does, thus forming part of a deterministic chain. It is rather the ability to deliberate in a genuine way which reveals the inadequacy of determinism (construed in terms of transeunt causation). (See, though, Chapter 8 above.)

Chisholm, in like manner, claims in 'Freedom and Action' that:

> ... perhaps more often than not, our desires do exist under conditions such that those conditions necessitate us to act. (p. 25)

Only *at times* does the agent have the power to act or not to act. Since the presence of this power is the necessary condition of responsibility, we are, on the agent-causation account, often not responsible. This is perfectly correct but I will endeavour to show that this correct claim cannot be *consistently* made by agent-causation theorists.[9]

Now let R stand for 'actions for which the agent is responsible', and NR for 'actions for which the agent is not responsible'. (In my terminology R stands for free actions and NR for voluntary but unfree actions.) Let P stand for 'actions that the agent had the power to perform or not to perform'. These are not necessitated, that is, they are not subject to causal law. Let NP stand for 'actions that the agent did not have it in his power to perform or not to perform'. These are necessitated, that is subject to causal law. Finally, let IC stand for 'immanent causation'.

There is no doubt that Chisholm interprets R and P as having the same denotation and, furthermore, NR and NP as well. In addition, there is no doubt that the possibility of exercising IC accounts for the possibility of P; so that all P are instances of IC. But does the reverse hold? Are all cases of IC also cases of P? Even though Chisholm does not, in fact, explicitly raise this question I do not think that he can answer either 'yes' or 'no'.

Let us assume first that he answers 'yes'. Then one must either deny the existence of any NR, which Chisholm explicitly asserts, or, alternatively, one must deny that actions are by definition instances of IC. Apart from the fact that he regards an act as *essentially* a case of IC,[10] he cannot deny that all actions are instances of IC without undermining his own explanation of the grounds of responsibility. If it *is* the case that actions are (analytically) instances of IC, then that accounts neatly for responsibility. But if that is *not* the case then what role does IC play? What determines its presence or absence in a given action? These questions indicate the doubt that hangs over the explanatory value of IC for until they are answered we seem to have only an empty statement to the effect that: IC if, and only if, P if, and only if, R.

We need now to assume the second possible answer to the question whether all cases of IC are also cases of P, namely that the answer is 'no'. This answer is compatible with the view that all actions, *qua* actions, are instances of IC. And, furthermore, it seems to account nicely for the existence of NR, for if some IC are not P and if all NP are NR then some IC are NR. In other words some of our actions are necessitated, even though they are *our actions*, caused by ourselves as agents.[11]

But such an admission would again have the effect of destroying the putative explanatory value of the notion of immanent causation as the ground of responsibility. For it amounts to saying that IC is not, after all, the difference between R and NR, rather IC is a necessary but not a sufficient condition for R. Certainly, then, at that rate, an essential element has been left out. Indeed, it is the very element whose presence underwrites responsibility and clearly that element is P.

Thus, neither answer does anything but show up the paucity of IC's explanatory role.

III

But perhaps there still remains an insight in the notion of agent-causation which has been missed up to now. Recall the claim that what distinguishes R from NR (our central interest, here) is the concept of a 'power to perform and not to perform an action'. Furthermore, recall that an action A is a member of the class of P-type actions if, and only if, there exists no set of conditions that determine the agent to do A *and* there exists no set of conditions that determine the agent not to do A. We clearly need to come up with some criterion, therefore, for distinguishing between cases of P and cases of NP without appealing to the criterion for the presence of R itself.

The problem emerges in its most interesting and crucial form when we consider the agent who had the power to resist his desires, inclinations and so on, but who did not exercise that power. How could we sort out those occasions when he did not overcome these inclinations but could have (and is, therefore, responsible), from those when he could not have (and is, therefore, not responsible)?

One common way (among libertarians) of making the required distinction (between cases of P and of NP) is to appeal to introspective knowledge. But any introspective awareness of a power is most likely to be of some positive ability or skill and only most implausibly an awareness of the *absence of causal determinants*. It is this latter condition which an agent-causation theorist must claim is fulfilled.

Perhaps someone might suggest that there is a second way of making the distinction, which is more effective, namely empirical investigation. But surely empirical investigation would only allow us to correlate a set of empirical conditions with actions, not possibilities. There just does not appear to be any way of recognising or exhibiting such possibilities empirically. Indeed, if there were, there would be no problem about freedom.

Thirdly, it might be suggested that there is some way of distinguishing the conditions that determine the presence of P, that is, some sufficient cause of P. This would amount to proving the truth of the expression that defines P (absence of causal determinants) for a given instance of immanent causation. But to produce such a proof one would have to exhaustively describe the external and internal conditions relative to the agent that exist at a given time *and*, furthermore, one would have to show that no combination of these is a sufficient condition for the action at that time. But this task is just impossible of fulfilment for one could never know that the description was complete, nor, for that matter, that the set of known laws relating antecedents and consequents was complete.

Finally, someone might make the response that even though we cannot find the conditions for the *presence* of P, yet we can know the cause of the *absence* of P. It might be said that our lack of power to act is due in all cases to the failings of the agent not to the presence of external causes. On this view then, we always have the power to act freely but on those occasions when our inclinations and desires necessitate our actions we would be said to have freely failed to exercise our freedom. Leaving aside the oddity of expression this still does not furnish a way out for on this view *all* actions are free actions and hence we are always responsible.[1][2]

Thus appeals by agent-causation theorists to the concept of a 'power to perform and not to perform an action' get us no further than the earlier appeal to the notion of 'immanent causation'. The theory, at least in the form in which it has been expounded to date, is shipwrecked by its inability to explain facts it purports to explain and which it is committed to explaining, namely, that men are sometimes properly held responsible, and that men are sometimes properly held not to be responsible.

One final criticism is in order. Let us allow for the sake of argument that the theory of agency can distinguish responsible from non-responsible conduct. (I shall set aside the argument to date.) Even making this allowance, the agent-causation standpoint, as it has been expounded by its advocates, seems to yield an all-or-nothing conception of moral responsibility. Previously I claimed that it is necessary to allow for degrees of responsibility. But, as I read him, Chisholm claims that desires or motives either necessitate or incline without necessitating.[13] It could be, of course, that the agent-causation theorist can modify his position to allow for degrees of responsibility.

My discussion has been extremely critical of present accounts of agent-causation freedom. Even so, there are some attractive aspects of such theories which lead me to believe them preferable to other forms of libertarianism. First, there is the stress on agents as possessors of causal power. As I shall suggest in my discussion of a compatibilist defence of freedom, the distinctive feature of human power is that *ceteris paribus* it is under the control of its possessor. This leads to a second attractive feature of the agent-causation view. If human beings have causal powers under their control, the claim that undetermined human behaviour must be random, pales. Thirdly, it could be said that grounding free action in persons significantly advances the freedom and determinism debate, because it is persons after all who are supposed to be free (not, for example, transempirical selves).

11 A Compatibilist Defence of Freedom

This chapter plays a strategic role in the essay and might well be thought of as the linch-pin of my discussion concerning the problem of freedom and determinism. If it can be established that freedom is compatible with a deterministic world, the incompatibilist stance of the hard determinist is rendered nugatory. Furthermore, in a thoroughly deterministic world, libertarian defences of freedom are knocked awry.

Having indicated the importance this chapter has, I propose now to outline the matters I shall consider in the chapter. I shall be defending the claim that even when there is a sufficient causal condition of the occurrence of some action which I perform, it does not follow that I am unable to perform some other action instead. In order to defend such a claim, it will be necessary to explicate the notion of 'ability' (or as I shall prefer, 'power') and then show that agents can possess and exercise the power to do other than they, in fact, do, causal necessitation notwithstanding.

Strictly, furnishing a compatibilist defence of freedom requires the completion of two tasks. The first is to show that a causal account of human decisions and actions is feasible. Within the limits permitted by the scope of this essay, I have tried to carry out this task in particular in Chapter 5, but also in Chapter 8. In this chapter I tackle the second task, namely, that of showing that those decisions and actions which can be causally accounted for, may, nevertheless, be free. Accordingly, the chapter has the following structure. In the first two sections I endeavour to combat certain highly esteemed attacks on compatibilism as a vital preliminary to the second task. These sections are thus somewhat negative. In the third and fourth sections, I attempt, more positively, to fill out the notion of 'power' as it bears upon human freedom.

One final explanatory point concerning my use of the term 'compatibilism' is in order. Elsewhere (in Chapter 9, Section II) I have spoken of the view that freedom entails determinism as 'hard compatibilism'. It requires us to assent to the implausible view that if there prove to be no deterministic laws governing human thought and behaviour, then there never have been, nor could have been, any free decisions and actions. The version of compatibilism which I shall be espousing might be called, in contrast, 'soft compatibilism'. It presupposes no such entailment relation between freedom and determinism, but only that there is no inconsistency in claiming that an action is both free and determined.

I

In his famous lecture on 'Ifs and Cans'[1], J. L. Austin argued that traditional compatibilist defences of freedom had failed to take two separate though related distinctions. The first is between what might be called a supplementation view of 'can' statements and an analysis view. The second between the categorical sense of 'can' or 'could' and the conditional sense. I want now to consider each of these claims in turn. My reason for concentrating on them is that they have come to be regarded as the apotheosis of attacks on the compatibilist position.

When 'can' statements are said to be in need of supplementation it is because they are thought to be elliptical, or incomplete, when they lack an appended 'if' clause. That is, in Austin's words, 'cans' are really constitutionally iffy. Thus 'He could have holed the putt' is incomplete, whereas 'He could have holed the putt if his wife had not attacked him with a fairway wood' is complete and meaningful. When, on the other hand, it is said that 'can' statements are in need of analysis, the claim is that some *other* verb in conjunction with an 'if' clause provides an adequate analysis. In particular, that 'can' is explicable in terms of what will happen (or would happen) if certain conditions were to hold true.

Austin maintained that both theses were false and, furthermore, 'quite distinct and incompatible'. Even if Austin was correct in pointing out that the theses have not always been differentiated, they certainly cannot be both false and incompatible, unless they are contraries. I do not think they are contraries. Indeed, they seem to me to be complementary, for if 'can' statements are disguised 'can if' statements, then in analysing locutions involving 'can' one must consider the entire non-elliptical expression. But it is more important to try to resolve the substantive issues raised by Austin's claims. There are two I want to consider here. Firstly, are 'cans' constitutionally iffy? Or, to put the same question in terms of the distinction drawn above, are 'can' statements in need of supplementation? The second substantive issue raised by Austin's contribution is whether 'can' statements are explicable in terms of the analysis thesis. I propose to consider these in turn.

On the first issue, Austin made use of at least three sorts of consideration in his endeavour to show that 'can' is not constitutionally iffy. I will contend that the first two of these considerations are quite indecisive against the position Austin attacks. The third matter will be discussed in two parts. The first part, I shall argue, is easily accommodated by the compatibilist regardless of whether he subscribes to the supplementation thesis or not. As for the second part, I will contend that it hinges on misconstruing the compatibilist position.

Firstly, Austin considered that his chosen opponents took 'can' to be constitutionally iffy because they in turn took 'could have' to be a past subjunctive, which he claimed 'is practically as much as to say that it needs a conditional clause with it'. On the contrary, argued Austin, 'could have' can be a past indicative, in which case the temptation to add a conditional clause disappears. But this argument is utterly indecisive. Though the temptation disappears, it may still *be the case* that 'could have', used as a past indicative, requires an 'if' clause.

Austin's second argument sets out to show that neither 'can' nor any other verb is such that it cannot occur without an 'if' clause. It goes as follows: let the verb be 'to X'. Then the supposition is that we can never say 'I X' *simpliciter* but must always say 'I X if I Y' or 'I X if conditions Y obtain'. But if we ever do Y, or if ever conditions Y obtain, we must be able to say that 'I X' *simpliciter*. Hence the supposition that English (or any natural language for that matter) does not countenance expressions of the form 'I X' for every verb in the language is false. However, there are at least two serious difficulties with the use of this test. First, it has been pointed out[2] that we have no reason to believe that the usual rule of detachment obtains for the 'if' clauses in question – we can get along quite well by treating 'I can if I choose' or 'I could have if I had chosen' as simple or atomic sentences. Secondly, as David Pears[3] has incisively shown, this test for hypotheticality sometimes yields divergent results from those produced by application of Austin's avowedly more important test: the contrapositive test for conditionality. I, therefore, set the detachment test aside, because it seems quite indecisive against the suggestion that 'cans' are constitutionally iffy.

The third consideration will, as previously indicated, be looked at in two parts. First, I have already spoken of Austin's contrapositive test for sorting out genuine conditionals from pseudo-conditionals. A hypothetical, he urged, is a conditional if, and only if, it entails its contrapositive. Underlying this claim is probably the belief that it is natural to call a hypothetical a conditional when, and only when, the truth of the antecedent is put forward as a sufficient condition of the truth of the consequent. This is the central and most frequent use of 'if', hence those 'hypotheticals' which fail the test may be termed pseudo-conditionals.[4] There is much more that could be said on these matters but my concern is with the philosophical point about freedom which Austin endeavoured to establish on the basis of his distinction between conditionals proper and pseudo-conditionals.

According to Austin not all 'if' clauses introduce causal conditions; some sentences in which 'if' is the main connective are causal conditionals and some are not. In particular, he drew attention to 'there are biscuits on the sideboard if you want them', as an example of a non-causal 'if', and argued that the 'if' in 'he can if he chooses (wants. . .)' was very similar. Now the compatibilist can agree that 'he *can* if he chooses (wants. . .)' is not a causal conditional, but baulk at the further claim that 'he *will* (would) if he chooses (chose)' is non-causal. This is a crucial, but often overlooked, distinction over which there has been some instructively confused debate in contemporary discussions of compatibilism.[5] I want to show why a compatibilist can react in the ways just described. I shall do so by looking at some formidable difficulties to which the view that 'he can if he chooses (wants. . .)' is a causal conditional, is open. These difficulties apply whether the 'if' clause is supposed to state a necessary or a sufficient condition.

D. J. O'Connor has argued that the legitimacy of the inference from 'I can if I choose' to 'I can whether I choose to or not', which was adduced by Austin to show that the 'if' could not be the 'if' of sufficient condition, does not dispose of the hypothesis that the 'if' is one of necessary condition. His contention is that because the 'can' in the first proposition means something different from the 'can' in the second, the 'if' may still be one of necessary condition. As it happens, O'Connor goes on to argue from phenomenological considerations that someone's choosing to do something is such as to render it incapable of being a necessary (and, presumably, a sufficient) condition of his doing it. I am not interested in pursuing this latter claim because there is a far more important way of seeing the weakness of the hypothesis that the 'if' is one of necessary condition.

It is vital not to elide the distinction between possession of a capacity and its exercise. O'Connor recognises it and, indeed, accepts Austin's argument to the conclusion that what is at stake is not a necessary (or sufficient) condition of the *possession* of a certain capacity or power, but of a person's *exercising* his power to act otherwise at the time and under the conditions referred to. But saying of someone who, in fact, did not-X, that he could have done X if he had chosen, won't involve one in asserting that his doing X was not possible *without* his choosing to do X. Obviously, the compatibilist can acknowledge that choosing and other 'initiating factors' (to use Pears' term) *sometimes* need to be activated if performance of a certain task like doing X is to ensue, but he need not assert that someone could have done X *only if* he had chosen. This would involve him in asserting that there could not be circumstances other than his choosing to do not-X, under which he also would have done not-X.

Surely, though, one could do something freely without choosing to do it (e.g. by doing it out of habit, or just unthinkingly).

Even so, O'Connor still needs to defend the claim that the 'could' in 'I could have done X, which I did not do, if I had wanted' *does not mean the same as* the 'could', in the following two statements entailed by it, namely, 'I could have done X, which I did not do, whether I had wanted to or not', and 'I could have done X, which I did not do'. This move is one I find quite unconvincing because it does not seem necessary at all to assign distinct senses to 'can' in order to account for the facts about the meanings of the sentences in which it occurs, and that would seem to be required if one is justifiably to assert the equivocality of 'can' (or any other term). Furthermore, the compatibilist does not need to resort to such a claim, as I think will become evident.

Does the 'if' clause in 'I can do X, if I choose' state a sufficient condition, then? Kurt Baier has argued that it does, but in the sense that adding '... if I choose' to 'I can do X...' implies that all necessary conditions constituting my possession of the ability and opportunity to do X are satisfied, and thus that the 'if' clause states the sufficient condition of my exercise of the power to do X.

Now it has been convincingly argued (by Keith Lehrer) that it is logically impossible for Baier's way of interpreting the 'if' clause to be correct, and determinism also to be true. His argument is as follows.

If my doing an action Y, were I to do it, would be a free action, then, were I not to do Y, it would nevertheless be true on a compatibilist account like Baier's, that I could have done it, if I had chosen. Now as Lehrer reminds us, if determinism is true, for any act, Y, which is not done, there will be a sufficient condition of its not being done. Before we proceed to the crunch, let us recall that on Baier's view, 'if I had chosen', when taken to state a sufficient condition, implies that all the necessary conditions of my doing an act have been satisfied. But, Lehrer argues in ' "Could" and Determinism':

If determinism is true, then ... if a person does not do X,

then there is some condition sufficient for his not doing X.
But if there is a sufficient condition for a person's not
doing X, then some condition necessary for his doing X is
not satisfied. The reason is that the non-occurrence of the
condition sufficient for his not doing X is a necessary
condition of his doing X, and that necessary condition is
not satisfied. (p. 160)

Thus it is a consequence of the truth of determinism, *pace*
Baier, that for anything which a person did not do, not all the
necessary conditions for his doing it were satisfied. The 'if'
cannot be that of sufficient condition in Baier's sense.

The upshot of the discussion is, I believe, that the 'if' in
'he can if he chooses (wants. . .)' should not be construed as a
causal conditional. What the compatibilist stresses, though, is
that it by no means follows from the foregoing considerations that the 'if' in 'he will (would) if he wants (wanted)' is
not a causal conditional.

Austin's second point may well be thought more daunting,
though. It may be put as follows. The supplementation
account confuses the categorical and conditional senses of
'can' and 'could'. This is not strictly a grammatical remark, I
admit, but Austin cites grammatical considerations as his
evidence for asserting that there is such a confusion.

Austin and others[6] contend that the supplementation
account treats sentences such as 'If A had chosen (wanted to
do. . .) otherwise, he could have done otherwise' as if they
were analogous to 'If A had found some fuel he could have
used the lamp'. The mistake, of which compatibilists are
allegedly guilty here, is that of treating 'A could have done X'
as being always conditional, instead of sometimes conditional
(as in the second of the two sentences above) and sometimes
categorical (as in the former of the two above sentences),
and, of not seeing that where the 'if' clause is equivalent to
'. . . if he had chosen (wanted. . .)' the 'could' will *always be
categorical*.

The same point can be put another way. What the
compatibilist allegedly does is to assimilate the case where a
man would have had something in his power if an unfulfilled
condition had been fulfilled, to that where something was in

fact categorically within his power. But this is just not true of all dispositional analyses of ascriptions of human power. The compatibilist can happily accede to the point that when someone who has the power to do an action and, who is not impeded by external factors such as the lack of means, or of entitlement, or of opportunity, and who is not ignorant of his power and so on, does not in fact do that action, that it still remains true to say he categorically could have done it. Furthermore, acceding to this point does not preclude his saying that if in fact he did not do the action, there may still be some true causal conditional to the effect that if he had wanted to do the action he would have exercised the needed power.

It might be said, though, that I have given Austin what he claimed. However, I do not see, if I have captured the Austinian complaint against the supplementation thesis, that that thesis has been shown to be false. Even so, it might be that the thesis is false, and that I have somehow contrived to defend it by incorporating elements of the analysis thesis into my defence against the final objection considered above. (I did say, as against Austin, that I believed them to be complementary theses.) I, therefore, turn immediately to consider the analysis thesis.

II

The issue in the debate about the analysis thesis is whether 'can' is analysable as 'will if' or some other similar variant. Consider the claim (call it (T)) that:

> For every person S and every individual action a, S can perform a (it is within S's power to perform a) if, and only if, S will perform a if he tries to perform a.

Obviously this claim could be paralleled in other tenses but its adequacy would remain unaffected. G. E. Moore in his *Ethics* (London, 1947), and P. Nowell-Smith[7] in his book of the same title (Harmondsworth, 1954) defend claims like the one above or some version of it in which 'chooses' replaces 'tries'. Austin argued against claims like it.

Moore wrote in his *Ethics*:

> I *could* have walked a mile in twenty minutes this
> morning, but I certainly could *not* have run two miles in
> five minutes. I did not, *in fact*, do either of these two
> things; but it is pure nonsense to say that the mere fact
> that I *did* not does away with the distinction between
> them, which I express by saying that one *was* within my
> powers, whereas the other was not. (p. 107, Moore's
> italics; cf. Nowell-Smith, p. 275)

Austin's main objection to (T) is that being able to do
something is consistent with trying and failing. Indeed he
claimed that a human ability or power or capacity is
inherently liable not to produce success, on occasion, and
that for no reason. The substance of his view is contained in
his well-known footnote concerning the golfer. Suppose that
a golfer tries to hole a very short putt but misses. It is,
nevertheless, true, argued Austin, that the particular golfer
could have made the putt — it was within his power to make
it. There is a large body of inductive evidence from circumstances in the past, similar to the present set in all relevant
respects, to show that he could have made the putt. Moreover, he might well return to the same spot and in similar
circumstances a short time later sink numbers of consecutive
putts. Hence the definiendum may be satisfied but the
definiens of (T) not be satisfied.

There are a number of things to be said about this
argument. First, though, a preliminary point. It might be said
that the claim that the golfer could have sunk the putt on the
particular occasion at issue is unjustified. Even though I do
not think Austin's argument achieves its purpose, I don't
consider this objection warranted. For, if we are to suppose,
as seems eminently reasonable, that there is some way of
justifying the claim that the golfer could have sunk the putt
when, in fact, he did not sink it, then *ex hypothesi* the
evidence in the case in question is sufficient to justify the
claim. While there may be no *entailment* relation between
'the golfer many times sank putts similar in all relevant
respects to the putt in question' and 'the golfer has the power

to sink the putt', the former statement surely constitutes *justifying evidence* for the latter.[8]

It seems clear to me that admitting that the foregoing ploy is unwarranted involves no untoward consequences for compatibilism. Nevertheless, it might be felt that it plays right into Austin's hands and allows him to press home the far more damaging point that the example of the golfer establishes the *indeterministic* sense of 'could have done otherwise'. But it does no such thing. The sort of justifying evidence referred to above might render highly probable the hypothesis that the golfer could have done otherwise, but it in no way renders highly probable the hypothesis that his action in putting was not causally determined. Nothing in Austin's argument can force the compatibilist to accede to the claim that abilities or powers are liable to fail their possessor on occasion *for no reason at all*.

Indeed, Austin's example raises peculiar difficulties for an indeterminist account of such abilities. When one ascribes some particular skill to a person (under conditions which are agreed to provide the opportunity to exercise the skill) it is frequently not required that there be an entailment relation *between* the presence of the skill coupled with the appropriate initiating factor *and* the performance. The antecedent and the consequent *will* have to be causally linked in a high enough proportion of relevant instances to warrant ascription of the skill. In those instances where performance fails to come up to expectations, we do not attribute such shortcomings to irrationality, undeterminedness or the like. In sports where a high degree of skill is demanded there are usually many elements of opposition confronting the sportsman. Sometimes the opposition comes in the form of human opponents, but sometimes, and golf seems to be a case in point, the 'opposition' stems from other factors such as the layout of the course, hazards, the speed of the green, indentations in the green, the lie of the ball, wind velocity and perhaps above all, psychological stress. Furthermore, many sporting activities involve highly complex actions.[9] The possibility of a sufficient degree of imprecision frustrating the genuine capacity of a participant, especially under conditions of stress is ever present. Clearly the compatibilist (on pain of ceasing to be a compatibilist) cannot concede Austin's indeterministic construction on the example. It is more than surprising, therefore, to find Nowell-Smith[10] appearing to do just that when he says:

> To accept the possibility of Austin's (golfer) example and the interpretation he puts on it is to reject the thesis that 'he can' in this sort of case means 'he *always* does, if. . .' but it invites, and I shall try to show that it requires, the thesis that 'he can' means 'he usually does, if. . .' This would be a crucial, indeed a fatal change, if the issue were between determinism and indeterminism; but it is not; the issue is the possibility of an hypothetical analysis of 'can'.

Subsequent sections of his essay may perhaps contain hints that he would be, in fact, unwilling to make his concession to Austin. But there is, nevertheless, no withdrawal of the concession as far as I can tell.

Furthermore, I would add to the claim that the compatibilist cannot concede Austin's interpretation, that he ought not, because Austin's argument for the indeterministic construction fails to convince. Austin wrote in 'Ifs and Cans':

> But if I tried my hardest, say, and missed, surely there *must* have been *something* that caused me to fail, that made me unable to succeed? So that I *could not* have holed it? Well, a modern belief in science, in there being an explanation of everything, may make us assent to this argument. But such a belief is not in line with the traditional beliefs enshrined in the word *can*: according to them, a human ability or power or capacity is inherently liable not to produce success, on occasion, and that for no reason (or are bad luck and bad form sometimes reasons?). (p. 119–20)

Firstly, not only a modern belief in science but a proper understanding of the notions of ability, power and capacity requires rejection of Austin's inference. I shall devote my efforts in showing this to a later part of the chapter. Secondly, in contrast to the situation with libertarianism, which I have previously defended against the charge that it makes free decisions and actions mere random happenings, Austin's claim is wide open to that very charge. Thirdly, why cannot the traditional view (if Austin's supposition is right) be subject to review by rational scientific inquiry? As Bruce Aune[11] has pointed out, there are words in our language which embody ancient errors (e.g. 'lunatic') but no one contends that the modern user of them thereby commits himself to endorsing the ancient but erroneous connotations.

If we return to the particular analysis embodied in (T), further criticisms of Austin's position are possible. To begin with I should think that a compatibilist ought to reject (T). I say this because a hypothetical analysis in terms of 'trying' must fail if there be any instances of what have been termed 'basic actions'. Raising one's arm at will has, for example, been used to illustrate the notion of a basic action. That the existence of such entities has been questioned I readily acknowledge, but, if the notion is defensible, a hypothetical analysis in terms of 'trying' must fail for such actions, since trying to do them is not something other than doing them, albeit with effort, on occasion. Further, an analysis like (T) cannot handle those cases where we speak with justification of a person's possessing power to do some act but go on to attribute his failure successfully to exercise it to the fact that he 'tried too hard'. Again, there are certain situations in which one can be said to have the power to perform a particular action which is not (in general, at least) a basic action but which one can nevertheless perform without any pre-action trying. For example, one can float without trying in a solution as saline as that of the Dead Sea. Finally, it must be borne in mind that it is plainly a mistake to claim that we can validly infer the shipwreck of *all and any* compatibilist analyses from the failure of (T). This is not to say that Austin made such a claim.[12]

The claim that all and any compatibilist analyses of the 'will if. . .' variety must fail has, however, been made on other grounds by M. R. Ayers[13] and also via a different argument mounted by Keith Lehrer[14] and independently by R. M. Chisholm.[15]

I take Ayers' objection first. He alleges that because the

antecedent of a causal conditional analysing freedom to decide or act cannot contain a verb of action as its dominant verb, no causal analysis is possible. The reason offered is that whereas in the case of action:

> ... that testing one's ability to do something is not the same kind of thing as testing the truth of a hypothesis, simply follows from the truism that in order to do something it is not always necessary to do something else first (p. 145)

in all other cases of causal conditionals, the antecedent *is* something that can be made true independently of the supposed effect. From this Ayers concludes that the possibility of any hypothetical analysis of personal power is ruled out.

But the conclusion is not sustained by his premise. From the obvious truth that 'in order to do something it is not always necessary to do something else first', all that follows surely is that the antecedent of a causal conditional offered in analysis of human freedom cannot have as its main verb a verb of action. Thus even though an agent cannot himself test the truth of the conditional by first doing something else, it doesn't follow that he can't test his powers in some other manner than that of doing something to create the conditions for actualising the power.

It is considerably more difficult to dispose of the arguments of Lehrer and Chisholm, who purport to show that no causal conditional statement of the form 'S will do A if C obtains' can entail the statement 'S can do A'. The arguments have given rise to a protracted debate.[16] I shall adopt the strategy of attempting to refute Lehrer's and Chisholm's claim by employing a *reductio ad absurdum* against their claim. Specifically, I will concentrate on Lehrer's contentions.

Lehrer's argument has the following structure. He claims that the statements reproduced below are consistent:

(1)   S would have done A if S had chosen:
(2)   S did not choose to do A;

(3)   If S did not choose to do A, S could not have done A.

But, continues Lehrer, the conjunction of these three statements entails that S *could not* have done A. Thus any argument designed to show that a causal conditional statement of the form 'S would have done A if C had obtained' entails the statement 'S could have done A', fails. We could substitute 'want' for 'choose'. Likewise it is clear that we could formulate the same argument using different tenses. The argument then is generalisable, and, if successful, precludes any compatibilist defence of the analysis thesis.

Lehrer offers, in effect, two lines of argument for the consistency of the three statements above. Firstly, he contends that it is surely logically possible that 'almost anything might happen as a result of my not willing to perform a certain action'.[17] In particular, that as a result of my not willing (or choosing, or wanting) to do some action, I might lose any of my powers, including my power to perform that action. If so, then (1), (2) and (3) are logically consistent and any analysis thesis fails.

Secondly, he furnishes an example which is supposed to illustrate the soundness of his argument. According to the example, a man might have a pathological aversion to a certain kind of candy, so that he could eat such candy *only if* he chose to do so. Assuming that he did not so choose, he might nevertheless be such that if he did so choose, he would have eaten the candy. He urges that these suppositions are surely and obviously consistent. Yet they imply the falsity of the analysis thesis in any manifestation.

As I have already indicated, I propose to deploy a *reductio* argument against Lehrer in order to show that his argument fails.[18] It does seem evident that there are at least some statements that can correctly be analysed in terms of conditionals. Paradigm cases of such statements are:

N: 'X is brittle',
which is analysable as something like
O: 'X will break if it is struck with a mild force by a hard object'

and

P: 'X is soluble in water',

which is analysable as something like

Q: 'X will dissolve if it is immersed in water'.

Indeed, a more accurate analysis would involve the use of a conditional like

Q_1 :   'X would dissolve if it were immersed in water'.

Now if Lehrer's argument be conceded for the moment, we can mount a *reductio* against him by using an argument of the same form as his to show that P, for instance, cannot be correctly analysed as Q or, better, Q_1 . Consider the following statements:

Q_1 :   'X would dissolve if it were immersed in water'.

R: 'If X is not immersed in water it is not soluble':

S: 'X is not immersed in water'.

R and S are jointly compatible with Q_1 (and, for that matter with Q). But someone might look askance at this suggestion. Here, like Lehrer, I will appeal to a logical possibility. Let X be a piece of sugar, and imagine a scientist who is a part-time magician and who, if X is not immersed in water, magically changes its molecular structure so as to make it non-soluble, whereas if X is immersed in water it is soluble. Under such logically possible circumstances, it seems clear that R and S are jointly compatible with Q_1 (or Q). But equally clearly R and S entail the negation of P. Hence Q_1 (or Q) does not entail P.

But this conclusion is very difficult to sustain for, either, we *can* analyse P as Q_1 or Q, or, if we cannot, then it is pretty certain that the trouble lies in some general worry about dispositional talk and, hence, constitutes a worry not peculiar to compatibilists. (It seems to me that the distress occasioned by talk of 'finkish' sugar has to be shared pretty widely.) Some further argument from Lehrer to the effect that there is a significant difference between the (1), (2), (3) case and the Q_1, R, S case, would be required before he could be held to have given a sound argument against every version of the analysis thesis.

III

I have attempted to defend a compatibilist position against certain attacks widely thought to refute it. One of the chief points which I have argued is that wanting (or some quasi-psychological condition of the agent such as trying, choosing or the like) is to be considered not so much in relation to an agent's *possessing* an ability as it is to his *exercising* it. But I imagine that incompatibilists will still not consider that I have made much headway, or answered all of their objections, but there *is* a positive contribution to be made in showing that the fact that an act was caused or causally necessitated does not entail that the agent was unable to do some other relevant act. So it is necessary to allay the suspicion of the incompatibilist that this can't be done.

At the outset it should be made clear or, admitted, if you like, that there is at least one sense of 'impossible' in which causal necessitation entails the impossibility of an agent's having acted otherwise. If A's not doing X (at t) is causally necessitated, it follows that it was causally incompossible relative to actual events prior to t that A do X (at t). (This sense of 'impossible' was, it will be recalled, defined in Chapter 8, Section I.) But it seems to me that this has no untoward consequences for a compatibilist account of 'power to do otherwise', a concept that has been prominent to date, albeit unanalysed.

It might be wondered why I consider there are no untoward consequences of this admission. The fact that A does not do X may stem from at least two sorts of factors. It could be that A is *unable* to do X or it could be that he is *disinclined* to do X. It is surely obvious that if prior events causally necessitate that S be *unable* to do X, that is quite a different matter from their causally necessitating his *disinclination* to do X. For in the latter but not the former circumstance, he is not rendered unable to do X and that fact is a crucial distinguishing feature.

An example might serve to clarify this point. It deliberately draws on a relatively uncomplicated power (in contrast to putting at golf or to performing successful heart transplants), in order to avoid problems arising from any gap between wanting to exercise some complex skill one does possess and actually doing so. If I do not switch on the radio because I know that there is nothing interesting on and because I prefer to read a new book instead, it seems to me that it would be silly to conclude from my conduct that I am *unable* to listen to the radio at the time. Given that I have a radio, that the needed electricity or batteries is available, that my physical well-being is such that I can turn the radio on, that I am not so tired that I will fall asleep as soon as the radio goes on, and so forth, it follows that I am *able* to listen to the radio at the time in question, even though I do not want to, and even though my not wanting to has prior causes.

However, an incompatibilist might well think this an opportune time to throw his strongest objection into the ring. He will no doubt contend that conditions of the sort indicated above do not show that I am able to listen to the radio at the time in question, simply because a further requirement has not been satisfied, namely that I be *able to want* to listen to the radio at the said time.

The first requirement in formulating a reply is to get clear about precisely what it would involve to be 'able to want'. The notion of ability is not ordinarily applied to wanting, though it may be that it could sensibly be spoken of in connection with choosing. 'Ability' is a notion which is, I think, overly restrictive anyway, since one can't use it to cover all the relevant issues in the problem at hand (e.g. it is far-fetched to speak of ability in relation to resisting temptation). Thus when it is said that we must be able to want, if my wanting to do x is a necessary condition of doing x, it is not an ability to want, so much as having the power to want, that is in question.[19] The notion of 'power' includes that of the more confined 'ability'. Other entities than human agents can have power, of course; for example, nitric acid has corrosive power. What is distinctive of human power is that *ceteris paribus* it is under the control of its possessor.

Even if we allow that there is a legitimate notion of lacking the power to want, its use would be pretty clearly *in contrast with* cases in which a person does not want to do something and, whose not wanting to do so is explicable in terms of 'standard' causes for not wanting to do it. Thus, if my not wanting to listen to the radio this afternoon is causally necessitated by such factors as my having been bored with the afternoon programmes on all past occasions, my wanting to write and so on, surely no one would seriously contend that I am unable to want to listen to the radio. By contrast, we do recognise that *some* causes hinder or preclude a man from wanting to carry out a particular course of action. If a man has been hypnotised and left with a post-hypnotic suggestion about not listening to the radio, his case is obviously different. Now I do not have a complete list of all the causes which fall into the second type of case, but I do know at least some of them. Hypnosis, pathological urges, uncontrollable impulses, brain-washing and the like, contrast clearly with the causes isolated in the first case and there is empirical evidence of great weight to substantiate the contrast.

Up to date I may have given the impression that all incompatibilists are united in saying that compatibilist analyses fail because they omit to account for the fact that the presence of causal ancestors of one's wants ensure that one lacks the power to want to do other than what one does, in fact. I must now, however, seek to 'divide and conquer' the incompatibilist opposition. What I have said in the preceding paragraph applies directly to both the hard determinist and the libertarian. What I want to point out now applies to the libertarian alone.

Libertarians insist against the compatibilist that people do not have power to want (choose), as opposed to power to do, except in the *absence* of causal determinants or, alternatively, when they act in *opposition* to these causal determinants but yet their acting is uncaused by prior causes.

The libertarian seems to me to introduce a 'power to choose' (or want) as simply a metaphysical presupposition of responsibility. Such a move is of no help in distinguishing responsible from non-responsible action, and thus stands in stark contrast with the fact that a compatibilist can indicate a plausible distinction in the two sorts of action by distinguishing different sorts of causes. In the libertarian strategy no attempt is made to describe the manifestation of the special sense of 'power to choose' employed, in any but phenomenological terms. In the compatibilist strategy an attempt is made to show that having the power to want is manifested in standard causal conditions.

I now turn briefly to the hard determinist, who claims that there is no distinction to be drawn between the effect on an agent of standard causes, and of the sorts of causes isolated above like hypnosis, pathological urges and so on. Now it is quite clear that in our actual practice we constantly and *systematically* make such a distinction and the onus of proof seems therefore to be on the hard determinist to show there is no basis for differentiating between the sorts of causes at all.

Clearly this is a difficult area and one can easily get bogged down in intuition-swapping. I propose instead to take an illustration from our approach to the responsibility of the mentally ill in an endeavour to show that our present systematic distinguishing between sorts of causes is based in part, at least, on criteria. The task of the hard determinist must, therefore, extend to showing that these criteria are misguided, inappropriate or somesuch, as the means to showing that all causes are to be assimilated.

It is a fact that the mentally ill sometimes perform voluntary crimes (where 'voluntary' is used, as elsewhere, so as not to beg the question about freedom). Why is it that we allow the presence of mental illness as the cause or even part of the cause of the mentally ill person's motives or desires as an exculpating consideration — even when these desires are not irresistible?[20] There are, I think, at least three reasons. Firstly, the mentally ill person's criminal behaviour tends to be contrary to his own interests — indeed to be frequently personally harmful and to that extent senseless. Secondly, the motives are apt to be not just senseless but incoherent because they seem *alien* and incapable of joint satisfaction with others which the person has. Thirdly, mentally ill persons characteristically lack insight into their own motives. The normal person can assess his motives in terms of their appeal or repugnance and so on. He can, of course, be mistaken. The true basis of appeal in the mentally ill criminal's motivation, by contrast, is obvious to the outsider, or may become obvious, but remains opaque to the agent. This ignorance appears to be a necessary consequence, or even a constituent, of the mental illness, which is an alien condition involuntarily suffered. Even so, it may be that sometimes the mentally ill are rightfully held to be responsible to some degree because of their contribution to the present alien condition.

The response to all this may well be: why should the incoherent, personally harmful and self-concealed character of the mentally ill man's motives be grounds for special consideration? My view is that it is because he is robbed of the power of moral assessment, but maybe one is reduced to saying that it is a brute fact that it does. But, at least, I should think, plausibility is on my side (whether or not I have to resort to bruteness) in saying that there *is* a distinction between standard and non-standard causes. I don't know how else to proceed at this stage simply because I cannot specify exhaustively what kinds of causes do, and what kinds of causes do not, void responsibility. That I cannot give a *complete* rationale for the distinction does not mean that there isn't one. Furthermore, I have given *some* indication of why and how the distinction is to be drawn. Finally, there is a fair degree of agreement among those who have considered the distinction between standard and non-standard causes as to which causes fall under which category.[21]

IV

In the preceding discussion I have been investigating what Chisholm[22] calls having something 'directly within one's power'. There is a need, however, to discuss what he calls having something 'indirectly within one's power'. As will emerge, the sort of objections levelled at compatibilist accounts of indirect power, also hinge on assimilating cases of powerlessness, to cases of causation, just as they do in connection with direct power.

In discussions about a person's having power to perform some act, we are more often than not interested in his capacity to do it *at a certain time*, or *by a certain time*.[23] Just as temporal references are required in specifying the time of the act, they are also required in specifying powers. For clearly, though someone may be unable, at t_2, to do A at

t_2, it does not follow that there was no earlier time t_1 at which he was able to do A by (or at) t_2. At 3.00 p.m. I may not be able to paint the house because I have no paint or paint brush. But I might well have been able to fetch a paint brush and some paint from the hardware store before they closed at 11.30 a.m. and thus be able to paint the house at 3.00 p.m. I let my opportunity pass by not creating the 'generational' conditions requisite for doing the painting. In the sense of having a *general* capacity to paint the house I had this at 3.00 p.m. even in the absence of the generational conditions. But in the far more important sense, as far as freedom is concerned, of having power to perform a task picked out by an *individuating* action description, it was only indirectly in my power at 3.00 p.m. to perform the task.

In general, in order for an agent to perform A by t_2, he must perform some acts prior to t_2 which together with the state of the rest of the world, cause him to be able, at some time t_1, where t_1 is either earlier than or simultaneous with t_2, to do A at t_1. (I include the notion of the opportunity to do A in 'the state of the rest of the world'.) Usually these preparatory acts are ones that would create generational conditions requisite for doing A (e.g. buying the paint and the brush). These acts, when taken in conjunction with the antecedently present house, fine weather and so on, cause a set of generational conditions such that the agent is empowered to paint the house at t_2. Some preparatory acts may serve to furnish the agent with new powers or to restore lost ones (e.g. having a kidney transplant).

Before going any further I must make a brief digression. M. C. Bradley has urged that the falsity of the antecedent of a hypothetical is compatible with the truth of the whole hypothetical analysis. Thus suppose that a hypothetical offered in analysis of 'x has the power to do y', is true, while the clause in the antecedent specifying x's ability to perform y happens to be false. In that event, says Bradley, x's power to do y surely lapses in view of x's simple inability to do it. ('Skill' could be substituted for 'ability' or 'power' to avoid any to-ings and fro-ings about the possible introduction of circularity into the analysis by the use of 'ability' *simpliciter*.) Bradley believes this circumstance would force

the compatibilist who relies on a hypothetical analysis of human power, to fall back on the line of thinking found in e.g. Schlick's writings on compatibilism where sentences about x's power can be rendered, roughly, in terms of x's actual actions not being performed under compulsion.

Now I am reluctant to pin my compatibilist hopes on this latter sort of understanding partly for reasons already considered in Chapter 2 in connection with the modifiability theory of responsibility — the two positions being closely linked. What I must contend, therefore, is *either* that the antecedent clause offered as a specification of x's power to perform y is correct (or very nearly so), *or* that even if the search for a correct analysis has so far proved frustrating and unfruitful that this does not show that there isn't a correct one. I am not so bold as to assert confidently that the former of ·these alternatives has certainly been realised, and better philosophers[24] than me express grave doubts even about the ultimate availability of such an analysis. Nevertheless, I do think some progress has been made and hence I remain guardedly optimistic about the proximity of the analysis offered to the correct one.

V

I have previously alluded to the issue of mental health, and I now want to draw on that area to illustrate the idea of having something indirectly within one's power. I suggested that sometimes the mentally ill are justly held responsible for certain of their acts provided that they have *contributed* to their alienated condition. Consider the following speculation. Let us allow that at some time in the future it becomes a well-established fact that taking certain drugs has, as a causal consequence, definitely specifiable mental illnesses. Let us allow that knowledge of this well-established fact is widely disseminated. It might well be that those who contribute to their mental illness by indulging in taking the drugs in question, will be justly held responsible for some of their acts done while mentally ill. The ground for holding them thus responsible would be that at the time of their criminal acts they had it indirectly in their power to avoid doing them.

There is a clear analogy here with the notions of culpable ignorance and wilful blindness.

If we say of an agent that his making a certain thing happen is within his power at time t_1 this will be true if, and only if, his making that thing happen is either directly within his power or indirectly within his power at that time. In the former case, if the agent wanted to do some act A at time t_1 then he would do A at t_1. In the latter case, he is able at t to do A by t_1, where t is either earlier than or simultaneous with t_1, if, and only if, there is a set of preparatory acts which, together with the state of the rest of the world (other than his own acts) would put him in a position (empower him) to perform the next preparatory act, and this series of preparatory acts would ultimately put him in a position at or before t_1, to perform the indicated act A.

On the account I have given, the agent's possessing power at a particular time does not depend on his actually performing the act at that time nor (in the case of his power being indirect) does it depend on his actually performing any requisite preparatory acts. In the latter case, if he fails to perform these preparatory acts he renders himself directly unable to perform the act for which they are prerequisites, but remains indirectly able to perform the act because he was able, at an earlier time, to do the act by the time in question. In other words, the fact that it is causally incompossible relative to actual events prior to t_1 for the agent to do S at t_1, does not bear on the fact that he possessed indirect power at t_1 to do S.

Two objections will be levelled at what I have had to say. Firstly, suppose that S is in a position, at t, to make himself a pavlova. It might be argued that it doesn't follow from this supposition taken in conjunction with the fact that he wants a pavlova that he *will* make one. This is, I think, correct. It may, for example, be that S does not *know* that he is in a position to make a pavlova. Though the ingredients are readily available, he may not know where to find them. To fill in the details, imagine that his wife has just been rushed to hospital a few hours earlier, and that he is quite ignorant of where she keeps the needed items. Now it appears that it is not true that if S wants to make the pavlova, that he will.

The objection then is that it would be false to say he is able to do so as the analysis would lead one to believe. But what these foregoing considerations should lead us to do is not abandon the analysis given but, rather, to distinguish between an epistemic and a non-epistemic sense of power. Thus we can say that it is within S's power to make the pavlova but that he doesn't know that it is. The non-epistemic sense of power or ability thus does not entail that the possessor of the power also possesses knowledge (or belief) of his power. Other examples could be given using an epistemic sense of power. The extent to which one's knowledge (or lack of it) is important in determining responsibility cannot be argued independently of circumstances. Sometimes it is directly and sometimes indirectly within one's power to acquire the requisite knowledge at or by a specified time.

The second objection brings us back into confrontation with the old worry about causal necessitation. It will predictably be objected that my account overlooks the following problem. Although an agent may be able (in either the epistemic or non-epistemic senses), at t_1, to do A by t_2, it may be causally necessitated by events at t_1, or, indeed, even earlier events, that the agent *will not want* to do A by t_2. It may be causally necessitated that at each of the intervening times between t_1 and t_2, he does not want to do A by or at t_2.

The compatibilist reply that I have been urging is that the fact that these desires are causally necessitated, by no means precludes the fact that he was *able* to do A by or at t_2. Nor, furthermore, does the fact that the agent's not doing A by or at t_2 was causally necessitated preclude the fact that he was able to do it by or at t_2.

Consider the following example, There may be events occurring now, at t_1 (or even earlier), which causally necessitate that I will not want (choose...) at t_3, to go to a lecture at t_5. Suppose, for instance, that some person is now making (at t_1), or has, at some time in the past made, plans to invite my wife and me to his place for dinner at t_5. This making of plans, together with a wide variety of other events at t_1, causally necessitates my being invited, at t_2, to go to the dinner party. Furthermore, it causally necessitates my wanting (choosing) to go to the dinner party at t_3, and hence my not wanting to attend the lecture.

None of this sequence of events and none of this causal necessitation need make me powerless (from t_1 through to t_5) to do other than go to the dinner party at t_5. I had the resources, the knowledge and so on to attend the lecture. My not going was not the outcome of lacking the power to attend, but simply of the fact that I was disinclined to go. Clearly, then, I had the power to do other than I, in fact, happened to do, and this satisfies the demands of freedom, provided only that there are present no non-standard causes (such as hypnosis, undue pressure from the inviter and so forth).

The bogy of determinism has been dealt with at great length. I am by no means sure that it has been laid to rest,[25] but I believe that what has been said to date is sufficiently cogent to allow me to proceed to the final two arguments outlined in Chapter 1. I should perhaps say, though, that for those who think there is an enormous discrepancy between the doctrine of determinism and the evidence available for its truth, and hence that the compatibilist position is just 'whistling in the dark', that it has been my concern to consider the compatibilist position on the assumption that determinism might be true. I have made such an assumption (even though it may go beyond present evidence) because it is the strongest possible one.

12 Omniscience and Freedom

I have contended that if the doctrine of determinism holds true, we have to deal with the fact that prior to every act conditions *empirically sufficient* for that act obtain. It has been frequently charged that if an omniscient God exists then prior to every act conditions *logically sufficient* for that act obtain. This latter consideration is further claimed to be ground for saying that we lack the power to refrain from certain acts and in turn to be ground for denying freedom of action sufficient for responsibility. At this point either of two charges may be laid. Firstly, it could be contended that because we are unfree and not responsible for our actions God cannot blame us and hence the whole Christian theological scheme with its talk of sin and culpability before God collapses. Alternatively, it might be urged that since we are responsible for our actions and do act freely God cannot exist.

An important discussion of this traditional problem has taken place in recent philosophy, which has permitted a considerable amount of progress to be made in resolving the problem. I first set out a rather elegant version of the problem and some underlying assumptions as these have been formulated by Nelson Pike.[1] The reader should note that these assumptions are put forward without challenge in order to set the problem up as fairly as possible. When possible resolutions are considered later in the chapter some of these matters will receive more critical attention.

I

The doctrine of God's omniscience is usually construed as involving:

(1) the claim that God is infallible,
(2) the claim that God knows the outcome of human actions in advance of their performance.

For present purposes we can best get clear about these two items if we go along with Pike in making the following assumptions. Firstly, I will assume that 'God is omniscient' is a necessary statement in the following sense. The title 'God' attaches to the attribute terms 'perfectly good', 'omnipotent', 'omniscient' and so on for all the standard attributes assigned to the Christian God, in such a way as to make the hypothetical functions 'If S is God, then S is omniscient' etc. necessary truths. That is, it is a logically necessary condition of bearing the title 'God' that an individual be omniscient and likewise for all the standard attributes assigned to the Christian God. It is, however logically even if not materially possible that an individual, Yahweh or Jesus, say, who is entitled 'God' might not have possessed that title since one might, for example, *entertain* the idea that God Yahweh (or, Jesus the Christ) is not, for instance, perfectly good. (In passing I should point out that because of the awkwardness involved in only using 'God' as it strictly should be used, namely as a title term, I often use it loosely as if it were a proper name.) It emerges from the foregoing that saying:

'If S is Yahweh, then S is perfectly good'
is to be distinguished from saying

'If S is God, then S is perfectly good'
precisely in that the latter (but not the former) is a necessary truth.[2]

Secondly, if an individual is omniscient that individual believes all true propositions. Hence

Necessarily, for any x and any P, if x is omniscient, then if P is true, x believes P.

Thirdly, if a given individual is omniscient, then that individual believes nothing that is false. This assumption goes beyond the immediately preceding one in that it is logically possible that an individual who believes all true propositions might also believe a false proposition in virtue of believing the negation of one of the other propositions that he believes.

It is worth pointing out at this stage that traditionally God's knowledge has been said to be non-inferential in that it is not based on evidence or grounds. Different models have been appealed to in support of this view, the chief ones being those of precognitive knowledge and a person's knowledge of his own actions. Each of these is, of course, controversial and to that extent the believer in God's non-inferential knowledge should be wary of placing too much weight on the soundness of the models themselves. Talk of God's knowledge of events as non-inferential has worried some believers, though. They have felt that such a view presupposes that God is 'outside of time'. Now it is true that adherents of the view that God's knowledge is non-inferential have generally believed that God, being outside of time, 'sees' the whole of history simultaneously, and, because of the immediacy of his perception of the whole, knows its contents non-inferentially. Boethius and later Aquinas and Calvin among others, subscribed to such a view. But the historically influential nature of this association does not appear to rest on a *conceptual* connection. Hence one can maintain that God's knowledge does not depend on his drawing evidentially grounded inferences, while avoiding commitment to the doctrine of God's timelessness. Later on I will take up the claim that among the attractions of the doctrine of timelessness is that it furnishes a solution to the problem of the relation between God's omniscience and human freedom.

If the second and third of the assumptions previously isolated are coupled together, they yield the conclusion that:

Necessarily, for any x and any P, if x is omniscient then if P is true x believes that P, and if x believes that P then P is true.

Fourthly, let us assume with Pike that omniscience is an essential property of any individual possessing it. That is, we are to assume that if a given individual is omniscient, that individual would not be the individual it is if it were not omniscient. Since it is impossible for God to hold a false belief, any individual holding a false belief could not be

God. The first, third and fourth assumptions taken together yield the doctrine of God's infallibility (or perhaps, unfailingness). Namely,

> Necessarily, for any x and any P, if x is God, then necessarily if x believes that P is true, P is true.

Fifthly, if a given individual is God, that individual has always existed and will always exist. This is the doctrine of God's everlastingness. God has time location in that it is not a category mistake to apply temporal predicates to him, and if God exists at any time, then he exists at all times (his duration extends indefinitely both forward and backward in time). He is, to speak technically, sempiternal.

Finally, assume that if an individual exists at a given moment in time, then in order to count as omniscient, that individual must hold any belief he holds at that moment in time. Thus:

> Necessarily, for any x and any P, if x is omniscient and exists at time t, then if x believes P is true, x believes P is true at time t.

Let us now consider the version of the argument proposed by Nelson Pike (which makes use of the above six assumptions).

(1)   'Yahweh is omniscient and Yahweh exists at t_1' entails 'If Brown does A at t_2, then Yahweh believes at t_1 that Brown does A at t_2' (from our second and sixth assumptions and further, where t_1 is prior to t_2).

(2)   If Yahweh is (essentially) omniscient, then 'Yahweh believes P' entails 'P' (from assumptions three and four — the doctrine of divine infallibility).

(3)   It is not within one's power at a given time so to act that both 'P' and '~P' are true. That is, one cannot do something having a description that is logically contradictory.

(4)   It is not within one's power at a given time so to act that something believed by an individual at a time

prior to the given time was not believed by that individual at the prior time.

(5)   It is not within one's power at a given time so to act that an individual existing at a time prior to the given time did not exist at the prior time. (The previous three items are considered by Pike to be part of the concept of 'ability' or 'power' as we use it when speaking of humans.)

(6)   If Yahweh believes at t_1 that Brown does A at t_2, then if it is within Brown's power at t_2 to refrain from doing A then either:

> (i) it was within Brown's power at t_2 so to act that Yahweh believed P at t_1 and 'P' is false;
>
> or (ii) it was within Brown's power at t_2 so to act that Yahweh did not believe as he did believe at t_1;
>
> or (iii) it was within Brown's power at t_2 so to act that Yahweh did not exist at t_1.

(Pike considers this item is a necessary truth in virtue of these three alternatives exhausting the possibilities.)

(7)   If Yahweh is (essentially) omniscient, then the first alternative in the consequent of (6) is false (from items (2) and (3)).

(8)   The second alternative in (6) is false (from (4)).

(9)   The third alternative in (6) is false (from (5)).

(10) Therefore, if Yahweh is (essentially) omniscient and believes at t_1 that Brown will do A at t_2, then it was not within Brown's power at t_2 to refrain from doing A (from (6) and (7) to (9)).

(11) Therefore, if Yahweh is (essentially) omniscient and exists at t_1, then if Brown does A at t_2, it was not within Brown's power at t_2 to refrain from doing A (from (10) and (1)). This conclusion could, of course, be generalised for all actions and all agents.

Notice, firstly, that Pike makes no mention of *causes* of Brown's action and this on purpose. Secondly, he acknowledges that the argument presupposes that it makes straightforward sense to suppose that God (or just anyone) held a true belief at some time prior to an action's occurring, but indicates that this is not to suppose that *what* God believed *was true at some time prior to the time of the action*.

II

Pike's version has the merit of clearly bringing out what historically has been thought to be crucial to the formulation of the problem, namely that God's knowledge is *in the past* relative to the human actions he foreknows. The standard contention has been that if, firstly, there is such divine foreknowledge the modality of the claim to such foreknowledge must take its colour from the pastness of God's knowledge not the reference to the future action. Secondly, it has been held that because propositions about the past are necessary in the sense that there is nothing one can now do about their truth value, nothing can be done about the truth value of propositions about future human actions known by God to be true or false sometime in the past. Pike's argument like all serious ones alleging an incompatibility between God's foreknowledge and human freedom is, at its core, an argument of the following form:

(1) If God is omniscient then if it is the case that p, God knows it is the case that p;

(2) If God knows that p, it must be the case that p;

(3) If it must be the case that p, then necessarily it is the case that p;

(4) If God knows that it is the case that p, then necessarily it is the case that p (from (2) and (3));

(5) If God is omniscient, every true proposition is necessarily true (from (1) and (4)).

Pike's argument, of course, introduces the notion of God's essential omniscience — a feature upon which I will remark · later. For the moment the important thing is to get clear about the construction to be placed on (2). If (2) is read as

(2′) Necessarily, if God knows that it is the case that p, it is the case that p,

the proposition is, I believe, true, but the inference from (2′) and (3) to (4) will founder. If, by contrast, (2) is taken as

(2″) If God knows that it is the case that p, then
  necessarily it is the case that p,
the inference follows but the question arises: 'Is (2″) true?'
Pike's version of the problem requires us to read (2″) as being
true. One can view the proposed solutions to the problem of
the alleged logical incompatibility between the divine
foreknowledge and human freedom as attempts to justify a
negative answer.

III

One proposal which has had wide support is that which
denies the antecedent of (2″).

It might be said that God (or anyone else) can only know
what will happen in the future if the events he foreknows are
'present in their causes' at the time of his foreknowing. But,
it might be continued, if future events (including free human
actions) are 'present in their causes' prior to their occurrence,
such events are necessary and any claim that human actions
are free, fails. Since, however, there are free human actions,
there can be no such order of causes and no foreknowledge
of the future.

It is evident that a view of this sort hinges on claiming that
God's foreknowledge of future events would be possible only
if he could predict on the basis of the present state of the
universe and of certain rigid laws of a causal kind governing
temporal events (cf. Laplace's calculating intelligence). An
adherent of this view would probably suggest that it is no
skin off God's nose that he could not know the outcome of
the future for he is only expected to know what is *knowable*
and *per impossibile* the future is not knowable.

Arthur Prior[3] attributed such a view to Aquinas though it
hardly seems consistent with Aquinas' more usual affirmation
(also acknowledged by Prior) that God timelessly 'sees' the
whole time-series at once in such a way that for him future
contingent events are present and hence not *fore*known.[4]
(Later on I will take up this second more influential way of
trying to resolve the problem.)

It is clearly presupposed in Pike's argument that it makes
straightforward sense to speak of holding a true belief about
some action, A, prior to A's occurring. This has been

disputed by Prior and others. The disputants allege that it makes no sense to speak of 'Brown does A at t_2' being true at an earlier time t_1 unless the action A, is present in its causes at t_1. Are statements of the form 'It is true at t_1 that Brown does A at t_2', sensible?

Notice first of all that the action, A, is dated (in that part of the statement which refers to it being performed) as being performed at t_2. There is, of course, a further (earlier) time mentioned in the statement. If one tries to date the truth value of the whole statement the mentioning of two distinct times poses a difficulty. One gets no help from considering what we do if a statement mentions distinct places (as against times). Thus

'"P" is true at S' (where S is a spatial location)

is restatable as

'"P at S" is true'.

If we assign two (incompatible) dates to the action we seem to end up with the nonsensical:

'At t_1 Brown does A at t_2'.

Attempts have been made to make sense of such statements. Ryle,[5] for example, urged that a statement of this form should be understood as affirming that if one guessed or asserted at t_1 that Brown does A at t_2 the guess or assertion would be correct. Richard Gale[6] has suggested that statements of the above form are to be read as affirming that at t_1 sufficient evidence was available upon which to base a well-reasoned prediction that Brown does A at t_2.

Recall that for Prior, God's foreknowledge of human actions presupposes the prior truth of propositions describing these actions. Under Ryle's interpretation

'It is true at t_1 that Brown does A at t_2'

is rendered trivially true if Brown does do A at t_2 and hence is insufficiently strong for Prior's purposes. Under Gale's interpretation the non-inferential knowledge attributed to God is precluded. It does seem to be a proposal like Gale's which Prior would support. In 'The Formalities of Omniscience' he wrote:

I cannot see in what way the alleged knowledge, even if it were God's, could be more than correct guessing. For there would be *ex hypothesi* nothing that could *make* it knowledge, no present *ground* for the guess's correctness. . . . (p. 122, Prior's italics)

Granted that, as in Pike's argument, no particular stance is taken on there being antecedently sufficient causal conditions for human actions — though it seems to me that Prior's stand demands a libertarian view of human freedom — this whole approach collapses if God's foreknowledge is, as I have taken it, non-inferential.[7]

IV

I turn now to consider a further proposal. In formulating the problem it was noted that the two items generating trouble were God's infallible foreknowledge and the claim that with respect to anything that was, is, or will be the case, God knew, *from eternity*, that it would be the case. Understood in a straightforward way, God's knowledge from eternity seems to entail his knowing the nature of certain states of affairs *in advance*.

But many philosophers and theologians have claimed that God 'exists outside of time' and hence that he bears no temporal relations to the events or circumstances of the natural world.[8] For these thinkers it would not be sensible to talk of God knowing 'in advance' for if he did know that a given event was going to happen before it happened, then at least this cognition would stand in a temporal relation to a natural event in the world just in virtue of its occurring *before* that event. This 'solution' then is an attack on the fifth assumption made earlier.

Now in what sense could God 'exist outside of time'? What this claim seems to mean is that time-location predicates (as well as space-location predicates) are not to be used when characterising God. Thus both *temporal extension* (with its idea of succession) and *temporal location* (with its idea of existing at a given moment) are inapplicable notions when God is being characterised. This could be stated more formally as the claim that:

Necessarily, for any x, if x is God, then necessarily x lacks temporal position and necessarily x lacks temporal extension.

First, an adherent of this view strictly speaking denies that God has *fore*knowledge. God knows of contingent events not as still future but as present. It might be thought that such a view has the advantage of not requiring us to talk of God undergoing change (in virtue of changes occurring in his states of knowledge). My own view is that God's unchangingness has to do with his attributes and the dispositions to certain kinds of behaviour to which they give rise, not with God's states of knowledge being mutable. Even so, there are certain costs attached to this denial of foreknowledge. Tobias Chapman[9] has argued that since Aquinas accepts the idea that the present is necessary in the same (Aristotelian) sense as the past, saying that God's knowledge is like knowledge of the present rather than foreknowledge, doesn't avoid the putative effects on human freedom. I do not think that Chapman could make this charge stick, chiefly because the seeing of someone doing something at the time he is doing it, cannot on its own be said to entail that the agent could not do anything other than what he is doing. At least, not in any interesting or relevant sense of 'could not'. But even allowing Chapman's contention, I think one could contend (as Chapman does) that Aquinas probably held a view, which, if defensible, would get him off the hook of the foregoing difficulty. Aquinas, like Plato and Boethius, certainly sometimes suggests that it is meaningless to say an *eternally* (timelessly) true statement like 'Brown does A at t_2' entails the further claim that the statement is true *sempiternally*. Chapman thinks that, consistent with this position, Aquinas could justifiably deny that 'necessarily true' means the same as 'always true'. Thus, if God's knowledge is exclusively of eternal truths, it will be meaningless to say his knowledge is the same at every moment, and propositions like 'Brown does A at t_2' can remain contingently rather than necessarily true. Two things need to be said at this juncture. First, even if these contentions are sound it is doubtful whether one could hold (as Aquinas would seem committed to holding) the consistency of the claim that God's *all at once* knowledge extends to knowledge of the truth and falsity of propositions *and* the denial that future contingent propositions can be said to be *now* true (or false) when the events to which they refer are taking place. Secondly, and more significantly, if Martha Kneale[10] is correct, it is a necessary condition for the expression of a timelessly true proposition that the sentence used to express it is true under all circumstances. Indeed, if she is right the notions of eternity and sempiternity are either identical or mutually entailing. These claims undercut the distinction to which Chapman thinks Aquinas would appeal. Nevertheless, if Mrs. Kneale is correct in her further contention (and she clearly is, I think) that while necessity entails sempiternity, the reverse entailment doesn't hold, the need to adopt Aquinas' dubious distinction disappears.

As well as the denial of *fore*knowledge, the appeal to timelessness has a further consequence. We have seen that on the timelessness view, there is no difference between God's knowledge of past and future. That is, no temporal operators can be applied to God's knowledge. But this seems to lead to a denial of God's *omniscience* because we humans could presumably know what would be outside the pale of God's cognition, namely that certain events are present (or past or future as the case may be). Further, the familiar image of God seeing the details of our world as though from a high mountain is useless, because the mountain-top perception cannot be of the successive movements but only of the particulars at a given moment in time. If the scene is taken as a four-dimensional continuant (*à la* Minkowski) difficulties re-enter when one tries to account for the percipient's *successive* awarenesses.

Nelson Pike[11] has argued with some plausibility that provided true statements in which temporal indexical expressions occur can be reformulated without such expressions and still report the same facts, a timeless being could be a knower. Thus his omniscience might be preservable though it would remain impossible for him to formulate his knowledge in certain ways, namely those prohibited to him *qua* timeless being.

Whatever vitality Pike's resuscitative operation might give to the notion of an omniscient timeless being, the supposed solution to our problem with which the view has been credited, must be bought at a theologically exorbitant price. We have already seen that the 'solution' is in fact a dissolution, because it consists in denying genuine *fore*-knowledge (and hence item (1) in Pike's version of the argument at issue). But even more damaging is the fact that the doctrine makes nonsense of much that is indispensable to the Judaeo-Christian understanding of the world. For instance, if the doctrine of creation is understood as asserting that the universe is not eternally extended backwards, that doctrine must go. Further, if God is 'outside of time' his capacity to act as an agent who brings things about in the way envisaged in accounts of the miraculous, may be questioned. Finally for our purposes, the Christian believer cannot square the doctrine with the incarnation involving as it does the datable events of Jesus' life, death, resurrection and ascension (and he, of course, bears the title 'God').[12]

V

Previously I indicated that the premise $(2'')$ of the argument given in Section II has been subjected to several lines of attack. In addition to the denial of its antecedent clause, which I have looked at already, the denial of its consequent must also be considered.

Let us call those facts about a time t 'hard' facts if they are not made true by any facts about a later time t_1, and those facts about a time t 'soft' facts if they are (at least in part) made true by what happens at a later time t_1. Thus, the holding of a belief will be a hard fact, but statements like 'Captain Cook discovered the east coast of Australia more than two hundred years before Young wrote his chapter on "Omniscience and Freedom"' or 'Smith believed at t_1 that Thompson does A at t_2' relate soft facts.

Consider the following principle:

(A)   One does not have the power (at a given time) so to act that the past (relative to that time) would be other than it was.[13]

I think it is fairly uncontroversial to claim that we often have the power so to act that 'soft' facts about the past would be different from what they are and hence that (A) is false at least in relation to 'soft' facts. I shall illustrate this claim by considering:

'Smith knew at t_1 that Thompson does A at t_2'

and in order to make the case as parallel as possible with one having God as subject, that Smith knew precognitively (or non-inferentially).[14] Here, because it is not evidentially grounded, knowledge is perhaps indistinguishable from true belief if Smith always believes rightly. (I shall, therefore, not be over-scrupulous in using one locution 'knows' rather than the other 'truly believes', in what follows.)

Why should we deny that it was within Thompson's power at t_2 to refrain from doing A? That is, why could he not have the power so to act that the belief held by Smith at t_1 was false? I have argued in Chapter 3 that statements of the above form are made true by what happens at t_2 and since the belief held by Smith at t_1 is not made true by any state of affairs prior to t_2, I see no reason (in the absence of defeating conditions) for denying his power to refrain from A. To assert otherwise is to engage in a question-begging denial that men ever have power to act in ways other than those in which they actually do.

It is, however, far more controversial to claim that (A) is false when applied to 'hard' facts. For the moment I will not be controversial and will accept for the sake of argument that (A) is true when applied to 'hard' facts. Thus while it is within Thompson's power at t_2 so to act that the belief held by Smith at t_1 was false, from the fact that the belief was made true by what happened at t_2 we can conclude that the power was not exercised. On the other hand in the light of (A) it is not within his power at t_2 so to act that Smith did not believe as he did at t_1. We must distinguish '*that* one believes' from '*what* one believes'. Likewise, taking it to be true for the moment that a person's existing at a time t is a 'hard' fact, he did not have the power so to act at t_2 that Smith did not exist at t_1.

Now to return to the case of divine foreknowledge. Suppose that God knows at t_1 that Brown does A at t_2, then, as in the human case, we can conclude that Brown does A for had he failed to do A at t_2, God could not be described as having known at t_1 that Brown would do A at t_2. This much is parallel. Just as before we also have to say that Brown did not have the power so to act at t_2 that God did not believe as he in fact believed at t_1.

But, and here is the disanalogy, according to the argument presented, if we assume that God held a certain belief at t_1 it is not just an additional contingent fact that what happens at t_2 makes it true, for unlike Smith in the human case, any individual who is God is infallible. Hence we cannot ascribe to Brown the power we gave to Thompson, namely the power to refrain from doing A at t_2. For, *on the analysis given previously*, to say that a given individual is infallible (e.g. Yahweh) is to say that 'Yahweh believes P' *entails* 'P'.

If we follow up Augustine's suggestion that there is a parallel between human and divine foreknowledge, it is clear that what has to be denied to ensure the parallel and avoid the argument's conclusion is God's infallibility. That is, the notion of God's infallibility specified at the beginning of our investigation. That notion was a direct consequence of assumptions two, three and four. What seems most problematic is assumption four about *essential* omniscience.

Let us suppose that Yahweh is omniscient; he therefore holds no false beliefs. But shall we go on to say that the consequence of holding a false belief would be that Yahweh isn't the person he was or that he is no longer the individual he was? Is the predicate 'omniscient' so related to personal identity that an omniscient being would not be the individual he is if he were not omniscient?[15] Thus suppose there was in the town of Z a man who had never been known to be unable to give a correct answer to any intelligible question and who was dubbed 'the infallible man'. One day someone asked him 'Will Brown do A at t_2?' and he said 'Yes, he will.' But Brown perversely spent the day in bed and failed to do A. In the face of this unprecedented situation what might the townsfolk of Z say?

Would they say that the individual in question had ceased to be the individual he was? I think not in the light of the fact that the criteria of personal identity have not been jettisoned or even threatened. Certainly,

'Z doesn't have an infallible man in it any longer'

is acceptable, but that is a different matter.

But, one might say, Pike's version of the problem stresses *essential* omniscience. That is surely true and forces us to recall that the predicate 'omniscient' is related to the title-term 'God' in such a way as to make 'God is omniscient' a necessary truth in the manner previously discussed. But it is a further claim (which goes beyond this assumption) to say that the individual who bears the title 'God' (i.e. Yahweh) would not be the individual he is if he were not omniscient. This solution[16] involves denying that omniscience is an essential property of any individual possessing it. At the same time it denies the consequent of the premise (2″) from Section II. Unlike the solution which depended on placing God outside of time, genuine *fore*knowledge is preserved by this solution.[17]

The time has come, however, to question an assumption made previously, namely that principle (A):

'One does not have the power (at a given time) so to act that the past (relative to that time) would be other than it was',

is true when applied to 'hard' facts about the past.[18]

Suppose that I buy my wife an anniversary present, that I have the ability (know-how and resources) to perform acts alternative to buying the present, and that conditions for the exercise of these abilities are normal. It follows that I have the power to refrain from making the purchase (call this act X). Suppose further that I know that my wife believes that I will do X, and that I am the sort of person who, in a situation like this, would not want to disappoint and would not disappoint my wife who believes that I am going to do X. Suppose that I am the sort of person who, in a situation like this, would want to refrain from X, and would refrain from X, only if my wife had not believed that I was going to do X. Then we may properly say that I would refrain from X only if the past had been different, only if my wife had not held a belief that in fact she did hold (which is a 'hard' fact) — I have the power to refrain from X, and this is a power that I would want to exercise, and would exercise, only if the past had been different in that a belief which was held had not been held. So my power to refrain from X is a power so to act that (to perform an act such that if it were performed) the past would have been different in that a belief that was held would not have been held. Is there any contradiction in having this power so to act that a 'hard' fact would have been other than it was? I think it is at the very least plausible to say there is no contradiction.

I now turn to the sort of case in which someone is said to have the power so to act that (to perform an act such that if one were to perform that act) a person who in fact did exist would not have existed.

Suppose, for example, that Robert Menzies would have been Leader of the Australian Federal Opposition only if Arthur Calwell had not existed.[19] Suppose that I am the sort of person who, in a normal situation, would assert that Menzies was Leader of the Federal Opposition only if Menzies had been Leader. It follows that I would assert that Menzies was Leader only if Calwell had not existed. I have the ability (know-how and resources) to make this assertion. I therefore have the power to perform an act that I would perform only if the past had been different in that a person who did exist had not existed. So long as we avoid thinking that my possession of this power permits me to cause alterations in the past, it is clear that there is nothing contradictory in having the power. It means only that one has the power to do something that one would want to do, and would do, only if the past had been different, in that something which took place at one time in the past would not have taken place at that time.

What if the person is God (allowing that the existence of God is a 'hard' fact *pace* Adams)? Suppose that at t_1 God knew, and hence believed, that I would do X at (a later time) t_2. Suppose I had the ability to do otherwise and conditions were normal. Then I had the power to refrain from X at t_2. If I had exercised this power then that belief at t_1 would not have been followed by my doing X at t_2. Thus it can properly be said that I had the power so to act that (to perform an act such that if I had performed that act) God's belief at t_1 would have been false. But if it was a belief held by God it could not have been false. Hence my power so to act that the belief would have been false was the power so to act that the person who held it would not have been 'God' — thus I had the power so to act that God, who in fact existed, would not have existed. The claim here then is that the power so to act is not merely a power so to act that a person who in fact was omniscient and divine would not have been omniscient or divine, but that he who in fact existed would not have existed (since we have assumed God's existence to be a 'hard' fact).

It is my contention, therefore, that the argument given in Section II is invalid when premise (2) is properly construed in the manner of (2′) and hence that Pike's particular version of this general argument fails. His introduction of the notion of essential omniscience gives the argument an air of toughness which dissipates upon the overthrowal of that notion. Thus his argument provides no grounds for an ontological disproof of God's existence or for denying the responsibility of men before God just in virtue of God's foreknowing what men will do.

13 'Omnipotence'

I have argued for the compatibility of the Judaeo-Christian God's omniscient foreknowledge with human freedom. I propose next to argue for the compatibility of God's omnipotence with human freedom. I think it is fair to say that the belief that omnipotence is incompatible with human freedom has greater intuitive force than the belief that omniscience is incompatible with free action and decision. There may be some value in pointing out, though, that a being that had whatever power was necessary for it to be regarded as omnipotent would not, in fact, be omnipotent, unless it were also omniscient. In at least one important sense, a god who could bring anything about, but did not always *know* the best way of bringing things about, would not be an omnipotent god.

The pre-analytic notion of omnipotence seems as straightforward as the comparable notion of omniscience. It would run something like this: to say that a given individual is omnipotent is to say that that individual has unlimited ('infinite') power. On investigation, however, the concept of omnipotence proves somewhat more troublesome that that of omniscience. Indeed, some philosophers have argued that the very notion of omnipotence is incoherent. It is necessary, first, therefore to deal with the matter of the coherence of the notion of omnipotence. This may seem a diversion. However, I believe that it is just as pressing to get clear about the doctrine of omnipotence as about, say, the doctrine of determinism, if one is profitably to discuss its connection with human freedom.

Before considering their connection, therefore, I shall make a prior study of the concept of omnipotence and I shall do so in the following way. First, I will discuss some candidate definitions of the concept which contain instructive errors. The final one considered will, I think, bring us quite near to an accurate understanding of the concept. But even though it, too, is probably deficient, I do not think that this should cause consternation. Many able philosophers have thought that even though the concept is not incoherent it nevertheless defies being finally and satisfactorily defined. So even if the end product of the investigation is not a finally satisfactory definition of 'omnipotence' the concept will not be shown thereby to be incoherent. I shall, therefore, endeavour in the latter part of the chapter to defend its coherence against the attack mounted by those who subscribe to the belief that there are unresolvable 'paradoxes of omnipotence'. In the succeeding chapter I will then try to show that the presence of omnipotence does not preclude men from acting freely and responsibly.

I

I said above that pre-analytically, to say that an individual is omnipotent, is to say that that individual has unlimited power (infinite power). One might begin to explicate the intuitive content of this idea along the following widely accepted lines: 'God is called omnipotent because he can do all things that are possible absolutely.'[1] Here 'possible absolutely' would mean that the description of a particular task is logically or (one might say) intrinsically consistent. A logically inconsistent description does not pick out a state of affairs difficult to produce, but fails to describe any state of affairs.

If we draw on this suggestion by Aquinas, we could put forward a first candidate definition.[2]

(D₁) S is omnipotent if, and only if, S has active power to do everything, x, such that 'x' represents a logically consistent description.

Now
 'Socrates sits'
 'Jezebel fornicates with the heathen'
 'Captain Cook discovers Australia's east coast'

are all seemingly intrinsically consistent. But S (an omnipotent being) cannot sit, fornicate, discover and so on unless it is the kind of being that can do such things and since, further, (D^1) imposes no *temporal restrictions* it would require an omnipotent being to be of a kind able to do all three acts simultaneously, were they all described as having taken place at the same time. But that seems an impossible demand and hence cannot be regarded as showing anything of consequence about 'omnipotence'. Furthermore, the introduction of any and every logically consistent description leads to other difficulties. One of these I will take up later in discussing the paradoxes, namely whether the inability of an omnipotent being to do some feat which ordinary mortals can do (like making something the maker can't subsequently destroy) renders 'omnipotence' incoherent. The other difficulty has in fact influenced many philosophers to the point where they have concluded there are insuperable worries in the way of defining 'omnipotence'. For there is dispute about how far the limitations which e.g. Yahweh's *moral nature* imposes on his choices, can be recognised without detracting from his power. This problem forces the abandonment of many initially plausible candidate definitions.

There is, for example, something logically incoherent about the statement 'God sins' (as far as Judaeo-Christian believers are concerned).[3] But the logical incoherence does not stem from Yahweh's creative power since, as Nelson Pike[4] has incisively shown, it is not because Yahweh lacks creative power to bring about states of affairs the production of which would be morally reprehensible, that the believer affirms Yahweh's impeccability. For if that were the case Yahweh *would be limited*. Rather, the one who bears the title 'God' cannot sin in that though he has the power to sin, it is not a power he could exercise and yet remain true to his firm and constant moral nature. He is of such a character that he *cannot bring himself* to act in a morally reprehensible way.

I previously alluded to the point that certain actions are such that they can only be performed by particular kinds of being. This point must now be developed further because I think it will promote a more informed understanding of the concept of omnipotence if the implications of that earlier remark are understood.[5] Consider then

(D$_2$) S is omnipotent if, and only if, S is able to perform
         any action of a kind which it is logically possible for
         a being of S's kind to do.

Clearly the proposal embedded in (D$_2$) faces an initial
difficulty in spelling out what sort or kind of being (D$_2$) is to
be taken to refer to. 'The sort of divine beings' would
obviously be open to the charge of circularity; 'the sort of
perfect beings' to the charge of vagueness to the point of
uninformativeness. What is more, because the notion of
'kinds of being' is unclear, if certain intuitively respectable
classifications of kinds be adopted, the analysis offered in
(D$_2$) will vacuously be fulfilled. Since, for example, it seems
sensible to talk of *inorganic* kinds of being, any being, S,
drawn from that kind will vacuously fulfil (D$_2$) simply
because it cannot (logically) perform any *action* at all. It will,
that is, be able to do every action of a kind which it is
logically possible for beings of its kind to do, namely none at
all.

II

Now James Ross has pointed out a readymade and acceptable
way out of a bit of the preceding worry. Instead of
conceiving of an omnipotent god's power in terms of *what he
can do*, we could say that the divine power extends to 'states
of affairs' and not to 'doings'. The latter is clearly far more
determinate language. Thus, the permissive 'do' should be
replaced by one of the so-called factitive verbs such as
'produce', 'effect', 'bring about'. Yahweh's ability, that is, is
in the realm of effectual power, it is purely intentional.[6]
Nevertheless, we are by no means out of the woods
because it is still incumbent upon us to specify the extent of
his effectual power. We still have to somehow limit the
substituend set of states of affairs he is required to have
within his power (without at the same time imposing
non-logical limits).
Ross, for example, notes that the power of an omnipotent
being can surely extend only to a sub-class of consistently
describable states of affairs, namely those which are *contingent*. This because omnipotent power could hardly be held

to range over consistent but necessary states of affairs. No being can *bring it about that* propositions such as that bachelors are unmarried, that plane triangles have three angles and so on are true. Hence 'consistent' must be understood as 'contingent and consistent'.

The upshot of Ross' discussion is a very strong definition of 'omnipotence':

> (D_3) S is omnipotent if, and only if, for every logically contingent (and consistent) state of affairs, p, whether p or $\sim p$ is the case is *logically equivalent* to the effective choice by S, that p or that $\sim p$ (respectively).

Ross contends that it is logical equivalence not material equivalence or simple entailment, which must characterise the connection between p and S's willing p. He urges that God's power is such that not only whatever he chooses is, in fact, the case, but also that whatever contrary to fact he *might* have chosen *must* then have been the case. Furthermore, not only must whatever God might have chosen (willed) have been the case, but nothing could have been the case had God not willed it.

There are some severe difficulties involved in Ross' definition and in the supporting arguments he advances for his definition, but before considering these I wish briefly to indicate its effectiveness in handling some of the conundrums raised about 'omnipotence' (and omnipotent beings). Consider

(a)   Can Yahweh[7] make a being he cannot control?

Under Ross' definition the only circumstance under which a state of affairs, q, is not determinable by the choice or will of Yahweh is if Nq or if $N \sim q$; further, it is inconsistent that he should choose that K exist where K causes q and q is necessarily the case. The existence of K falls within his power only if it is contingent. It is inconsistent that a being whose existence is contingent should be the cause of q where q is necessarily true. Thus it is impossible that Yahweh make a being he cannot control because it is impossible that K should exist and be able to cause a state of affairs which does not fall within his determining will.

Likewise consider

(b)   Can Yahweh make a stone he cannot lift?

Deleting the metaphor we get

(b')   Can Yahweh bring it about that there is a stone, x, which is such that 'x moves' is not a state of affairs he can bring about?

Only if 'x moves' is inconsistent or necessarily true could it not be a state of affairs which God could produce. But it is obviously contingent, hence falls within Yahweh's effectual choice.

Clearly Ross' definition is a powerful one — but is it too strong? If it is then it would be preferable to try and solve any worries about 'omnipotence' without committing ourselves to difficulties endemic in this approach. I think there are such difficulties.

First, his account of 'omnipotence' poses problems about the freedom of agents. Ross does recognise the difficulty his account poses for freedom, but endeavours to show that the problem is not intractable. Initially he points out that it is a mistake to infer from

$$N \, (SWp \supset p) \quad \text{by way of}$$
$$SWp \qquad \qquad \text{to}$$
$$Np$$

(Where SWp stands for S effectively wills (chooses) that p be the case.)

The modal operators do not transfer, a point which was argued in Section II of the previous chapter. With this much we can agree. But Ross claims that there is still something mysterious even though the modal operators do not transfer. He claims that corresponding to the logical equivalence between the divine choice and certain states of affairs, there must be an ontological dependence of the states of affairs.[8]

According to Ross, if one rests an argument against God's determining providence upon supposing an incompatibility between God's being a sufficient cause of a free act and the agent's also being its sufficient cause, then one must be (falsely) treating God and the agent as being of *the same level of reality*.[9] It is his contention that *natural* causal sufficiency can obtain only among beings of the same level of reality, while at the same time with regard to a being of higher level, *metaphysical* causal sufficiency can also obtain. The creator-creature relation and the author-character relation are equally instances of the same relation, namely, metaphysical dependence. Thus Macbeth is the sufficient natural cause of Duncan's death, while at the same time Shakespeare is the sufficient cause both of Macbeth's doing what he did and of its having that effect. Macbeth remains a free agent because on a different level of reality.

Hence in order to establish the incompatibility of God's sufficiency and man's sufficiency for the same event, one must appeal to something like the following proposition.

> R: That for anything A, which acts freely, it is false that A is metaphysically dependent upon something else.

In order to then proceed to lay the blame for the world's moral evil at God's door, one would have further to affirm

> R_3:   When a being of higher level is sufficient cause for the free evil action of a being of a lower level, the higher being is morally defective and ought not to have done so.

Yet according to Ross, both R and R_3 are known to be false. For, he urges, if R were true it would be impossible for *any* being to create a free being. But the Shakespeare-Macbeth relation and the author-character relation in general, fulfil the conditions for reality level difference and of metaphysical dependence.[10] They stand as counter-examples to R. Hence if the relation God bears to men is such that they are metaphysically dependent, there can be no incompatibility between God's providence and human freedom. To assert otherwise is to equivocate between the two distinct kinds of causality: 'metaphysical' and 'natural'.

Despite Ross' protestations and despite his appeal to 'metaphysical dependence' and 'levels of reality', his account fails to preserve any genuine human freedom. He contends that God's willing a certain event (like a human action) is necessary and sufficient for its occurrence *and* that the act is a humanly free one if the person who performs it can be said also to be the sufficient condition of its occurrence. Now at first sight this seems to be a case involving over-determination and hence Ross' position may appear defensible. But if God's willing some act is both *necessary*[11] and sufficient for its coming about it seems that it cannot be a case of over-determination we have here at all. For clearly one must say of any such human act that it *could not* have taken place were God not to have willed it. But the sense of 'could not' involved here is surely not that which in Chapters 8 and 11 was dubbed 'causal incompossibility relative to actual prior events' and which I argued does not vitiate human freedom. There the human agent *did* seem to have something within his power which, were he to want to exercise it, he would.

Predictably (from remarks he makes) Ross would say I have simply begged the question against him (and, for his part, orthodoxy[12] as well). I do not think this is the case because I have provided *an argument* in support of my position and one which doesn't appear to hinge on anything as controversial as, for instance, 'metaphysical dependence'. But I want to go on now to make some further points about his definition of 'omnipotence' because, even though his position on freedom seems to be a consequence of it and hence to raise some doubt about the account, that account cannot be overthrown just for that reason. Perhaps, in other words, any defensible account of omnipotence would have that result.

Now while Ross' definition has some admirable features it is unacceptable. First, it depends very heavily on his (more that usually) controversial idea of 'necessary being' and on such obscure notions as 'metaphysical causation' and 'reality level differences'. Second, and more crucially, as far as I can see, Ross gives no good reason (nor does one seem otherwise available) for believing that there cannot be contingent states of affairs described by propositions which do not have *entailments* about the effective choice of some omnipotent being, S. Certainly no religious believer who is a libertarian about human freedom could agree to Ross' proposal and only a compatibilist of the kind I have previously referred to as a 'hard compatibilist' could accept Ross' position. And even leaving aside questions of human freedom, Ross' view *demands* commitment to an implausible position on the notion of 'necessary being'. Should anyone think that Ross' definition of 'omnipotence' could be used while treating 'S exists' as contingent[13,14] the problem of how to restrict the states of affairs falling within the decision of S to a sub-class of the contingent rears its ugly head again.

III

Recently Richard Swinburne[15] has put forward an interesting analysis of 'omnipotence' which, like Ross', is in terms of effectual power rather than in terms of doings. First I want to single out some of the difficulties which Swinburne's account tries to allow for. One has already been considered, namely the requirement that omnipotence range over the contingent. Another has also been mentioned in passing in Section I – the need for temporal indicators. As Swinburne points out, it is logically impossible to bring about a past state (as was seen in Chapter 3). Hence no omnipotent being can be required to bring about any logically contingent state of affairs, x, unless it is future to the time at which the power to bring it about is being assessed. Further, no omnipotent being can be expected to bring about a completely uncaused state of affairs or some state of affairs not in fact brought about by it (like e.g. 'the bringing into existence of a table not brought into existence by an omnipotent being').

Having taken account of such matters Swinburne offers:

(D₄) S is omnipotent if, and only if, for all times, t, S is able at t to bring about any *x* which is a logically contingent state of affairs after t *and* the occurrence of which after t does not entail that S did not bring it about at t.

(In this definition S ranges over all existent beings[16]: *x* over all logically possible states of affairs; and '*x* is a logically contingent state of affairs after t' is to be understood as claiming that x is a state of affairs logically compatible with what has happened at and before t.)

Swinburne's definition is a decided improvement on the earlier ones considered. It does, however, have the interesting consequence (acknowledged by Swinburne) that 'a God who now has unlimited power . . . could, if he chose, abandon that power tomorrow, or even commit suicide' (p. 236). I think the final clause of this claim gives pause for reflection about the accuracy of Swinburne's definition because it does not seem to me that an omnipotent being's committing suicide is at all like abandoning his power. Might Swinburne be envisaging these as distinct but successive happenings? Nevertheless, I do not want to delay to quarrel with him over the details, for I think that the alleged incoherence of 'omnipotence' which the so-called 'paradoxes of omnipotence' are supposed to establish, can be got around irrespective of the availability of a finally satisfactory definition. Thus, like Swinburne, I wish to turn my attention to these paradoxes.

IV

The charge has been levelled in recent years that the concept of omnipotence is revealed as incoherent in the light of the so-called 'paradoxes of omnipotence'. Some versions of these paradoxes (e.g. Ziff's[17]), are specious. Of the significant paradoxes, not all serve the purpose for which they were intended. I want first of all to consider the most discussed of the paradoxes in a form which is designed to lead to the conclusion that the Judaeo-Christian God is not omnipotent. I want to show that under the assumptions generally made in connection with this version, this 'paradox' disappears. I then will show that a version of the paradox leading to the conclusion that the existence of any omnipotent being is logically impossible, is non-specious but, nevertheless, resolvable.

J. L. Mackie[18] stated a paradox of omnipotence in the following way:

Can an omnipotent being make things which he cannot control? Or, what is practically equivalent to this, can an omnipotent being make rules which then bind himself? (p. 210)

At the time Mackie's view was that neither a negative nor an affirmative answer could prevent a denial that the being in question was omnipotent. He has subsequently accepted criticisms of his presentation by Bernard Mayo.[19] Mayo pointed out that since 'things which an omnipotent being cannot control' is a self-contradictory phrase, making such things is logically impossible and failure to bring about logical impossibilities does not count against omnipotence. Mackie thinks that while his presentation was wrong, the problem, for one affirming God's omnipotence, remains, for he is unconvinced that the affirmative answer to the paradox is not equally plausible (as the negative answer supported by Mayo, *et al.*).

Both Mayo and George Mavrodes reason in pseudo-dilemma fashion so that (assuming the existence of God) they say he is either omnipotent or he is not. If we assume he is not omnipotent, the task of, say, creating a stone which he cannot lift (or a being he cannot control) is not self-contradictory. Thus we can conclude that God is not omnipotent on the grounds that both his ability (to create the stone) and his inability (to perform the lifting) imply that he is not omnipotent. But to prove his non-omnipotence in this way is trivial. Mavrodes puts it this way:

> To be significant (the paradoxical argument) . . . must derive this same conclusion *from the assumption that God is omnipotent;* that is, it must show that the assumption of the omnipotence of God leads to a *reductio.* (p. 222)

However, on the assumption that God is omnipotent, the task is self-contradictory. But this implies no limitation on the part of the agent. The paradoxical argument is in consequence, either insignificant or unsound.

Despite Mackie's back-down this reply is open to several objections. Firstly, and crucially, 'a stone which God cannot lift' is self-contradictory — on the assumption that God is omnipotent — *only* *if* 'God is omnipotent' is *necessarily true*.[20] Otherwise, creating a stone which he cannot lift would only be a task which God *in fact* could not perform. Now Mayo and Mavrodes fail to make this assumption explicit and they offer no argument for it. But, when it is brought to the surface we see that the assumption begs the question, because assuming that God exists and that 'God is omnipotent' is necessarily true, ensures that the paradox which seeks to prove that God is not omnipotent will turn out to be either unsound or insignificant.

Secondly it is not the case that the paradoxical argument need be represented as a *reductio ad absurdum*. Mavrodes' reasoning implies that the paradoxical argument must either assume that God is omnipotent or assume that he is not omnipotent. But this is false, for neither assumption need be made (and I do not think, furthermore, that the versions criticised by him make either assumption).

But something important has emerged from our discussion. Mackie in his original piece, and his successive critics, have all concentrated on a version of the paradox which seeks to prove that God is not omnipotent. God may exist but if he does he is not omnipotent. Yet if one takes it that God is by definition omnipotent, the paradox is obviously going to turn out to be ineffective.

A version of the paradox can be drawn up which seeks to prove that the notion of an omnipotent being is logically inconsistent, that is, that the existence of an omnipotent being is logically impossible. It tries to do this by focusing on the perfectly consistent task of creating a stone, say, which the creator cannot lift.[21]

Consider a version such as the following, which employs a (D_1) type definition of 'omnipotence' rather than one like (D_4):

(1) Either x can create a stone which x cannot lift, or x cannot create a stone which x cannot lift;

(2) If x can create a stone which x cannot lift, then, necessarily, there is at least one task which x cannot perform (namely, lift the stone in question);

(3) If x cannot create a stone which x cannot lift, then, necessarily, there is at least one task which x cannot perform (namely, create the stone in question);

(4) Hence, there is at least one task which x cannot perform;

(5) If x is an omnipotent being, then x can perform any task;

(6) Therefore, x is not omnipotent (and since x is any being, the existence of an omnipotent being is logically impossible).[22]

Now Savage argues that the fallacy in this, the most significant version of the paradox, lies in (3). He writes

... 'x can create a stone which x cannot lift' does indeed entail that there is a task which x cannot perform, and consequently, does entail that x is not omnipotent. However, 'x cannot create a stone which x cannot lift' does not entail that there is a task which x cannot perform and, consequently does not entail that x is not omnipotent. That the entailment *seems* to hold is explained by the misleading character of the statement 'x cannot create a stone which x cannot lift'. . . 'x cannot create a stone which x cannot lift' can only mean 'If x can create a stone, then x can lift it'. (p. 77)

This move has not been found convincing by Cowan or by Swinburne. Each objects that it remains true that there is a task (which satisfies a (D_1) type account of 'omnipotence') that x cannot perform — namely to bring into existence a stone to which he gives the power to resist subsequent lifting by himself. But all that seems to me to follow from this is that a (D_1) type account of 'omnipotence' won't do, and there's nothing new in that, because, in Section III, I pointed out that, for instance, 'the bringing into existence of a table not brought into existence by an omnipotent being' could not be held to show that some putatively omnipotent being, S, was less than omnipotent. Yet such a task seems within the range of many men's powers.

Savage does have a further card up his sleeve, to which

Swinburne also objects. Savage contends that whether x = y
or x ≠ y, x's inability to create a stone which y cannot lift
constitutes a limitation on x's power only if, either

   (1)   x is unable to create stones of some poundage;
or
   (2)   y is unable to lift stones of some poundage.

Since either (1) or (2) may be false 'x cannot create a
stone which y cannot lift', does not entail 'x is limited in
power'.

The fact that discussions of abilities and inabilities normally take place in contexts restricted to discussions of beings
limited in various ways, may lead to the illusion that a being's
inability to create a stone which he himself or some other
being cannot lift, *necessarily* constitutes a limitation on his
power. That is, that

   (a)   x cannot create a stone which y cannot lift (where
         either x = y or x ≠ y)
entails
   (b)   x is limited in power.

But to succumb to this belief, says Savage, would be to
succumb to an illusion *if one is discussing God's power.* For
God's inability to create a stone which he cannot lift is a
limitation on his power only if:

   (1)   he is unable to create stones of some poundage;
or
   (2)   he is unable to lift stones of some poundage.

Swinburne claims that factors other than weight, such as
great bulk or slitheriness, might limit y's lifting ability. He
contends that the claim that S cannot create a stone which y
cannot lift is the claim that he cannot give to a stone any
property which will defeat y's lifting powers, and that means
y's future lifting powers. Thus if S could make some stone of
any poundage but not a stone with that property he would
be limited in power. And, further, S might, Swinburne

claims, have the ability to make a stone with the required property, even though at the present instant y could lift any stone at all. According to Swinburne this shows the failure of Savage's additional argument. It seems to me, though, that Savage could reply by asking why we should suppose that S suffers from any of these possible limitations? If he is omnipotent, Savage could reply, then he must be able to create stones of any poundage, bulk, slitheriness and so on, and lift stones of any poundage, bulk or slitheriness. And this surely entails that God cannot create a stone which he cannot lift. Again the weaknesses of a (D_1) type account appear, but nothing more.

In fact Swinburne (despite crediting Savage's argument with less force than I do) doesn't think the paradoxical argument reproduced above reveals an incoherence in 'omnipotence' either. He objects to the alleged necessary truth of (5) which could only be such if a (D_1) type definition were defensible. Should anyone substitute for 'task' in the argument formulated above, the locution 'task which it is logically possible for x to perform' then (5) would be reinstated as a necessary truth but only at the expense of the necessary truth of (2).[2][3]

So it appears that the most stringent formulation of the paradox does not reveal any incoherence in 'omnipotence', regardless of the ultimate satisfactoriness of a (D_4) type definition. Whatever *real* problems arise in considering the concept of omnipotence, arise from the need to preserve the consistency of the concept of an omnipotent being and at the same time the believer's (informed) conception of the power of God. It is in the relation of the concept of omnipotence with human freedom that one finds the greatest challenge to the simultaneous preservation of these two conceptions.

14 Omnipotence and Freedom

In the course of recent discussions of the problem of evil, it has been claimed that the proposition 'God is omnipotent, omniscient and wholly good' entails the proposition 'God creates no persons who perform morally wrong actions'.[1] (Once again, 'God' shouldn't be used as it is here as a proper name, but as long as there are no illegitimate switches between the use of the term as a proper name and its use as a definite description, no harm should eventuate.) The following argument might be suggested[2] as underpinning the alleged entailment.

(1) God is omniscient, omnipotent, and wholly good;
(2) For any free possible person P who, if created, would perform morally evil actions, there is another free possible person P_1 who is exactly like P except that P_1, if created, would never perform morally evil actions;
(3) If God is omniscient then he knows as regards any free possible person whether that person, if created, would or would not perform morally evil actions;
(4) If he is omnipotent then he can create those free possible persons who, if created, would never perform any morally evil actions;
(5) If he can create those free possible persons who, if created, would never perform any morally evil actions, and if he is wholly good and omniscient, then any free persons created by him never perform a morally evil action;
(6) No free person created by God ever performs a morally evil action (from $(1) - (5)$)

Since it is further alleged that (2), (3), (4) and (5) are *necessary* truths, there is established an entailment between the propositions previously cited, which are just (1) and (6) in the above formulation.

Obviously if it can be shown that (2), (3), (4) and (5) are necessary truths, traditional Christian theism is in all sorts of bother. In this chapter I propose to consider the above argument. This will require chiefly, though not only, a consideration of what has been termed 'the free will defence' against the argument outlined. Now it should be clear that I consider the most plausible approach to the problem of freedom and determinism is a compatibilist approach. It should, furthermore, be clear that my discussions have had a secondary goal, namely, that of showing that a failure on the part of the compatibilist thesis would most likely drive us in the direction of some version of libertarianism. With this dual claim in mind my strategy in this chapter will involve consideration of both libertarian and compatibilist accounts of freedom and their relation to the free will defence. Nevertheless, my central concern in this chapter is the relation of omnipotence and freedom.

I

The free will defence is usually stated in something like the following way. A world containing creatures who freely perform both good and evil actions — and do impressively more good than evil — is more valuable than a world containing beings who always do what is right because they are unable to do otherwise. For if someone really cannot help doing what he should, if moral wickedness is in fact not possible for him, then he cannot be said to choose virtue rather than vice, and so cannot be said to be a fully responsible and morally good person. Now the free will defender urges from this that while God can create free persons, he cannot *guarantee* that they only do what is right, for if he does so then they do not do what is right, *freely*. To create beings capable of moral good, therefore, he must create beings capable of moral evil. But he cannot create the possibility of moral evil and at the same time prohibit its actuality. As it turned out, some[3] of the free beings God created, exercised their freedom to do what is wrong, hence moral evil. The fact that free creatures sometimes err, however, in no way tells against God's omnipotence (or his goodness) for he could prevent the occurrence of moral evil only by removing the freedom needed for genuine moral good.

Thus, this traditional plank in the Christian explanation and justification of part of the evil that occurs, hinges on the claim that perhaps there are certain good states of affairs that an omnipotent God cannot bring about without permitting evil. This despite the fact that these goods are not a logically sufficient condition of any evil at all.

Those who have opposed the free will defence have agreed that the point is not one about moral evil being made impossible for men. They have acknowledged that the point is about moral evil not in fact being done, notwithstanding that men still remain perfectly capable of doing it.[4] There is a related point on which they have been agreed with most[5] free will defenders. It is that even though one must insist that moral virtue logically presupposes temptation and a practical possibility of succumbing, it does not follow that if there are to be temptations there must necessarily be lapses.

II

In some extremely rigorous and demanding work, Alvin Plantinga has recently done a good deal of the spadework for at least part of what I have indicated I shall be trying to do in this chapter.[6] Even though this spadework has been done, a great deal of interesting and important work remains. In particular, I shall be considering the implications for the doctrine of God's omnipotence, should Plantinga's version of the free will defence prove successful.

His version probably fits either a contra-causal libertarian or an agent-causation libertarian view. In *God and Other Minds* he writes:

When we say that Jones acts freely on a given occasion, what we say entails, I should think, that either his action on that occasion is not causally determined or else he has previously performed an undetermined action that is a causal ancestor of the one in question. (p. 134)

I leave until Section IV objections which might be raised against Plantinga's whole programme on the ground that his account of freedom is unacceptable.

Plantinga makes the following points. First, that God (or anyone else) determines or brings about an action of another agent, is incompatible with that action being a free action. Second, that it is possible that God cannot instantiate any 'possible person' containing the property *always freely does what is right* and also possible that he can instantiate some such possible persons. But that he can, if indeed he can, is a contingent truth. Third, since the anti-theists require an entailment relation between the proposition 'God is omnipotent, omniscient and all-good' and the proposition 'God creates no persons who perform morally wrong actions', they cannot employ such a contingent truth and hence their argument fails.

It is evident that the second point is crucial and most in need of discussion. What could the notion of a 'possible person' mean? What are we to make of the suggestion that God could have created 'possible persons'? This technical terminology can be explicated in the following way. Consider first the set of all those properties which it is logically possible for human beings to have. The properties in this set will be called H properties from now on. Included in the set of H properties will be 'having auburn hair', 'being six feet tall'. Moral properties, too, such as 'being a liar', and 'performing at least one wrong action' will be included. The complement $\bar{P}$ of an H property P, is the property a thing has if, and only if, it does not have P. Hence a *consistent* set of H properties is a set of H properties such that it is logically possible that there be a human being having every property in the set. And there can be, at most, one instantiation of any possible person, A, because among the members of the set which is A will be some such (determinate) individuating properties as 'is the third child of Frederick and Marjorie Young'. Next, call an H property, Q, *indeterminate* if 'God creates a person and causes him to have Q' is necessarily false. Otherwise it is determinate. Properties such as 'freely refrains from doing W', where W is some specified wrong act, or 'always freely does what is right' will obviously be indeterminate.

Now take any free possible person, F. Can God instantiate F as the instantiation of a perfect possible person? Clearly F contains the property 'is free to do what is wrong'. Hence we know that there is some action W such that F contains the properties 'free to perform W' and 'free to refrain from performing W', and such that if F were to be instantiated, its instantiation (call it FI) would be doing something wrong were it to perform W. According to the anti-theists, an omniscient God would know certain relevant facts about F. He would know what sorts of free choices FI would make if F were instantiated, and presumably, on the basis of this knowledge would decide whether or not to instantiate a given possible person such as F.[7] (It may be worth noting in passing that those who believe God's foreknowledge must be inferential, would be entitled to question the truth of this premise. As far as I can tell, Plantinga doesn't.)

In the case where God knows that FI will refrain from W he can instantiate F with no unhappy results. He will be creating an actual person who he knows in advance will perform only right actions. On the other hand, in the case where what God knows is that if FI is left free to perform W, he *will* perform W, then God cannot instantiate F as the instantiation of a perfect possible person. For if he instantiates F and allows FI to remain free with respect to W, then FI will perform W, thus doing something wrong. But if God instantiates F and does not allow FI to remain free with respect to W, then FI is not free with respect to W and hence not the instantiation of F at all. So if F has the indeterminate property of performing W, God could not instantiate F as the instantiation of a perfect possible person. It is possible, furthermore, that F *does* have the indeterminate property of performing W and hence it is possible that God cannot instantiate F as a perfect possible person. Finally, evidently it is also possible that *every* possible person containing the property 'always freely does what is right' is such that neither God nor anyone else can instantiate it. It is also possible of course that he can instantiate some such possible persons. What the foregoing argument reveals is that if indeed he can instantiate such persons it will only be contingently true that he can. Thus Plantinga's argument, if sound, undermines the *necessary* truth of item (4) in the argument outlined at the head of the chapter.

Notice that the H properties which make trouble for the objector to the free will defence are the *indeterminate* properties. It is because of them that God is restricted — he cannot instantiate just any possible person he chooses, since possible persons have these indeterminate properties. So perhaps the anti-theist might try to formulate a definition of 'possible person' in which a possible person is a consistent set S of *determinate* properties such that for any determinate H property P, either P or P̄ is a member of S. This, however, is too loose, for it still lets in some possible persons whom God cannot instantiate. For where I is any indeterminate H property and D is a determinate H property, the disjunction D-or-I is determinate (like D). Clearly, however, God cannot instantiate persons containing both the property 'has red hair or is not created by God' and the property 'does not have red hair'. We must, therefore, stipulate the condition that no possible person entails an indeterminate property.

But as Plantinga reveals, even this further modified definition is unacceptable because it entails that there are no possible free persons. We may see this as follows. Let F be a possible free person, thus having the property of being free with respect to some action, W. Furthermore, F would have either the property of performing W (a determinate property) or the property of refraining from performing W. But if F has the property of performing W and the property of being free with respect to W, then F entails the property of freely performing W, which is an indeterminate property. The same holds in the case where F has the property of refraining from performing W. Hence in either case F entails an indeterminate property and accordingly is not a possible person.

The objector to the free will defence must, therefore, urge that for any action with respect to which a given possible person F is free, F contains neither the property of performing that action nor the property of refraining from performing it. This may be accomplished by saying, first, that a person is *free with respect to a property P*, if, and only if, he can freely choose whether or not to have P. Second, by saying that a set of properties is free with respect to a given

property P, if, and only if, it contains the property *is free
with respect to P.*

With the addition of these points it now seems apparent
that God, if he is omnipotent, can instantiate any possible
person, and any compossible set of possible persons, he
chooses. The objector will continue that, if God is also
all-good, he will, presumably, instantiate only those possible
persons that have some such indeterminate H property as
that of always freely doing what is right.

Here Plantinga[8] raises the crucial question:

> ... what reason is there for supposing that there are *any*
> possible persons, in the present sense of 'possible person',
> having the indeterminate property in question?

It is clear that the proposition 'Every possible free person
is such that if he were instantiated he would perform at least
one morally wrong action' is possibly true. Now, if every
possible free person would, if instantiated, perform at least
one wrong action, then every actual free person also freely
performs at least one wrong action. Hence, if every possible
free person does perform at least one wrong action, God
could create a universe without moral evil only by refusing to
create any persons at all. The free will defender claims,
though, that a world containing free persons and moral evil
(provided that it contained impressively more moral good
than moral evil) would be superior to one lacking both free
persons and moral good and moral evil.

There is one other point I want briefly to make in this
context. Against Plantinga's argument for the contingency of
(4), William Rowe has offered the following counter-claim.
Rowe alleges that if one assumes Plantinga's own account of
'omnipotence', all that follows from his argument is the
contingency not of (4) but of the *consequent* of the proposition that 'If God is omnipotent then he can instantiate
possible persons containing the property of "always freely
doing what is right" '. But the account of 'omnipotence'
Rowe attributes to Plantinga, namely that 'If God is omnipotent then God can create any state of affairs S such that
"God creates S" is consistent', is not in fact one that

Plantinga subscribes to, as emerges from remarks he makes (in *God and Other Minds*, pp. 137, 170 and notes thereto). And, furthermore, not one that he *needs* to accept, as should be clear from the arguments given already in the immediately preceding chapter.

III

Should Plantinga's argument go through (and I believe that it does so within the context of his account of freedom), it would appear that what God can do is partially determined by a set of contingent facts describing how the members of sets of persons would behave if those sets were instantiated. This might appear to be incompatible with God's omnipotence.

We must be clear at the outset that the limitation apparently involved here is not God's inability to determine free actions. If the point made by Plantinga, that it is logically impossible that God (or anyone else) determine the *free* actions of free agents, is correct, then this will be in no way incompatible with his omnipotence. For, as was pointed out previously in considering the doctrine of omnipotence, 'omnipotence' has not usually been defined in such a way as to require the ability to perform logically impossible tasks.

The limitation (if limitation it be) with which we are concerned is of an essentially different kind. Namely, that given that a particular set of contingent facts of the kind in question obtains, the range of options open to God is limited. Now it does not appear to be logically necessary that God be limited in this way because it is not logically necessary that *that* set of contingent facts obtain. For example, given the realisation of the logical possibility that every possible set of free persons contains members who would freely (morally) fail if that set were created, then God cannot create a world which contains free persons but no moral failures. But it is, of course, not necessary that it be the case. Thus, that God creates a world in which free persons never fail would appear to be logically possible, and therefore God's failure to do this cannot be traced to the logical impossibility of the task or the logical impossibility of God's performing the task. What *is* logically impossible on Plantinga's account is that it be the case that every possible set of free persons contain members who would freely (morally) fail if that set were created, *and* that God create a world in which free beings never fail.

An objector might claim that if the contingent facts were different, so that it were true, say, that there are possible sets of free persons which are such that all members of those sets will always freely do what is right if those sets are created (and which are such that the worlds containing them, would, if created, contain a more favourable balance of good over evil than those worlds which contain failures), then God would be *less limited than he is in fact*. That is, he would be better able to do what he wants to do. If it is simply a contingent fact that all possible sets of free persons include members who would freely fail if the set were created, then God is subject to a limitation to which he need not be subject (i.e. an alternative set of contingent facts might have been true) and, therefore, he is not the most powerful possible being.

How might the free will defender counter this objection? Wainwright[9] suggests that one way he might endeavour to do so is as follows. First, he could point out that power sometimes attaches to ability to do what one wants, sometimes to an agent's skill or strength. From this he could then concede that the objector's conclusion is correct if the power referred to by 'omnipotence' is the ability to do whatever one wants (assuming, naturally, that the circumstances in which one is placed have to be taken as providing untrammelled opportunity to exercise such ability). For, clearly, given that certain contingent facts obtain, namely that every possible set of free persons contains members who would freely fail if that set were created, God may be less able to do what he wants than he would be if certain other contingent facts obtained. On the other hand, he might continue, the conclusion is incorrect if the power in question is measured by the difficulty of the task or the skill or strength of the agent. A God-like being placed in more favourable circumstances might be better able to do what he wants, better able to achieve a result in accordance with his purposes, but it is not clear that a being who created a world populated by free but morally perfect persons, when placed in those circumstances would deserve to be called more skilful, stronger or the like. Such a being would simply be more favourably situated. While this counter isn't entirely adequate it does raise a point I shall come back to in a moment.

Plantinga's version of the free will defence appears, one might say, to prevent God from freely realising his desires. Even though no being could, given the facts, more fully realise his purposes and even though whether or not these facts obtain, no being could be intrinsically more powerful in the sense of being more skilled, stronger, better able to perform difficult tasks, it does appear to be logically possible that there be a being freer from restrictions than God is, in fact. Perhaps then, the limitation, which is not self-imposed in the way that sovereign parliaments, for example, restrict themselves, precludes the Judaeo-Christian God from being believed omnipotent. Are Plantinga and those who would use his version of the free will defence open to the charge of being 'revisionists'? I do not think this is the case. Unfortunately I possess no decisive argument which refutes the charge but I shall now try to show why I think it plausible to rebut the charge.

Firstly, the concept of omnipotence is not an entirely clear one. Indeed, as emerged in the previous chapter, it is an extremely difficult one to isolate. There is no agreed definition to which one can appeal in an effort to sort out what comes legitimately within the scope of 'omnipotence'. It seems to me that we should be chary of saying, therefore, that the restriction on God involved in Plantinga's version of the free will defence, is incompatible with the Judaeo-Christian notion of omnipotence.

Secondly, it has frequently been contended in Judaeo-Christian thought that God is somehow limited by human freedom of action.[10] I think that many who have so thought have considered the limitation self-imposed (along the lines of the example of parliament mentioned above), though such thinkers probably were not working with a model as carefully spelled-out as Plantinga's. There is a note of caution again in this second point against abandonment of Plantinga's position.

Thirdly, I wish to come back to a point foreshadowed above in making the distinction between senses of 'power'. One reason (perhaps the chief) for saying that God must be omnipotent is that if he were not he would be less than perfect. In view of this it may be the case that if God were free from a restriction like that discussed, he might be regarded as *more fortunate* but it is not clear that he should be regarded as *more perfected*. He would undoubtedly be *better off* but it does not follow, and is not clear, that he would be any *better*. It seems that our notion of God's omnipotence is closely aligned with that of our notion of his perfection and hence that this third point is of undoubted significance. Perhaps, then, nothing has to be sacrificed concerning God's omnipotence if Plantinga is right about the limitation man's use of freedom may (and, in fact, does) impose on God. The charge of revisionism is plausibly rebutted, therefore.

IV

It is important to realise that there are other areas in which challenges might be offered to Plantinga's account of the free will defence than its relation to God's omnipotence. That particular matter has occupied us because of its crucial connection with the central interests of this essay. There are two broad regions in which further ramifications of Plantinga's defence might well be explored. One is a distinctively theological region which might give rise to certain *ad hominem* objections. For example, objections concerning the doctrine of election, and objections concerning the position of the blessed in glory. I shall illustrate the sort of *ad hominem* objections I have in mind from this latter category. Flew has argued in his paper 'Possibility, Creation and Temptation' that since the blessed in glory are human they can thus only be characterised by a human goodness. Yet to have this they must be both exposed to temptation and capable of sin. Now, if their salvation is to be truly consummated then it must be the case: both that they still are exposed to temptation; and that they are reliably assured that they will never again in fact succumb. The objection goes on: if Plantinga is right about God's situation *vis-à-vis* men always freely choosing the right in this world, the same situation must ensue in the world of resurrection glory. Alternatively, if God is better equipped to handle the situation there, how is it not possible for him to deal with it in the same way in our world? Thus, according to the objection, Plantinga is impaled on the horns of a dilemma occasioned by his own (presumed) commitments.

I do not have the space needed to pursue such objections any further here. Nevertheless, I should indicate that I believe there are adequate replies open to Plantinga which hinge on the notion of 'grace' and on the redundancy of any divine purposes of 'soul-making' in the resurrection world (God's transforming work being by then accomplished).

Secondly, there is Plantinga's stated commitment to a libertarian freedom. I have to date contended that, within the context of his account of freedom, Plantinga's defence holds up against his stated opponents. It has recently been argued[11] that the defence Plantinga offers must be counted a failure just because the account of freedom it presupposes is mistaken.

In *God and Other Minds* Plantinga uses the term 'free action' in such a way that the sentence 'All of Sammy's actions are causally determined and some of them are free' expresses a necessarily false proposition. Now Flew[12] claims there is an ordinary use of the locution 'free action' according to which the sentence above expresses a consistent proposition. Faced with this claim, Plantinga decides to give Flew the term 'free' and to state his own case using the term 'unfettered' which he defines as follows: an action A is unfettered just in case it is free in Flew's sense and not causally determined. He then advocates that the free will defence be restated, substituting 'unfettered' for 'free' throughout. This manoeuvre is designed to disarm Flew's comments on the ordinary use of the term 'free' by rendering them irrelevant.

Now Tomberlin, in the paper referred to, demurs:

... but a free action, for Flew, *just is* a causally determined action. So this verbal manoeuvre does not accomplish very much. For Flew would now deny that a world in which people perform both good and evil unfettered actions (and do more good than evil) is more valuable than a world in which they perform only good but fettered actions. And I fail to see how Plantinga could meet this reply. (p. 375)

In a subsequent reply to Tomberlin, Plantinga reiterates the claim he made in *God and Other Minds* concerning the idea of an 'unfettered' action.[13] He does so, though, in a little more detail and thereby draws attention to the ingenuity of his point — an ingenuity that seems to have been overlooked. He contends that the construction Tomberlin has put on Flew's remarks makes the proposition 'If a man's action is free, it is causally determined', a necessary truth. That is, Tomberlin takes Flew to be a 'hard' compatibilist. If this be the case then it is not possible that there be persons who perform free but unfettered actions on Flew's account. Hence a world in which people perform both good and evil unfettered actions, being an impossible world, would not be more valuable than a world in which people perform only good but fettered actions.

But, says Plantinga, this is an error, for Flew maintains that freedom and determinism are compatible, not that freedom entails determinism. It is clear that an action could meet this condition without being causally determined. (This is not to go back on my claim that it *less plausibly* meets this condition when it is causally undetermined in one or other of the libertarian senses I have examined.) So it seems legitimately open to Plantinga to charge that it just isn't true in Flew's sense that an action can be free *only if* it is determined. Were it possible to establish (with a semblance of probability) a hard compatibilist position, Plantinga would be in strife. As it is not, he is, I suggest, able to evade the objection I have considered.

V

Earlier I observed that both opponents and proponents of the free will defence agree that the notion of God's making men freely choose the good is inconsistent. The dispute between the opposed forces, hinges, rather, on whether the quite different notion of God's making men such that they always freely choose the good, is consistent. I indicated that there is also agreement that evil must not be made impossible for men. They are to remain, in other words, liable to temptation, to be endowed with inclinations, to tend to assert themselves and so on. The great divide emerges when the question is considered whether an omnipotent, omniscient (and all-good) God is able so to arrange his creation that all men in fact always freely choose the right. . . to create people who, no matter what the temptations, always freely refrain from evil.

If the argument to date goes through, a libertarian Christian theist seems able to appeal to a sort of lacuna, in that it is a contingent matter whether the men that God makes, always freely choose the good. But it would seem that a compatibilist Christian theist must needs be debarred from talk of such a lacuna — for on his account selves or agents who act in opposition to prior causes or who initiate new causal chains, do not get in on the act. No doubt the attraction of libertarian accounts of freedom for Christian theists, has had something to do with the belief that some such lacuna is demanded, if a fully-fledged version of Christian theism is to be viable. But I have argued at great length that given certain (plausible) beliefs about the nature of our world, a compatibilist account of freedom is a deal more convincing than current libertarian accounts. It is, therefore, necessary to give attention to what follows for the free will defence in a genuinely compatibilist world. I must confess that this seems to me to be one of the most difficult exercises in Christian apologetics. Hence some of what I shall say is advanced tentatively.

VI

In the sort of world envisaged by a libertarian, causal conditions are often not sufficient for a man's decisions or actions. But in that envisaged by the compatibilist there are always causally sufficient conditions for decisions and actions and these conditions are not necessarily internal to a man. Thus, in attempting to construct a world like that the sceptic has in mind and which is compatibilist in nature, one must reckon on the fact that whereas in our world the presence of certain conditions is sufficient for wrongdoing, they will not have such an effect in the world the sceptic has in mind, which I shall call W. We know, for example, that certain evils and pains sometimes are sufficient for bringing about evil-doing. The libertarian, of course, can always contend that the individual could avoid the doing of evil in such cases because his response to his circumstances is not totally caused.

If it be allowed that there is some such distinction as that between natural evil and moral evil, then, in the compatibilist W envisaged by the sceptic, the natural evils that might be present (for some purpose, let us say, which God wishes to fulfil[14]) will never be sufficient to bring about a morally evil response. I am well aware, of course, that the sceptic doesn't believe natural evil can be justified any more than he believes moral evil can. But for present purposes I want to abstract from the natural evils because their continuance will be instructive in helping see what sort of alterations there would need to be in W from our world (assuming it to be compatibilist).

Before proceeding to my speculations about W, there is one further preliminary. Whereas Mackie resists the suggestion that *he* should give any content to his alternative evil-free world, Flew holds that people in the world he imagines will be naturally inclined to do evil in the sense that they will have a tendency to do so. 'Tendencies' in this context are causes which, operating unimpeded, would produce the thing tended to. Flew gives no indication of what is to do the impeding. But he frequently talks of men having a stronger sense of duty and a greater strength of character (and in a manner very like that of the moral libertarian who views the resisting of temptation as duty gaining ascendancy over desire).

Let us make a start by recalling that it is agreed that men are to have the power and the desire to do evil. What the sceptic must recognise is that if, in a compatibilist world, people are always to resist the temptation to do evil (whether by omission or commission), this amounts simply to the conditions that would be causally sufficient for their exercising these powers or for their desires getting out of control (and hence for the performance of a morally wrong act), never eventuating. Whether these unexercised capacities would survive as genuine capacities is, I think, dubious, at least. Presumably God would be required to ensure their continuing vitality. In light of the fact that we are increasingly in possession of knowledge of the conditions sufficient for certain wrong-doings in our world, if W is to be a compatibilist one, it must be *possible* to stipulate just what would constitute conditions sufficient for the free performance of a morally wrong act.

One is tempted to say that in W, whenever anyone's plans and hopes are thwarted he will want to curse, be angry, rail upon others and so on, but never will, because his strength of character or sense of duty will outweigh the inclination. It has been suggested to me, though, that the thwarting of hopes is unpleasant and therefore ought not to be in the scheme of things in W. Here we are up against a serious difficulty. It appears that the actions of an individual (or individuals) which, if taken in isolation, are reasonable, could have deleterious effects on others. Thus noise from a party or gathering might itself be reasonable, but anger and annoy a nearby person who desires to sleep. Now it may be said that it is always morally wrong to act in such a way that someone else is caused pain or annoyance or the like. But this certainly doesn't seem obvious to me. Later on I will consider situations where there is resource scarcity, but it will serve well for the present purpose also. Even where distribution of such resources has been carried out morally rightly (because perfectly justly) some may have their hopes or desires (reasonable in themselves and not, say, selfish and hence evil) thwarted. Furthermore, there are cases where natural conditions may thwart a man's morally reasonable hopes or desires which would seem certain still to arise in W. The man who has looked forward all year to his holiday in the sun may in fact find the weather turns out to be utterly inclement. It seems to me fanciful to suggest that the world could be so arranged that he could have all his desires satisfied, and yet the farmer who lives at the back of the hill adjacent to the beach and who desires rain, have all his desires fulfilled too. Of course that might just be possible were there no others to take into account, and were the world not to be a law-governed one but one subject to *ad hoc* improvisation, yet when the set of events required to be causally compossible is enormously large, there seems every reason for believing it could not be thus compossible. Rather it seems to me that what must be said is that even when one's hopes, ambitions or wants (as opposed to needs) be thwarted, what W would require is that the temptation to assert oneself, swear, curse and be disagreeable because of the disappointment suffered, will always be resisted.

Couples who want casual intercourse, but not an enduring relationship will stifle their desires by calling on the resources of their strong character and sense of duty. The point I am urging does not depend on conventionalism, but on the presence of (mutual) exploitation. To whom the sense of duty is to be directed is, of course, problematic — but no doubt Flew can nominate a suitable repository.

Anyone tempted to be jealous of another's greater attributes will refuse to succumb. Even though men will still form groups (families, nations, etc.) they will not allow these ties to lead them into behaviour hurtful or unjust to those not of their group. The groupings which emerge will not produce arrangements that place their members under serious stress. Nor will those with more 'advanced' technology and those who have greater attributes of intelligence or command over material resources, yield to the temptation to make use of other people to further the interests of those near and dear to them. Short term expedients, which involve soft-pedalling on the demands of morality, will always be forsaken regardless of the importance of obtaining immediate benefits.

In making use of the natural resources, no one will ever spoil them for others in a morally culpable way. (Some illnesses are induced by environmental despoliation — hence a deal of natural evil may be the result of moral evil.) In the distribution of resources, domestically, nationally and internationally, no one will ever be unjustly treated. When there is not enough to go around without rationing, reason will prevail to ensure justice is done. (I presume resources will still be limited in the sorts of ways they currently are.) No one, of course, will become lazy, even though they know they will be treated justly whatever they do.

Whenever the beings of W intelligently develop their

resources so as to cope with the world, what they develop (fire, knives, alcohol, guns, atomic power) will never be misused or abused, nor ever give rise to fear that they might be. Whenever serious disagreements arise which could be settled by the swift application of violence or force they will not be thus settled but, amicably, by reasoned debate.

None of W's inhabitants will ever become tired and strained to a degree sufficient for irritability, anger, and so on to be vented upon others. It goes without saying, of course, that proud and smug thoughts in connection with their resistance to temptation will never gain sway in the minds of the beings of W. People will always go out of their way to befriend others. The aged, the less attractive, the less talented would thus never be left out and become lonely.

Further details of the thought experiment can I think be spared. It appears that W *is* conceivable despite its extraordinary complexity. My chief ground for arriving at such a conclusion is that there seems to be no obvious reason to believe that it cannot be consistent. I shall now take up a few, but by no means all, the points that seem to be entailed by the conception which is W. It will emerge, I think, that sceptics like Flew seriously underestimate the number of changes required from our world, and hence the difficulty of assessing the superiority of such a world over ours.

In W all inductive evidence would point to the fact that other members are self-effacing, though these beings will (contrary to this evidence) be prone to being very self-assertive. Of course, should anyone wonder whether another member of W really was as self-effacing as he appeared, his being told by the member that really he was prone to violent temptation, would not lead the questioner to do more than entertain a doubt about the other's truthfulness. There is something a little queer about this.

Second, whereas in our world some labour under the characteristic known as 'weakness of will', many in W will suffer from the malady of 'strength of character'. It will never occasion a degree of frustration sufficient for moral wrong, though. It is important to point out that the inhabitants would never do their duty *because* so doing would lead to their flourishing. Even a mere perfect correlation might give rise (on inductive grounds) to people doing their duty because of the pay-off. Hopefully everything could be arranged so as to permit genuinely disinterested moral goodness. Despite its attractions such men as *enjoy* their 'sin', may look askance at the suggestion that they should prefer W to the present world. Of course, it will be said, war, murder, robbery, rape and so on should be eliminated from W, but not swearing, exploitation, laziness, drunkenness[15], 'free' enterprise, gambling, pollution. Where will its inhabitants get any 'enjoyment'? At least some men may not think W a straightforwardly superior world to our present one. It is well to remember that it is men as now constituted who are supposed to favour W over the present world.

Third, in W people will never make mistakes (of omission or commission) which have any but morally innocuous consequences. Men and women will never let others down or hurt them by breaking promises or abusing trust. Nor will they misuse cars or make culpable errors of judgement when driving them that lead to injury. Most competitiveness and the associated spite and bitterness will be eliminated. People will always choose the right marriage partner (whether there is any legal institution by that name the practice seems certain to endure), there will never be any bitter recriminations or soul-destroying arguments – they will be just as blissfully happy anyway. Children will be raised free of any obstructions to their growth as mature, perfect beings. My only comment at the moment is that the changes in men envisaged here go far beyond mere boosting of their consciousness of duty and their strength of character. At the very least, the sceptics seem wrong about what changes need to be made from our world.

I earlier indicated that, in a compatibilist world, account must be taken of the fact that natural conditions are frequently sufficient for occasioning a morally evil response. Death is one important natural condition and its place in W needs to be considered. If there is to be death, to ease the ecological strain, whenever anyone does die, despite the fact that love and devotion are supreme moral virtues, there will be no resentment, depression or venting of spleen. This does seem a little odd.

Human freedom would have to be severely restricted, I think. For those who stress the social nature of man this will (to some extent) be clearly desirable, but it is likely to raise the hackles of the individualistically oriented. (I can only note here that the deep divisions among men about moral rightness, even among objectivists like myself, may require more resolution than seems available if one is to speculate reliably.) Even though it pre-empts certain matters of the kind alluded to, consider just how much moral evil could be removed if steps were taken to relieve modern man of the anomie, not to say, alienation, occasioned by the sort of urbanisation and industrialisation capitalist economies and some would-be socialist ones, too, have brought in their train. At the same time one should recognise what restrictions on human freedom such moves would entail.

Fifth, the complexion placed on moral maturation in W will be somewhat altered. On the one hand, it will have to be tied to quantitative temptations overcome, and (oddly) the development of new possibilities of temptations. On the other, it will involve development of capacities (greatly removed from those just mentioned) such as that of moral discrimination and the opening up of new levels of social interaction. Moral advice and exhortation would disappear, because, by all appearances, morality is destined to be an innate idea. Ninian Smart, like F. R. Tennant earlier this century, thinks this is unrealistic. Perhaps it is, but I frankly don't know whether it is or not. But if, as it seems it *must* be, it is realistic, then the inhabitants of W would enter the world with a highly developed consciousness of their duty and strong characters. They would possibly be able to advance in widening the sphere of operation of these characteristics during their sojourn. The categorical imperative: 'do your duty and be of strong character', would be emblazoned on their minds along with an unerring sense of rightness. Again, if this is feasible, it seems to go beyond Flew's characterisation.

Sixth, and from here on I leave the filling out of further details to the reader, it is worth remembering that while the inhabitants of W would not be moral pygmies, they probably wouldn't even be of moderate moral stature because they wouldn't be faced, for example, with needing to forgive or with the difficult task we presently·have of acting rightly even when morally wronged. They are quite removed from men as we know them in other ways, too. Highly gifted in some regards (e.g. rationality, their unerring sense of morality as an overriding consideration, their ability to avoid morally weak judgements and so on), they are also rather limited and restricted in other ways. Indeed I should say that many moderns and a lot of ancients would think them conformists, sycophantic and repressed.

It is time to ask how W rates against our world. The sceptic seems committed to rating W very highly. Now whether he must support it as the *best* of all possible worlds may well depend on the coherence of that notion. Many, from Aquinas on, have not thought it a coherent idea.[16] The sceptic certainly will have to say it is a *better* possible world than ours. Ascertaining how to rate worlds in terms of moral value is itself a problem. Anti-theists seem to have conveniently overlooked the difficulties of ranking such qualitatively different worlds.

Up until now I have taken it as obvious that if W is, in fact, to be given the nod over our present world, it will not be because men are any freer (in a compatibilist sense) in W than they are in our world (if it, too, is compatibilist). Before I endeavour to wind up my discussion of the comparative merits of W and our world, it may be useful to acknowledge that many readers could well think that the characterisation of W shows that compatibilism is, as they suspected all along, a hollow option and, hence, that we should therefore embrace libertarianism. I certainly have, I must admit, nagging doubts. But I still believe it seems more reasonable to claim that there may well be differing *ranges* of freedom as between alternative (compatibilist) possible worlds. One could say that, in the light of my investigations, men are freer over a greater range of activities in the present world than they would be in W. Libertarians, of course, will probably think this exposes a chink. Nevertheless, if my immediately preceding speculation is on the right track no serious gap remains open.

I shall proceed, therefore, on the assumption that if an

omnipotent, omniscient and all-good God exists, and has established the initial conditions and deterministic laws of our world, men will still do what they do (whether evil or good) freely. Provided I am right, there is no obvious ground for believing that he could not have so established the world that men were always caused (by standard causes) to freely do the right, and, should he exist, it is manifest that he didn't do what he could have done.

Bearing in mind that the compatibilist maintains that just as it remains possible for men always freely to do the morally right thing in our world, given that standard causes are in operation, and possible also for those in W to do moral evil, what, if anything, follows from my speculations about W and my remarks about the difficulty of adjudging it to be clearly a superior possible world? If these speculations and remarks have had any force, what seems to follow for anyone crediting them with such force is that they must acknowledge it would not be unreasonable for God to prefer our world (with its moral evil) over W in virtue of its more valuable features for those who inhabit it. I am not putting this claim forward as a solution to the problem of all evil — I have not been trying to resolve that problem, which accounts for my neglect, for instance, of the difficulties associated with the existence of natural evils like those which antedate human habitation.

My contention has been, then, that it is not an obvious truth, let alone a necessary truth (and hence is no indispensable tenet of revealed Christian theism), that W is morally a more valuable world than our present one. Furthermore, if God does have a reason or reasons for not having instantiated people such as the inhabitants of W in preference to the sinners he has, that reason or those reasons could not be left out of any assessment of the moral value of the alternative worlds. No such comparisons could afford to neglect the creator's purposes. Thus, thirdly, even if it is necessary to side with the sceptics and say that God could have instantiated beings such as those in W, the argument with which we began is arguably unsound even if a compatibilist account of freedom is espoused.

While I have not been trying to solve the problem of the presence of all the evils there are, it may have occurred to readers that what I have been saying is somewhat akin to what Nelson Pike[17] has urged in relation to the alleged incompatibility between the existence of an omniscient, omnipotent and wholly good God and the presence of all and any evil. For he has pointed out that no such incompatibility can be established without a premise to the effect that God could have no morally sufficient reasons for allowing evil in any world he created. Now my point has been in line with his but is a much more limited one. Even so, if my claims about the unobvious preferability of W aren't plausible, there seems to be nothing to disbar a Christian theist from retreating to a position like Pike's. In reply it may be said that the onus is not on the sceptic to furnish such reasons, but on the Christian theist to give some content to the claim that God would morally be justified in creating a (compatibilist) world like ours, rather than one in which men always freely do the right. Now I think there is *something to be said for* this sceptical reply — indeed that is why I have written at such length about W. But, since I do not think it controversial to claim that nobody *comes to* a belief in, or *continues* to believe in, Christian theism, just because he has resolved all his doubts about the availability of reasons justifying God's preference for a world like ours (with its moral evils), but rather because he believes God has communicated his self-revelation to him, I do not think it is *all* that can sensibly be said.

The position is, I think, that the factors inclining one to believe in Christian theism (stemming from God's alleged self-revelation) must be ranged against those (such as the presence of moral evil) inclining one to disbelieve. What the Christian theist contends is that the positive evidence holds sufficient sway as to make it reasonable to claim *that* God has morally sufficient reasons (for natural as well as moral evil), even though he doesn't know just *what* those reasons are in detail. The Christian may point out that often enough men have good reason for believing that a certain person has a justification for some action, even though they may not know in any but the vaguest detail what it is. The sceptic is liable, of course, to claim that in such cases independent reasons are available for believing that that person has a justification but such independent reasons are ruled out in the case of God. The reader will recognise familiar territory. It is my conviction that the charge that the Christian does not have independent grounds for his claim cannot be sustained. Nevertheless, interesting and crucial as this territory of dispute happens to be, it lies outside the scope of this present inquiry.[18] I recognise that this leaves the debate in a rather desultory state, but one cannot hope to solve every problem in one essay — indeed it would be presumptuous on my part to even pretend I could *solve* those I have directly tackled.

Notes

CHAPTER 2 MORAL RESPONSIBILITY

1. The most perceptive recent work on responsibility has been produced by writers who have been concerned with questions both of moral responsibility and legal responsibility. It is almost superfluous to add that such writers have studiously avoided the trap I have been discussing. Cf. H. L. A. Hart, *Punishment and Responsibility* (Oxford, 1968); J. Feinberg, *Doing and Deserving* (Princeton, N.J., 1970); J. Glover, *Responsibility* (London, 1970).

2. Cf. A. Kaufman, 'Moral Responsibility and the Use of "Could Have"', *Philosophical Quarterly*, 1962, pp. 120–8, and 'Responsibility, Moral and Legal' in P. Edwards (ed.), *The Encyclopedia of Philosophy* (New York, 1967), vol. 7; R. J. Richman, 'Responsibility and the Causation of Actions', *American Philosophical Quarterly*, 1969, pp. 186–97; H. Frankfurt, 'Alternate Possibilities and Moral Responsibility', *Journal of Philosophy*, 1969, pp. 829–39; J. Glover, op. cit.

3. While this sort of position has in the main been championed by compatibilists, especially those compatibilists who believe it is necessary for an act to be determined if it is to be free, it could be espoused by 'hard determinists' who believe that all actions are determined and, therefore, unfree. On the hard determinist view, blame and punishment can never be deserved *in principle,* whereas with most of the compatibilists it is ruled out as a matter of moral *taste.* 'Moral' education and social engineering might be engaged in by a hard determinist with the aid of 'blame' and 'punishment', but no *moral* significance would attach to their use.

4. In section III of 'Is "Free Will" a Pseudo-Problem?' reprinted in Campbell's essays *In Defence of Free Will, with Other Philosophical Essays* (London, 1967).

5. David Blumenfeld and Gerald Dworkin, 'Necessity, Contingency, and Punishment', *Philosophical Studies*, 1965, pp. 91–4, try to reveal what they consider is a basic confusion in the theory which makes it possible to generate counter-examples like these.

6. P. F. Strawson's 'Freedom and Resentment', *Proceedings of the British Academy*, 1962, pp. 187–211, makes some interesting points of relevance here.

7. See Michael Stocker's stimulating ' "Ought" and "Can" ', *Australasian Journal of Philosophy*, 1971, pp. 303–16; Alvin Goldman, *A Theory of Human Action* (Englewood Cliffs, N.J., 1970) pp. 208ff. In addition William Frankena's 'Obligation and Ability' in M. Black (ed.), *Philosophical Analysis* (Englewood Cliffs, N.J., 1963) and J. Margolis, 'One Last Time: "Ought" Implies "Can" ', *The Personalist*, 1967, pp. 33–41, are also worth consulting.

8. It will be obvious that the content of these formulae will bear differing moral convictions.

9. It might well be thought that, in general, philosophers exclude ignorance in the way Aristotle did, by writing its absence into the conception of voluntariness or freedom. Perhaps this is so, but I separate it out for two reasons. Firstly, it highlights the need to take account of it, and, secondly, as my discussion of slogans should have made clear, much the greater part of discussions of freedom ignore ignorance.

CHAPTER 3 FATALISM AND FREEDOM

1. S. M. Cahn, *Fate, Logic and Time* (New Haven and London, 1967), Chapter 2, goes to some pains to show that some notable contemporary philosophers have succumbed to this misunderstanding. In fairness to such philosophers, though, it should be said that the sorts of fatalism which they have charged with these consequences haven't always been of the sophisticated philosophical kinds that Cahn and I are interested in.

2. *De Interpretatione*, Chapter 9, 18a 34–19b 4.

3. V. McKim's, 'Fatalism and the Future: Aristotle's Way Out', *Review of Metaphysics*, 1971–2, pp. 80–111 provides a valuable discussion.

4. This argument, known as the 'Master Argument of Diodorus', has been discussed extensively in the literature. See S. M. Cahn, op. cit., Chapter 4 for a defence of a reconstruction of it and for other references.

5. I am indebted to a review of Cahn, op. cit., by Storrs McCall contained in *Journal of Philosophy*, 1968, pp. 742–6 for this formulation.

6. 'Fatalism and Ordinary Language', *Journal of Philosophy*, 1965, pp. 211–22.

7. Op. cit., pp. 745f.

8. McCall considers Cahn's proposal of differentiating an analytic formulation of the law of excluded middle (logically undeniable) and a synthetic one (empirically deniable) as approaching his own suggestion. However, he thinks Cahn's *imaginary* distinction side-tracked him from finding a way out from fatalism.

9. 'Excluded Middle, Bivalence and Fatalism', *Inquiry*, 1966, pp. 384–6. He presents a philosophical treatment of 'time' in his 'Temporal Flux', *American Philosophical Quarterly*, 1966, pp. 270–81. Section VI of that paper develops the distinction between bivalence and excluded middle, which is then drawn on in Sections VII and VIII to elucidate the asymmetry of past and future.

10. So, for instance, McCall, ibid., p. 279, where he claims propositions about the past but not those about the future are subject to the law of bivalence.

11. Cf. R. Taylor's 'The Problem of Future Contingencies', *Philosophical Review*, 1957, pp. 1–28. He does not, however, make use of the distinction to explain the passage of time.

12. I am indebted to Paul Fitzgerald's, 'Is the Future Partly Unreal?', *Review of Metaphysics*, 1967–8, pp. 421–46 in the following two paragraphs, as well as at other points acknowledged in the chapter.

13. Fitzgerald, ibid., p. 444 cites a number of references. For a different view see R. Swinburne, *Space and Time* (London, 1968), p. 169.

14. 'Present Truth and Future Contingency', *Philosophical Review*, 1957, pp. 29–46 (esp. pp. 29–34).

15. In adopting this criterion I am following R. Gale and I. Thalberg in their 'The Generality of Predictions', *Journal*

of Philosophy, 1965, pp. 195–210. While I arrive at a different conclusion, my discussion profits from theirs.

16. For a clear statement and spirited defence of this thesis (which claims Peirce, Broad and Ryle as adherents) see B. Mayo, 'The Open Future', *Mind*, 1962, pp. 1–14.

17. Cf. Fitzgerald, op. cit., pp. 431–40. The formulation of this and the following argument is mine, though drawn from Fitzgerald's paper.

18. P. Fitzgerald, 'The Truth About Tomorrow's Sea-Fight', *Journal of Philosophy*, 1969, pp. 307–29. The qualification 'pre-relativistic' is mine not Fitzgerald's for, as I shall later observe, non-full theories may be open to relativistic restatement. Fitzgerald's paper has been criticised by T. Chapman in his 'Special Relativity and Indeterminism', *Ratio*, 1973, pp. 107–10.

19. It is interesting to note that McCall backs the halfway theory on ordinary language grounds simply because he (rightly) regards the question of the truth of fatalism or of determinism as independent of whether the universe is 'block'.

20. Cf. J. J. C. Smart's article 'Time' in *The Encyclopedia of Philosophy*, vol. 8, pp. 132–3 and compare also R. D. Bradley, 'Must the Future Be What It Is Going to Be?', *Mind*, 1959, pp. 193–208. Bradley claims that logical determinism doesn't entail fatalism. See also 'The Sea Fight Tomorrow', p. 274, reprinted in D. Williams, *Principles of Empirical Realism* (Springfield, Illinois, 1966).

21. Cf. Saunders, op. cit., and two further papers of his to which I am indebted, 'Of God and Freedom', *Philosophical Review*, 1966, pp. 219–25 and 'The Temptations of Powerlessness', *American Philosophical Quarterly*, 1968, pp. 100–8.

CHAPTER 4 DETERMINISM

1. Some of the work needed has recently been done by Bernard Berofsky in his *Determinism* (Princeton, N.J., 1971). See also D. Wiggins, 'Towards a Credible Libertarianism', esp. Section II; and T. Honderich, 'One Deter-

minism', both in Honderich (ed.), *Essays on Freedom of Action* (London and Boston, 1973).

2. 'Indeterminism in Quantum Physics and Classical Physics', *British Journal for the Philosophy of Science*, 1950—1, pp. 117—33; 173—95.

3. The notion of 'predictability in principle' has been vigorously attacked by D. J. O'Connor in *Free Will* (New York, 1971), pp. 68—70.

4. Cf. B. Berofsky (ed.), *Free Will and Determinism* (New York, 1966), p. 5.

5. 'Causal Relations', *Journal of Philosophy*, 1967, pp. 691—703. Cf. also his 'The Logical Form of Action Sentences' in N. Rescher (ed.), *The Logic of Decision and Action* (Pittsburgh, 1967), and 'The Individuation of Events' in N. Rescher and others (eds.), *Essays in Honor of Carl G. Hempel* (Dordrecht, Holland, 1969).

6. Cf. G. J. Warnock, 'Every Event Has a Cause' in Antony Flew (ed.), *Logic and Language*, Second Series (Oxford, 1953), pp. 95—111.

7. Cf. R. G. Swinburne, 'Physical Determinism', in G. N. A. Vesey (ed.), *Knowledge and Necessity* (London, 1970); H. Margenau, *Scientific Indeterminism and Human Freedom* (La Trobe, Pennsylvania, 1968).

8. James Jordan, 'Determinism's Dilemma', *Review of Metaphysics*, 1969—70, pp. 48—66. He provides references to those from Kant on whom he regards as having put forward similar arguments. See also J. R. Lucas, 'Freedom and Prediction', *Proceedings of the Aristotelian Society*, 1967, pp. 163—72.

9. M. C. Bradley's, 'A Note on Mr. MacIntyre's Determinism', *Mind*, 1959, pp. 521—5; and J. J. C. Smart, *Between Science and Philosophy* (New York, 1968), pp. 300—4 seem to take this sort of way with related arguments.

10. 'Freedom, Knowledge, Belief and Causality' in Vesey (ed.), op. cit., (esp. pp. 137ff).

11. An interesting argument in this connection is J. M. Boyle, G. Grisez and O. Tollefsen, 'Determinism, Freedom and Self-Referential Arguments', *Review of Metaphysics*, 1972—3, pp. 3—37. For critical discussion see

my reply 'A Sound Self-Referential Argument?' *Review of Metaphysics*, 1973—4, pp. 111—8.

12. The culmination is his book, *The Freedom of the Will* (Oxford, 1970). References to his earlier papers, and to critical discussions, can be found in the bibliography of that work. More recent criticism is contained in C. D. Chihara, 'On Alleged Refutations of Mechanism Using Gödel's Incompleteness Results', *Journal of Philosophy*, 1972, pp. 507—26 and D. C. Dennett's, 'Review of *The Freedom of the Will*', *Journal of Philosophy*, 1972, pp. 527—31.

13. 'Minds, Machines and Gödel', *Philosophy*, 1961, pp. 112—27 (esp. pp. 113—4).

14. 'Minds and Machines' in S. Hook (ed.), *Dimensions of Mind* (New York, 1960). Cf. P. Benacerraf, 'God, The Devil and Gödel', *The Monist*, 1967, pp. 9—32 (esp. pp. 20ff).

CHAPTER 5 'TWO-DOMAINISM' AND FREEDOM

1. It may well be that someone more sympathetic, than I, to the views of Melden (and others) will consider that I do them a disservice by discussing their views in the context of an attempt to evade the problem of freedom and determinism. There may well be a case for the claim that it would be misleading to impute a desire to escape the clutches of determinism to those who have sought to furnish an account of *action*. But, whatever the *motives* of 'two-domainists' they have certainly claimed it is a *consequence* of their views that the determinist problem is set aside.

2. I have added this qualification because some of the 'two-domainists' (e.g. Melden) claim the identification is, on occasion, possible provided we take into account the context of rules and practices in which the movement occurs. More of this in Section IV.

3. According to Ryle, *The Concept of Mind* (London, 1949), pp. 67ff, this sense of 'voluntary' is not the normal one but a device of philosophers. For reasons that will emerge I will substitute the term 'free' for his normal sense.

4. Pp. 66ff. Cf. also Melden, op. cit., pp. 47ff.

5. There have been two recent attempts to partially re-instate 'volitions'. Cf. J. R. Silber, 'Human Action and the Language of Volitions', *Proceedings of the Aristotelian Society*, 1964, pp. 199–220 and W. R. F. Hardie, 'Willing and Acting', *Philosophical Quarterly*, 1971, pp. 193–206.

6. May Brodbeck, 'Meaning and Action', *Philosophy of Science*, 1963, pp. 309–24 has remarked on the 'incongruity' of this claim. See further p. 311.

7. *The Explanation of Behaviour* (London, 1964), p. 10. Unlike Melden, op. cit., pp. 105ff, and R. S. Peters, *The Concept of Motivation* (London, 1958), pp. 27ff, Taylor considers the choice between teleological and causal or physicalistic explanations is not just a conceptual issue but depends on both empirical investigations and analysis.

8. Cf. C. Landesman, 'The New Dualism in the Philosophy of Mind', *Review of Metaphysics*, 1964–5, pp. 329–45 (esp. pp. 336ff).

9. Op. cit., p. 98.

10. *Thought and Action* (London, 1959), p. 98.

11. *The Idea of a Social Science* (London, 1958), p. 52.

12. 'Actions, Reasons and Causes', *Journal of Philosophy*, 1963, pp. 685–700. With this article one should compare W. D. Gean, 'Reasons and Causes', *Review of Metaphysics*, 1965–6, pp. 667–88, and R. Brandt and J. Kim, 'Wants as Explanations of Action', *Journal of Philosophy*, 1963, pp. 425–35 for similar views.

13. 'Motives, Causal Necessity and Moral Accountability', *Australasian Journal of Philosophy*, 1964, pp. 322–34.

14. Brian Medlin, 'Materialism and the Argument from Distinct Existences', in J. J. MacIntosh and S. C. Coval (eds.), *The Business of Reason* (London, 1969), pp. 168–85.

15. Op. cit., pp. 695f.

16. D. Pears, 'Are Reasons for Actions Causes?' in A. Stroll (ed.), *Epistemology* (New York, 1967) argues that fairy stories which treat wishes as causes *and* describe a wish simply as concentrated willing, counter this claim.

17. The following appraisal of the argument owes much to Gean, op. cit., pp. 679ff.

18. Op. cit., p. 699. See also R. Hancock, 'Interpersonal and Physical Causation', *Philosophical Review*, 1962, pp. 369—76.

19. Cf. also R. J. Richman, 'Reasons and Causes: Some Puzzles', *Australasian Journal of Philosophy*, 1969, pp. 42—50; M. Brand (ed.), *The Nature of Human Action* (Glenview, Illinois, 1970), p. 12. For further discussion see my 'Reasons as Causes', *Australasian Journal of Philosophy*, 1971, pp. 90—5.

20. Daniel Bennett, 'Action, Reason and Purpose', *Journal of Philosophy*, 1965, p. 87 has argued that making causing intentionally and causing rationally, relative to the expression 'under the description' has two counter-intuitive consequences. It seems to mean that agency entails a language and that an action would only be done for a reason if it were actually described. These are matters worthy of attention but are beyond the scope of this essay. The important point for our purposes is one Bennett recognises, namely that the description-relative device overcomes the argument considered above.

21. Cf. Davidson, op. cit., p. 700.

22. Cf. Landesman, op. cit., pp. 344f.

23. D. M. Armstrong has suggested to me that against Melden, 'appropriate circumstances' must not only exist but be known (or believed) by the agent to exist. If this is so the knowledge or belief then looks like a causal factor in his action.

24. Cf. M. Brand (ed.), op. cit., p. 17.

25. May Brodbeck, op cit., and Ruth Macklin, 'Explanation and Action', *Synthese*, 1969, pp. 388—415.

CHAPTER 6 'ARISTOTLE'S VIEW' AND FREEDOM

1. 'A Plea for Excuses', *Proceedings of the Aristotelian Society*, 1956—7, pp. 1—30. Cf. P. Nowell-Smith, *Ethics* (Harmondsworth, 1954); R. Bronaugh, 'Freedom as the Absence of an Excuse', *Ethics*, 1964, pp. 161—73; Austin's own 'Three Ways of Spilling Ink', *Philosophical Review*, 1966, pp. 427—40; and J. F. M. Hunter, 'Acting Freely and Being Held Responsible', *Dialogue,* 1973, pp. 233—45.

2. Cf. H. L. A. Hart's, 'The Ascription of Responsibility and Rights', *Proceedings of the Aristotelian Society*, 1949, pp. 171—94 and 'Legal Responsibility and Excuses' in S. Hook (ed.), *Determinism and Freedom in the Age of Modern Science* (New York, 1958).

3. I am indebted to D. Holdcroft, 'A Plea for Excuses?', *Philosophical Quarterly*, 1969, pp. 314—30 for these formulations.

4. Cf. V. Haksar, 'Responsibility', *Aristotelian Society Supplementary Volume*, 1966, pp. 187—222.

5. Even though it appears irreconcilable to argue that there is a general criterion for distinguishing free from unfree actions *and* that 'free' is a defeasible concept, some philosophers, perhaps Hart included, have endeavoured to do just that. Thus, in his *Ethics*, Nowell-Smith not only says that 'free' is a defeasible concept but also offers a general criterion for distinguishing free from unfree actions, namely that free actions are modifiable by blame and punishment, unfree ones not. For similar reasons, Aristotle too would be involved in an inconsistency, if Austin and Hart are right in attributing the defeasibility theory to him, for he said free actions are those where the moving principle is in the man himself, unfree ones being those 'whose moving principle is outside, the person compelled contributing nothing'.

6. Cf. Bronaugh, op. cit., pp. 164f.

7. Cf. Holdcroft, op. cit., pp. 316ff.

8. 'Prolegomenon to the Principles of Punishment' in Hart's *Punishment and Responsibility*, op cit., p. 14.

9. In Hart's contribution to Hook (ed.), op. cit., he disavows any intent to say anything about responsibility, other than legal responsibility. To that extent he should be read as saying something different from at least some others who have appealed to his writings.

10. Cf. Holdcroft, op. cit., pp. 327f.

11. Cf. Nowell-Smith, *Ethics*, op cit., '. . . we use the word "compulsion" not because we have identified the object which caused him to do what he did, but because we want to excuse him . . .' (p. 296).

12. Bronaugh, op. cit., pp. 164f (Bronaugh's italics). One

feature of his paper is that (remarkably) when he actually considers 'determinism', he considers only what amounts to the 'hard determinist' view and neglects the compatibilist altogether.

13. I must acknowledge the help of V. Haksar's, 'Responsibility', op. cit., pp. 206ff, in considering Bronaugh's paper.

CHAPTER 7 'HARD DETERMINISM' AND FREEDOM

1. In his 'Hard and Soft Determinism' in S. Hook (ed.), *Determinism and Freedom in the Age of Modern Science*, op. cit.

2. Cf. J. Hospers, 'What Means this Freedom?' in ibid., pp. 113–30, (esp. pp. 119–20).

3. Notably Hospers, ibid., and W. Matson, 'On the Irrelevance of Free-Will to Moral Responsibility and the Vacuity of the Latter', *Mind*, 1956, pp. 489–97. See also R. Taylor, *Metaphysics* (Englewood Cliffs, N.J., 1963).

4. This is, I think, symptomatic of several confusions found in the article. One illustration comes in his failure to be clear about whether what should occasion concern is our lack of control over the formative influences on our character, or whether it is that these influences work deterministically.

5. Cf. Hospers, op. cit., p. 135. One should notice that for a determinist 'luck' must be used euphemistically and certainly can't be used to signify that some event or state is uncaused.

6. Cf. S. Hook, 'Necessity, Indeterminism and Sentimentalism' in Hook (ed.), op. cit., pp. 187–92.

7. Both Hospers and Edwards oscillate between holding that it is self-contradictory to assert that we are free in the sense required by the demands of moral responsibility, and that we seldom, if ever, are free in the required sense.

8. 'Psychoanalytic Explanation and Rationality', *Journal of Philosophy*, 1971, pp. 413–26 (esp. pp. 425f). Cf. G. Pitcher, 'Necessitarianism', *Philosophical Quarterly*, 1961, pp. 201–12.

9. Cf. R. G. Henson, 'Responsibility for Character and Conduct', *Australasian Journal of Philosophy*, 1965, pp. 311—20. This is quite like the point made by Hook on another matter — see note 6 above.
10. Cf. Henson, ibid.
11. Ronald J. Glossop has recently argued (to my mind quite unconvincingly) that the hard determinist is committed to a dualistic self and hence could not, presumably, avail himself of the way out I have sketched. See his 'Beneath the Surface of the Free-Will Problem', *Journal of Value Inquiry*, 1970, pp. 24—34.

CHAPTER 8 EPISTEMIC INDETERMINISM AND FREEDOM

1. In distinguishing these species of possibility and, indeed, for much else in this chapter, I am indebted to Alvin Goldman's discussion in 'Actions, Predictions and Books of Life', *American Philosophical Quarterly*, 1968, pp. 135—51 (esp. pp. 136f). That paper is substantially incorporated into Chapter 6 of Goldman's, *A Theory of Human Action*.
2. Cf. M. Cranston, *Freedom: A New Analysis* (London, 1953), p. 118.
3. Cf. similar claims in Goldman, op. cit., pp. 138f.
4. I have in mind Carl Ginet's, 'Can The Will Be Caused?', *Philosophical Review*, 1962, pp. 49—55. But compare also, for example, S. Hampshire and H. L. A. Hart, 'Decision, Intention and Certainty', *Mind*, 1958, pp. 1—12, and Richard Taylor, 'Deliberation and Foreknowledge', *American Philosophical Quarterly*, 1964, pp. 73—80.
5. Cf. J. W. Roxbee Cox, 'Can I Know Beforehand What I Am Going to Decide?', *Philosophical Review*, 1963, pp. 88—92; M. Stocker, 'Knowledge, Causation and Decision', *Nous*, 1968, pp. 65—73.
6. Cf. Roxbee Cox, op. cit., p. 90; Stocker, op. cit., pp. 66ff; John Canfield, 'Knowing About Decisions', *Analysis*, 1961—2, pp. 127—9.
7. For some valuable suggestions in this regard see Stocker, op. cit., p. 67 note 2.

8. Cf. Stocker, ibid., p. 69.

9. *Freedom of the Individual* (London, 1965), p. 54. Goldman, art. cit., p. 149 furnishes an extended example which also constitutes a counter to Hampshire's position.

10. Cf. Stocker, op. cit., pp. 70ff, and A. Kaufman, 'Practical Decision', *Mind*, 1966, pp. 25–44 (esp. 28–9).

11. Cf. 'Indeterminism in Quantum Physics and in Classical Physics', *British Journal for the Philosophy of Science*, 1950–1, pp. 117–33; 173–95.

12. On the figures given above, the equation yielding the band-waggon effect is $V = 60 + .2 (P - 50)$, where P is the percentage vote for A publicly predicted by the pollster and V is the actual resultant vote for A. The pollster must calculate (and then predict) a value for P which will make $P = V$, namely sixty-two and a half per cent. Cf. Herbert Simon, 'Bandwagon and Underdog Effects of Election Prediction' reprinted in *Models of Man* (New York, 1957). My discussion over the next couple of pages is heavily dependent upon Goldman's discussion of the same issues.

13. Ibid., pp. 146f.

14. This is relevant to the claim by D. M. MacKay that there is a 'logical indeterminacy' involved in the fact that any communicated prediction becomes only a further factor for the agent to consider. Since consideration of this information can be absorbed only at the cost of changes in the brain, even if the brain is a completely clockwork mechanism, no completely detailed present or future description of a man's brain can be equally accurate whether the man believes it or not. Cf. MacKay, 'On the Logical Indeterminacy of a Free Choice', *Mind*, 1960, pp. 31–40; *Freedom of Action in a Mechanistic Universe* (Cambridge, 1967). MacKay, like quite a few others, appears to confuse epistemic with ontic considerations – a common enough confusion in the freedom-determinism debate, but a confusion all the same.

CHAPTER 9 CONTRA-CAUSAL LIBERTARIANISM AND FREEDOM

1. *On Selfhood and Godhood* (London, 1957), Lecture IX

(incl. Appendix B); *In Defence of Free Will with Other Philosophical Essays* (London, 1967); 'Free-Will: A Reply to Mr. R. D. Bradley', *Australasian Journal of Philosophy*, 1958, pp. 46—56; 'Moral Libertarianism: A Reply to Mr. Franklin', *Philosophical Quarterly*, 1962, pp. 337—47.

2. E.g. R. E. Hobart, 'Free Will as Involving Determination and Inconceivable without It', *Mind*, 1934, pp. 1—27. M. Schlick, *Problems of Ethics* (New York, 1962), pp. 281ff. J. J. C. Smart, 'Free Will, Praise and Blame', *Mind*, 1961, pp. 291—306. Smart does seem to concede elsewhere that libertarians have sought to circumvent this charge. See his *Between Science and Philosophy* (New York, 1968), pp. 300—4. For criticism of the 'randomness' contention, see Philippa Foot, 'Free Will as Involving Determinism', *Philosophical Review*, 1957, pp. 439—50.

3. Cf. Smart, art. cit., p. 294.

4. Cf. P. Nowell-Smith, *Ethics*, op. cit., pp. 282f; Hobart, op. cit., pp. 3ff.

5. 'Is "Free-Will" a Pseudo-Problem?', Section VI.

6. A similar argument may be found in E. D'Angelo, *The Problem of Freedom and Determinism* (Columbia, 1968), pp. 14f.

7. So Richard Taylor, 'Determinism and the Theory of Agency' in S. Hook (ed.), *Determinism and Freedom In the Age of Modern Science*, p. 228.

8. See, e.g., Nowell-Smith, op. cit., esp. p. 281; R. D. Bradley, 'Freewill: Problem or Pseudo-Problem?', *Australasian Journal of Philosophy*, 1958, pp. 33—45, esp. pp. 41—2.

9. *On Selfhood and Godhood*, p. 216. Cf. 'Free Will: A Reply to Mr. R. D. Bradley', *Australasian Journal of Philosophy*, 1958, pp. 46—56, esp. p. 52.

10. Cf. R. L. Franklin, *Freewill and Determinism* (London, 1968), Appendix I, p. 328.

11. K. Lehrer, 'Can We Know We Have Free Will by Introspection?', *Journal of Philosophy*, 1960, pp. 145—57 has suggested this defence.

12. 'Free Will: A Reply to Mr. R. D. Bradley', op. cit., pp. 50—1 (Campbell's italics).

13. Franklin, op cit., pp. 329ff argues in a similar way.
14. Cf. M. C. Bradley's review of Campbell's *In Defence of Free Will etc.* in *Journal of Philosophy*, 1968, pp. 344ff. I attempt some of the philosophical reflection below in Chapter 11, and some has already been offered in Chapter 2.
15. Franklin's discussion (op. cit., pp. 325ff) has been of great help in this section and I follow him closely.
16. *Freewill and Determinism.* The book has been favourably reviewed by Bernard Berofsky in his helpful review article 'Conceptions of Freedom', *Journal of Philosophy*, 1970, pp. 208–20.
17. In drawing attention to this affinity I do not wish to minimise the important differences that exist between these views.

CHAPTER 10 AGENT-CAUSATION LIBERTARIANISM AND FREEDOM

1. In particular R. M. Chisholm, *Human Freedom and the Self* (Lindley Lecture for 1964) (Kansas, 1964); 'Freedom and Action' in K. Lehrer (ed.), *Freedom and Determinism* (New York, 1966); 'He Could Have Done Otherwise', *Journal of Philosophy*, 1967, pp. 409–17; and 'Some Puzzles About Agency' in K. Lambert (ed.), *The Logical Way of Doing Things* (New Haven, 1969).
   Cf. R. Taylor, *Action and Purpose* (Englewood Cliffs, N.J., 1966); D. Wiggins, 'Towards a Reasonable Libertarianism' in T. Honderich (ed.), *Essays on Freedom of Action*, op. cit.
2. I say 'revive' because Thomas Reid in his *Essays on the Active Powers of Man* and Berkeley in his *De Motu* long ago defended agency theories.
3. Richard Taylor's views on this point appear to have altered. See 'Thought and Action', *Inquiry*, 1969, pp. 149–69 where he claims the element of purposiveness is absent in simple actions. His position has been criticised by M. Brand in *The Nature of Human Action*, op. cit., pp. 228ff.
4. 'Freedom and Action', op. cit., p. 17. Even though he adopts different terminology, Richard Taylor, op. cit.,

Ch. 3 claims with Chisholm that if we did not already have the idea of immanent causation, we could not understand that of transeunt causation.

5. 'Freedom and Action', pp. 20ff.

6. 'Agency' in R. Binkley, R. Bronaugh and A. Marras (eds.), *Agent, Action and Reason* (Oxford, 1971), esp. pp. 14ff.

7. Further criticism of agent-causation views may be found in Donald Davidson, 'The Logical Form of Action Sentences' in N. Rescher (ed.), *The Logic of Decision and Action*, op. cit.; I. Thalberg, 'Do We Cause Our Own Actions?' as reprinted in his *Enigmas of Agency* (London and New York, 1972).

8. *Action and Purpose* (e.g. pp. 114, 143f, 146, 151).

9. My argument in the remainder of this chapter owes much to Nani L. Ranken's, 'The "Unmoved" Agent and the Ground of Responsibility', *Journal of Philosophy*, 1967, pp. 403–8.

10. Op. cit.; p. 29 (my italics). This quotation obviously contradicts Chisholm's remark quoted a moment ago, but at this stage I shall not do more than just indicate the fact.

11. Cf. Richard Taylor, op. cit., pp. 140f, though not in a context dealing with the question of responsibility. Again notice the discrepancy with Chisholm's comments and, indeed, with those of Taylor himself as cited in note 8.

12. Fundamentally, this is indicative of the inability of agent-causation theories to handle cases of over-determination. Since it is alleged to be impossible for an action to be brought about by an agent *and* for there also to be a sufficient condition that does not include the agent, it would have to be said of a case of over-determination that the presence of a sufficient condition not involving the agent (e.g. a heart attack bringing about A's death at t) makes it impossible for the agent to, say, cause A's death at t by shooting him. This is just false.

13. The reader may well think that Chisholm has allowed for 'degrees of responsibility' in his notion of 'inclination without necessitation'. But Chisholm's case of the public

official (see 'Freedom and Action', op. cit., pp. 24ff) does not lend itself to any convincing interpretation permitting of degrees of responsibility that I can envisage.

CHAPTER 11 A COMPATIBILIST DEFENCE OF FREEDOM

1. Reprinted in Austin's, *Philosophical Papers* (Oxford, 1961), pp. 153—80 from *The Proceedings of the British Academy*, 1956, pp. 109—32.
2. M. Brand in Brand (ed.), op. cit., p. 130.
3. 'Ifs and Cans', *Canadian Journal of Philosophy*, 1971—2, pp. 249—74; 369—91 (esp. Part I).
4. Pears, ibid., argues interestingly for a way of unifying the theory of the conditional 'if' which includes even the pseudos (especially those he terms 'integrated pseudos'). For a very different view see I. Thalberg, 'Austin on Abilities' in K. T. Fann (ed.), *Symposium on J. L. Austin* (London, 1969), (reprinted in *Enigmas of Agency*, op. cit.). Pears' view is undoubtedly more convincing than Thalberg's.
5. Cf. D. J. O'Connor, 'Possibility and Choice', *Proceedings of the Aristotelian Society* (Supplementary Volume), 1960, pp. 1—24; K. Baier, 'Could and Would', *Analysis Supplement*, 1963, pp. 20—9; K. Lehrer, ' "Could" and Determinism', *Analysis*, 1963—4, pp. 159—60; W. D. Hudson, *Modern Moral Philosophy* (London, 1970), pp. 340—5.
6. For example, R. L. Franklin, *Freewill and Determinism*, p. 118; 336f.
7. Cf. also 'Ifs and Cans', *Theoria*, 1960, pp. 85—101. Moore's and Nowell-Smith's analyses are discussed in Bruce Aune, 'Abilities, Modalities and Free Will', *Philosophy and Phenomenological Research*, 1962—3, pp. 397—413; D. Pears, op. cit.; Donald Davidson, 'Freedom to Act' in Honderich (ed.), op. cit.; and in R. D. Bradley, ' "Ifs", "Cans" and Determinism', *Australasian Journal of Philosophy*, 1962, pp. 146—58 (esp. 155ff).
8. Cf. Keith Lehrer's discussion of the availability of ade-

quate empirical evidence in such matters in his 'An Empirical Disproof of Determinism?' in K. Lehrer (ed.), *Freedom and Determinism*. I should add that Lehrer takes a somewhat different (and tougher) line than I have.

9. Cf. Thalberg's example of rifle-shooting (op. cit., pp. 187ff) and Pears' discussion of the same skill (op. cit., pp. 380ff).

10. 'Ifs and Cans', op. cit., p. 96 (and also the whole of Sections II and III).

11. Op. cit., pp. 401f.

12. I shall now leave consideration of (T). Austin's historically and philosophically important objections are not the only ones which have been levelled at it. Keith Lehrer has also raised an interesting objection. See his 'Ifs, Cans and Causes', *Analysis*, 1959—60, pp. 122—4, and his 'Cans and Conditionals: A Rejoinder', *Analysis*, 1961—2, pp. 23—4. The latter is a response (I think an inadequate one) to criticism by B. Goldberg and H. Heidelberger, 'Mr. Lehrer on the Constitution of Cans', *Analysis*, 1960—1, p. 96. See, too, Myles Brand (ed.), *The Nature of Human Action*, pp. 131—3.

13. *The Refutation of Determinism* (London, 1968).

14. 'An Empirical Disproof of Determinism?', op. cit. (esp. section X); 'Cans Without Ifs', *Analysis*, 1968—9, pp. 29—32.

15. 'J. L. Austin's "Philosophical Papers" ', *Mind*, 1964, pp. 20—5; 'He Could Have Done Otherwise', *Journal of Philosophy*, 1967, pp. 409—17 (reprinted in revised form in Brand (ed.), op. cit.).

16. E.g. B. Aune, 'Hypotheticals and "Can": Another Look', *Analysis*, 1966—7, pp. 191—5; 'Free Will, "Can", and Ethics: A Reply to Lehrer', *Analysis*, 1969—70, pp. 77—83; I. Thalberg, op. cit.; A Goldman, op. cit., pp. 199—200; Clement Dore, 'On a Recent Discussion of If's and Can's', *Philosophical Studies*, 1970, pp. 33—7; D. Pears, op. cit., Part II.

17. 'Cans Without Ifs', op. cit., p. 31.

18. Cf. Goldman, op. cit., pp. 199—200. Different (and, I believe, less decisive) strategies are employed by Bruce

Aune in 'Free Will, "Can" and Ethics: A Reply to Lehrer', op. cit. and by David Pears, op. cit., pp. 376ff.

19. Bernard Gert and Timothy Duggan in their 'Voluntary Abilities', *American Philosophical Quarterly*, 1967, pp. 127–35 have, however, argued that there is such an ability as 'the ability to will'.

20. Cf. the interesting papers in this area by Joel Feinberg in his recent collection *Doing and Deserving* (esp. papers 10, 11), and by Jonathan Glover in his *Responsibility*. Glover believes that the concept of mental illness can be regarded as an objective one (the most important condition being that the person is in a state which is personally harmful) but, interestingly, also contends that the selection of the conditions is morally motivated.

21. Even Strawson in 'Freedom and Resentment', op. cit., makes use of a similar kind of distinction in his discussion of human normality.

22. 'He Could Have Done Otherwise', op. cit.

23. Cf. Goldman, op. cit., pp. 200ff and Chisholm, ibid., Section IV. Goldman's discussion has been particularly helpful. Some aspects of his position have been attacked, though, by Donald Davidson in 'Freedom to Act', op. cit., pp. 151f.

24. E.g. Davidson, ibid., p. 154.

25. In fact one is frequently given pause to reconsider one's position. Most recently perhaps by Wiggins, 'Towards a Reasonable Libertarianism', op. cit., and by Theodore Guleserian's, 'Factual Necessity and the Libertarian', *Philosophy and Phenomenological Research*, 1971–2, pp. 188–204. Unfortunately space does not permit my taking up the points they raise in any detail, though I might be permitted to say that their *positive* contributions from a libertarian standpoint are very thin.

CHAPTER 12 OMNISCIENCE AND FREEDOM

1. In 'Divine Omniscience and Voluntary Action', *Philosophical Review*, 1965, pp. 27–46, and in *God and Timelessness* (London, 1970), pp. 53–86. Cf. S. M. Cahn, *Fate, Logic and Time*, op. cit., pp. 69ff.

2. For an illuminating discussion on the preceding matter

and in particular of the relations between titles, proper names and descriptions see Pike's, *God and Timelessness*, pp. 17—38. See also C. B. Martin, *Religious Belief* (Ithaca, N.Y., 1959), pp. 33—63, and G. E. Hughes in 'Mr. Martin on the Incarnation', *Australasian Journal of Philosophy*, 1962, pp. 208—11.

3. Cf. 'The Formalities of Omniscience', *Philosophy*, 1962, pp. 114—29. Prior cites Part I, Lectio 13 of the *Peri Hermeneias* commentary. See also *Past, Present and Future* (Oxford, 1967), Ch. 7, and *Papers on Time and Tense* (Oxford, 1968), Ch. 3.

4. Cf. *Summa Theologica*, 1a, Q14, A13, ad.3; *De Veritate*, Q2, A12. Anthony Kenny's, 'Divine Foreknowledge and Human Freedom' in Kenny (ed.), *Aquinas* (London, 1970) is helpful.

5. 'It Was To Be' in *Dilemmas* (Cambridge, 1966), pp. 15—35.

6. 'Endorsing Predictions', *Philosophical Review*, 1961, pp. 367—78.

7. This is a difficulty, too, for Richard Taylor's 'Deliberation and Foreknowledge', *American Philosophical Quarterly*, 1964, pp. 73—80.

8. Cf. Boethius, *The Consolation of Philosophy*, Bk. 5, Sections 4—6; Anselm, *Proslogion*, Ch. 19; *Monologion*, Chs. 21—22; Aquinas, *Summa Theologica*, Pt. 1, Q10; Schleiermacher, *The Christian Faith*, Pt. 1, Sect. 2, para. 51. On the doctrine of God's timelessness see Pike, *God and Timelessness*.

9. 'Determinism and Omniscience', *Dialogue*, 1970, pp. 366—73.

10. 'Eternity and Sempiternity', *Proceedings of the Aristotelian Society*, 1969, pp. 223—38. See also W. Kneale, 'Time and Eternity in Theology', *Proceedings of the Aristotelian Society*, 1961, pp. 87—108. Mrs. Kneale's analysis of 'timelessness' has the counter-intuitive consequence of leaving open the possibility of there being timeless physical objects (e.g., in the event of there being a constant number of Epicurean atoms). See further pp. 230—1.

11. Op. cit., chapters 5, 7 (esp. pp. 94f, 125ff).

12. Some of these unsatisfactory consequences are discussed in Pike, ibid., Chs. 6, 9 (esp. pp. 172ff); P. Geach, *God and the Soul* (London, 1969) p. 93.

13. Cf. J. T. Saunders, 'Of God and Freedom', *Philosophical Review*, 1966, pp. 219–25; N. Pike, 'Of God and Freedom: A Rejoinder', *Philosophical Review*, 1966, pp. 369–79; M. McCord Adams, 'Is the Existence of God a "Hard" Fact?', *Philosophical Review*, 1967, pp. 492–503.

14. This also serves to bring out what has been noticed at least since Augustine, namely that the problem is raised by any and all foreknowledge, divine or otherwise. Cf. Augustine, *On Free Will*, Bk. 3. For a discussion of Augustine's own unsatisfactory response see William Rowe, 'Augustine on Foreknowledge and Free Will', *Review of Metaphysics*, 1963–4, pp. 356–63. Cf. also Leibniz, *Theodicy*, Pt. 1, Section 37.

15. G. E. Hughes has suggested that the worry about 'Would God be the same individual if he weren't omniscient?' might be diminished if we compared it with 'Would the number 7 be the same individual if it ceased to be prime?'. He remarks that even if one is hesitant about calling a number an individual some have been equally hesitant about calling God an individual since he is a person in at most a highly 'analogical' sense. I owe the illustration of the 'infallible man' to Professor Hughes.

16. This solution is favoured by Pike in *God and Time-lessness*, Ch. 4.

17. Marilyn McCord Adams, op. cit., has challenged the claim that a person's existing at a time t is a 'hard' fact in the case where the person is God. Space precludes further discussion of her position, but it achieves only a slight advance on that discussed in the text.

18. Cf. J. T. Saunders, 'The Temptations of Powerlessness', op. cit.

19. For those not familiar with the machinations of post-war Australian politics, this proposition would not be without support.

CHAPTER 13 'OMNIPOTENCE'

1. Cf. Aquinas, *Summa Theologica*, Pt. 1, Q25, a.3. (This

represents only one strand of his thinking on the topic. For some discussion of his overall position see P. Geach, 'Omnipotence', *Philosophy*, 1973, pp. 7–20.) Descartes' standpoint on this issue was very different. It is helpfully discussed in H. Frankfurt, 'The Logic of Omnipotence', *Philosophical Review*, 1964, pp. 262–3 and by C. Wade Savage in 'The Paradox of the Stone', *Philosophical Review*, 1967, pp. 74–9.

2. For other interesting criticisms of this and related analyses see James F. Ross, *Philosophical Theology* (Indianapolis and New York, 1969), pp. 203ff.

3. Geach, op. cit., thinks it 'frivolous' to talk of God sinning (because of this incoherence) but it seems to me he has not taken the measure of the difficulty at all. See p. 15f.

4. 'Omnipotence and God's Ability to Sin', *American Philosophical Quarterly*, 1969, pp. 208–16.

5. My discussion is heavily indebted to Ross, op. cit., and to Richard Swinburne, 'Omnipotence', *American Philosophical Quarterly*, 1973, pp. 231–7.

6. Cf. also Geach, op. cit., who distinguishes 'almightiness' from 'omnipotence'.

7. I employ the proper name 'Yahweh' here in place of Ross' use of 'God', which is not a proper name, to avoid any charge of smuggling in a reference to omnipotence such as would occur if 'God' were used as a definite description.

8. Op. cit., p. 212.

9. Roughly, b is of a lower *level of reality* than a, if, and only if, b belongs by essence to a class of things, B, such that no member of that class could exist unless:

1. some member of the class of things, A, to which a belongs by essence, actually exists;

2. some member of class A actually produces the existing members of class B;

3. some member of class A maintains a conserving relationship to that member of B throughout its existence; and

4. no member of class B has any property whatever that is not bestowed upon it by some member of class A or some member of some class of things to which the members of class A stand in relations (1), (2) and (3).

Metaphysical dependence, then, is a relation which obtains between particular effects and their causes where the effects are of a lower level of reality than their causes. This is not simple causal dependence, for particular effects can perdure when all members of the class to which their cause belonged have ceased to exist. Nor is it logical dependence, for reality level difference requires the logical dependence of the classes (as well as the individuals) so that the lower cannot have members if the other does not (but not conversely).

10. I shall heed his protestations that the author-character relation is not an analogy for God's to the world. Since they are both instances of the same putative relation, though, there must be some analogous features.

11. This alone differentiates God's creating something from Shakespeare's doing so, because it seems perfectly reasonable to say that *someone else* (say Marlowe) could have created a character identical with Macbeth and yet have so created him that he refused to murder Duncan.

12. Cf. also Dewey Hoitenga's, 'Logic and the Problem of Evil', *American Philosophical Quarterly*, 1967, pp. 111–26; contrast G. Mavrodes, 'Some Recent Philosophical Theology', *Review of Metaphysics*, 1970–1, pp. 82–111.

13. Cf. T. Penelhum, 'Divine Necessity', *Mind*, 1960, p. 185.

14. Cf. A. Plantinga, 'Necessary Being', in Plantinga (ed.), *Faith and Philosophy* (Grand Rapids, Michigan, 1964), p. 107.

15. Op. cit., esp. pp. 231–3. (A formal statement of the definition he espouses may be found on p. 233.)

16. Swinburne recognises the point made earlier that substitutions for S will have to be via *proper names* not definite descriptions. Cf. also A. Plantinga, *God and Other Minds* (Ithaca, N.Y., 1967), p. 170.

17. 'About "God" ' in S. Hook (ed.), *Religious Experience and Truth* (New York, 1962).

18. 'Evil and Omnipotence', *Mind*, 1955, pp. 200–12, and 'Omnipotence', *Sophia*, 1963, (no. 2), pp. 13–25.

19. 'Mr. Keene on Omnipotence', *Mind*, 1961, pp. 249–50. Cf. also G. Mavrodes, 'Some Puzzles Concerning Om-

nipotence', *Philosophical Review*, 1963, pp. 221—3 for arguments with similar import.

20. Cf. Savage, op. cit.; Plantinga, *God and Other Minds*, op. cit., esp. p. 171.

21. Cf. Savage, op. cit., pp. 75f. The following formulation is due to him. Cp. J. L. Cowan, 'The Paradox of Omnipotence', *Analysis*, 1964—5, pp. 102—8. While Cowan correctly rejects the Mavrodes-type solution, he nevertheless fails to recognise that there are other approaches not subject to his criticisms. He is led to conclude (mistakenly) that any actual God *must be limited*.

22. It should be noticed that in Savage's version no critic can maintain that it is assumed that God is omnipotent. Likewise the point that 'a stone which God cannot lift' is self-contradictory, is irrelevant to an argument which does not even include a reference to the word 'God'.

23. For details see Swinburne, op. cit., p. 235.

CHAPTER 14 OMNIPOTENCE AND FREEDOM

1. E.g. J. L. Mackie, 'Evil and Omnipotence', op. cit.; A. Flew, 'Divine Omnipotence and Human Freedom' in A. Flew and A. McIntyre (eds.), *New Essays in Philosophical Theology* (London, 1955).

2. Cf. W. Rowe, 'God and Other Minds', *Nous*, 1969, pp. 259—84 (esp. pp. 274—7).

3. 'Some', of course, may mean 'all'.

4. *Pace* J. E. Barnhart, 'Omnipotence and Moral Goodness', *The Personalist*, 1971, pp. 107—110.

5. Ninian Smart may be an exception. See his 'Omnipotence, Evil and Supermen', *Philosophy*, 1961, pp. 188—95. See also replies in subsequent issues by A. Flew, 'Are Ninian Smart's Temptations Irresistible?', 1962, pp. 57—60 and J. L. Mackie, 'Theism and Utopia', 1962, pp. 153—8. Smart also has a rejoinder entitled 'Probably' which is found at the same place as Flew's reply. In this he argues *inter alia* that if there were a psychologically significant chance of failure, some men some time would be *empirically certain* to fail.

6. See his 'The Free Will Defence' in M. Black (ed.), *Philosophy in America* (London, 1965), which is basic-

ally Chapter 6 of Plantinga's, *God and Other Minds*, op. cit. He has elaborated on certain of his claims in responses to criticisms. See 'Pike and Possible Persons', *Journal of Philosophy*, 1965, pp. 104–8, and 'The Incompatibility of Freedom with Determinism', *Philosophical Forum* (Boston), 1970, pp. 141–8.

7. Clement Dore, 'Plantinga on the Free Will Defence', *Review of Metaphysics*, 1970–1, pp. 690–706 provides a stimulating alternative response to that (of Plantinga) which I discuss.

8. *God and Other Minds*, op. cit., p. 146.

9. William J. Wainwright, 'Freedom and Omnipotence', *Nous*, 1968, pp. 293–301 (esp. Section III). I am indebted to his valuable paper.

10. I do not intend to deny that some Christian thinkers have rejected such a view. See Ross, *Philosophical Theology,* op. cit., pp. 246ff; Hoitenga, op. cit.

11. Cf. James E. Tomberlin, 'Plantinga's Puzzles About God and Other Minds', *The Philosophical Forum* (Boston), 1969, pp. 365–91 (esp. 372–5).

12. Cf. 'Divine Omnipotence and Human Freedom', op. cit.; 'Possibility, Creation and Temptation', *The Personalist*, 1971, pp. 111–3 and 'Compatibilism, Free Will and God', *Philosophy*, 1973, pp. 231–44. Cf. also Philip W. Bennett, 'Evil, God and The Free Will Defence', *Australasian Journal of Philosophy*, 1973, pp. 39–50.

13. Cf. 'The Incompatibility of Freedom with Determinism: A Reply', op. cit., pp. 146ff.

14. For discussion of this matter see e.g. C. Dore, 'An Examination of the "Soul-Making" Theodicy', *American Philosophical Quarterly*, 1970, pp. 119–30 and W. Wainwright, 'God and the Necessity of Physical Evil', *Sophia*, 1972, (no. 2), pp. 16–19.

15. Quite apart from its general moral wrongness, drunkenness often occasions wrongdoing in our world. While the wrongdoing thus brought about may not be freely done, it is culpable because of the free action of getting drunk. The creator of W could not be *required* to intervene to save the drunken from wrongdoing, hence the only way to guarantee that drinking to excess

doesn't produce evil, is to preclude drunkenness from W by ensuring conditions are never sufficient for it. The same surely applies to certain drugs. Once the set-up in W were even partially broken down, further evils would infiltrate.

16. Cf. G. Schlesinger, 'The Problem of Evil and the Problem of Suffering', *American Philosophical Quarterly*, 1964, pp. 244–7 and 'Omnipotence and Evil: An Incoherent Problem', *Sophia*, 1965, (no. 3), pp. 21–4.

17. 'Hume on Evil', *Philosophical Review*, 1963, pp. 180–97.

18. A little of the story is given in my 'Miracles and Epistemology', *Religious Studies*, 1972, pp. 113–25 and 'Petitioning God', *American Philosophical Quarterly*, 1974(forthcoming). References on the debate about evil can be found in e.g. my 'Omnipotence and Compatibilism', *Philosophia*, 1975 (forthcoming), where I also consider several other aspects of the relation between omnipotence and freedom for which no space could be found in the present work.

Index